PERSONS AND INSTITUTIONS IN EARLY RABBINIC JUDAISM

BROWN UNIVERSITY
BROWN JUDAIC STUDIES

Number 3

PERSONS AND INSTITUTIONS IN EARLY RABBINIC JUDAISM

edited
by
William Scott Green

SCHOLARS PRESS
Missoula, Montana

PERSONS AND INSTITUTIONS IN EARLY RABBINIC JUDAISM

edited
by
William Scott Green

Published by
SCHOLARS PRESS
for
Brown University

Distributed by

SCHOLARS PRESS
Missoula, Montana 59806

PERSONS AND INSTITUTIONS IN EARLY RABBINIC JUDAISM

edited
by
William Scott Green

Library of Congress Cataloging in Publication Data

Main entry under title:

Persons and institutions in early rabbinic Judaism.

(Brown Judaic studies ; no. 3-)
Includes bibliographical references and indexes.
1. Rabbinical literature—History and criticism—Addresses, essays, lectures. 2. Tannaim—Addresses, essays, lectures. I. Green, William Scott. II. Series.
BM496.5.P47 296.1 76-52503
ISBN 0-89130-131-3

Printed the United States of America
1 2 3 4 5

For Joel Zaiman

TABLE OF CONTENTS

PREFACE

During the preparation of this volume, I benefitted from the counsel of my teacher, Jacob Neusner, and his assistance helped in many ways to make the appearance of this book a certainty. My thanks go to him for this and for much else.

I again am delighted to acknowledge the generosity of the Jewish Community Federation of Rochester, New York, whose support made possible the publication of this volume. At a time when it confronts a host of problems of urgent human need, the Federation's continued interest in scholarly Judaica is another demonstration of the authentic commitment to and appreciation for the enterprise of learning which characterizes the Jewish Community of Rochester. Once again my gratitude goes to Mr. Irving Ruderman, the Federation's President, and Mr. Darrell D. Friedman, its Executive Director.

The indices for this volume were compiled by Paul V. Flesher. He and Daniel Goldblatt, both students at the University of Rochester, kindly assisted in the completion of several tasks, both mechanical and substantive, essential to this project. I thank them both.

I have tried to maintain uniformity in the transliteration of unvocalized Hebrew and Aramaic terms. The transliteration of vocalized terms, as well as other matters of style and notation, reflect the preferences of the various authors.

Robert Goldenberg's "The Deposition of Rabban Gamaliel II: An Examination of the Sources" appeared originally in the *Journal of Jewish Studies*, 23 (Autumn, 1972), pp. 167-190. The original version of David Goodblatt's "The Beruriah Traditions" appeared in the *Journal of Jewish Studies*, 26 (Spring-Autumn, 1975), pp. 68-85. Both are reprinted here by permission, with minor technical alterations.

Rabbi Joel Zaiman, Temple Emanu-El, Providence, Rhode Island, made important contributions to the education of the editor and some of the authors, as well as to the Program of the History of Religions: Judaism, Department of Religious Studies, Brown University. It is a pleasure to dedicate this collection to a valued friend and teacher.

W.S.G.

Rochester, New York
November 23, 1976
Erev Rosh Ḥodesh Kislev, 5737

ABBREVIATIONS

Albeck	Ch. Albeck (ed.), *Sheshah Sidré Mishnah*
Albeck, *Mo'ed*	Ch. Albeck, *Sheshah Sidré Mishnah: Seder Mo'ed*
Albeck, *Nashim*	Ch. Albeck, *Sheshah Sidré Mishnah: Seder Nashim*
Albeck, *Nezikin*	Ch. Albeck, *Sheshah Sidré Mishnah: Seder Nezikin*
Albeck, *Qodashim*	Ch. Albeck, *Sheshah Sidré Mishnah: Seder Qodashim*
Albeck, *Ṭohorot*	Ch. Albeck, *Sheshah Sidré Mishnah: Seder Ṭohorot*
Albeck, *Zera'im*	Ch. Albeck, *Sheshah Sidré Mishnah: Seder Zera'im*
ARN	Abot deR. Nathan
ARNa, ARNb, ed Schechter	S. Schechter (ed.), *Aboth de Rabbi Nathan, Version A, Version B*
A.Z.	'Avodah Zarah
b.	*Talmud Bavli*
B.B.	Bava' Batra'
Bekh.	Bekhorot
Ber.	Berakhot
Bertinoro	Mishnah Commentary by Obadiah Bertinoro
B.M.	Bava' Meṣi'a'
B.Q.	Bava' Qama'
Braude	W. G. Braude (trans.), *The Midrash on Psalms*
Chron.	Chronicles
Dan.	Daniel
Danby	H. Danby (trans.), *The Mishnah*
Deut.	Deuteronomy
'Ed.	'Eduyyot
Enc. Jud.	*Encyclopaedia Judaica*
Epstein, *Tan.*	J. N. Epstein, *Mevo'ot leSifrut HaTannaim* (*Introduction to the Tannaitic Literature*)

'Eruv.	'Eruvin
Esth.	Esther
Esth. R.	Esther Rabbah
Ex.	Exodus
Ex. R.	Exodus Rabbah
Gen.	Genesis
Gen. R.	Genesis Rabbah
Giṭ.	Giṭṭin
Ḥag.	Ḥagigah
Hist.	J. Neusner, *A History of the Jews in Babylonia*, Vols. I-V
Is.	Isaiah
Jastrow, *Dict.*	M. Jastrow, *A Dictionary of the Targumim, the Talmud Babli and Yerushalmi and the Midrashic Literature*
Jer.	Jeremiah
Josh.	Joshua
Kanter,	S. Kanter, *Gamaliel of Yavneh*
Kaufmann	J. Beer (ed.), *Faksimile-Ausgabe des Mischna Codex Kaufmann A50*
Kel.	Kelim
Ket.	Ketuvot
Kip.	Kippurim
Lam.	Lamentations
Lam. R.	Lamentations Rabbah
Lam. R. ed. Buber	S. Buber (ed.), *Midrasch Echa Rabbati*
Lauterbach	J. Z. Lauterbach (trans.), *Mekhilta de Rabbi Ishmael*
Lev.	Leviticus
Lieberman, *Tos. Kif. Mo'ed*	S. Lieberman, *Tosefta Kifshutah: Seder Mo'ed*
Lieberman, *Tos. Kif. Nashim*	S. Lieberman, *Tosefta Kifshutah: Seder Nashim*
Lieberman, *Tos. Kif. Zera'im*	S. Lieberman, *Tosefta Kifshutah: Seder Zera'im*

Lightstone, *Ṣadoq*	J. Lightstone, *Ṣadoq the Yavnean*
Lk.	Luke
Lowe	W. H. Lowe (ed.), *The Mishnah on which the Palestinian Talmud Rests*
M.	Mishnah
Ma.	Ma'aserot
Maimonides	Mishnah 'im Perush Rabbenu Moshe ben Maimon. Trans. Joseph David Qappah (Jerusalem, 1968)
Maksh.	Makshirin
Meg.	Megillah
Mekh. Ish.	Mekhilta deRabbi Ishmael
Mekh. Ish. eds. Horovitz, Rabin	H. S. Horovitz and I. A. Rabin (eds.), *Mekhilta d'Rabbi Ishmael*
Mekh. Sim.	Mekhilta deRabbi Simeon b. Yoḥai
Mekh. Sim. ed. Epstein	Y. N. Epstein and E. Z. Melamed (eds.), *Mechilta d'Rabbi Šim'on b. Jochai*
Miq.	Miqva'ot
Mishnah Aḥaronah	Ephraim Isaac of Premysla. Published in 1882.
Mk.	Mark
M.Q.	Mo'ed Qaṭan
Mt.	Matthew
M.T.	Midrash Tannaim
MT	*Mayim Tahorim*. Judah Leb Edel Halevi of Bialystok, 5577 [=1817]. From reprint of Mishnah in Babylonian Talmud.
Munich	*Babylonian Talmud: Codex Munich 95*
Naples	*Mishnah 'im Perush HaRambam, Defus Rishon: Napoli 1942*, with an introduction by A. M. Haberman
Ned.	Nedarim

Neg.	Nega'im
Neh.	Nehemiah
Neusner, *Development*	J. Neusner, *Development of a Legend*
Neusner, *Eliezer* I, II	J. Neusner, *Eliezer b. Hyrcanus: The Traditions and the Man.* Vol. I, Vol. II
Neusner, *Pharisees*	J. Neusner, *The Rabbinic Traditions about the Pharisees before 70*
Nid.	Niddah
Num.	Numbers
Par.	Parah
Parma	*Mishnah Codex Parma (deRossi 138)*
Pes.	Pesaḥim
Pesiqta R.	Pesiqta Rabbati
Pesiqta Rabbati ed. Friedmann	M. Friedmann (ed.), *Pesikta Rabbati*
Porton, *Ishmael*	G. Porton, *The Legal Traditions of Rabbi Ishmael*
Ps.	Psalms
Qid.	Qiddushin
Qoh.	Qohelet
Qoh. R.	Qohelet Rabbah
Rabad	Commentary to Sifra of Abraham b. David of Posquieres (1125-1198) in Sifra, ed. I. H. Weiss
R.H.	Rosh Hashanah
Ruth R.	Ruth Rabbah
Sanh.	Sanhedrin
Sem.	Semaḥot
Sem. ed. Higger	M. Higger (ed.), *Treatise Semaḥot and Treatise Semaḥot of R. Ḥiyya and Sefer Ḥibbuṭ ha-Keber*
Sens	Samson ben Abraham of Sens, ca. 1150-1230
Shab.	Shabbat

Shevu.	Shevu'ot
Sheq.	Sheqalim
Sifra ed. Weiss	I. H. Weiss (ed.), *Sifra debe Rab of Sefer Torat Kohanim*
Sifré Deut.	Sifré Deuteronomy
Sifré Deut. ed. Finkelstein	L. Finkelstein (ed.), *Sifré on Deuteronomy*
Song	Song of Songs
Song R.	Song of Songs Rabbah
Suk.	Sukkah
Ta.	Ta'anit
Tem.	Temurah
Ter.	Terumot
Ṭoh.	Ṭohorot
Tos.	Tosefta
Tos. ed. Lieberman	S. Lieberman (ed.), *The Tosefta*
Tos. ed. Zuckermandel	M. S. Zuckermandel (ed.), *The Tosefta: Based on the Erfurt and Vienna Codices*
Tyy	*Tiferet Yisrael, Yakhin.* Israel Gedaliah Lipschutz
y.	Talmud Yerushalmi
Yad.	Yadayim
Yev.	Yevamot
Zab.	Zabim
Zev.	Zevaḥim

TRANSLITERATION OF HEBREW

א = ʼ	מ ם = M
ב = B	נ ן = N
ג = G	ס = S
ד = D	ע = ʻ
ה = H	פ ף = P
ו = W	צ ץ = Ṣ
ז = Z	ק = Q
ח = Ḥ	ר = R
ט = Ṭ	שׁ = Š
י = Y	שׂ = Ś
כ ך = K	ת = T
ל = L	

INTRODUCTION

William Scott Green

A formidable obstacle to historical research into rabbinic Judaism is the highly interpretive, non-historical character of rabbinic literature. The product of men striving to live the holy life according to God's revelation, Torah, believed by them to have been given orally and in writing to Moses at Mount Sinai, rabbinic literature is designed principally to explain, invigorate and transmit Torah, to render it contemporary and demonstrate its pertinence. The materials contained in rabbinic documents were deemed important not because they dispassionately recounted the past or told in the mundane sense "what actually happened," but because they were regarded by rabbinic authorities as paradigmatic, possessing some teaching or message that offered meaningful instruction about living in the present. In rabbinic documents we confront neither history nor biography, but rather a literature of religious tradition, and this deliberately traditional character of rabbinic materials makes the historical reconstruction of rabbinic Judaism problematic. Tradition is hardly neutral, and as Gershom Scholem notes, a distinctive feature is its selectivity.

> Tradition is not simply the totality of that which the community possesses as its cultural patrimony and which it bequeaths to its posterity; it is a *specific selection from this patrimony* which is elevated and garbed with religious authority. It proclaims certain things, sentences, or insights to be Torah, and thus connects them with the revelation.[1]

Moreover, as Jacob Neusner points out, we err drastically if we expect the materials of a tradition to supply answers to conventional historical questions.

> The intense concern to locate the actual words of a given authority, to be able to make a determination of whether or not something really

> happened commits outrage on the materials of a tradition. For those materials to begin with do not allege concerning themselves the sort of historical interest, let alone historical accuracy, implicit in such a question.[2]

Because of the failure fully to appreciate this fundamental characteristic of rabbinic literature, historical research into rabbinic Judaism has yet to produce convincing theories of the formation and transmission of that literature or coherent accounts of the persons and institutions which stand behind it in its present form.[3] Acceptance of the basically theological outlook of rabbinic tradition has led many investigators to view rabbinic Judaism as a substantive monolith, to presuppose a uniform, linear development of a single, unitary rabbinic law, and to regard all early rabbinic figures and groups as mere subsets of the otherwise undifferentiated "rabbis" or "sages," all of whom allegedly shared a common heritage, world-view and religious purpose.[4] Descriptions of the various parties and individuals consequently have been fashioned largely out of the narrative biographical materials in the post-Mishnaic exegetical and aggadic literature, and these narratives too often are treated as essentially reliable representations of the events or persons they depict. This approach to the reconstruction of the history of rabbinism has two difficulties. First, the goal of most rabbinic narrative is exhortation or edification, and it consequently is extrinsic to the central activity of rabbinic Judaism, the study of law. Studies of individual rabbinic figures must begin with the legal traditions ascribed to them, and descriptions which rely heavily on the non-legal narratives lose credibility because they are constructed of materials which gloss others more essential to the rabbinic enterprise. Second, as the studies below demonstrate, it is routine for later authorities to revise or invent narratives to suit their own purposes, and passages in late collections consequently have a stereotyped, embellished and, hence, a legendary quality.

Recent research has shown, on the other hand, that rabbinic materials, both legal and non-legal, have been manipulated by various tradental, redactional and editorial circles, each with its own agendum. It therefore is impossible to begin research into rabbinic Judaism with the presupposition that in their present form rabbinic narratives or legal sayings accurately reflect the original concerns, much less represent the original language, of the authorities who initially told them or the figures to whom they are attributed. To the contrary, the study of individual figures must begin with the careful and systematic exegesis of the traditions ascribed to or reported about them. The need for exegesis, unfortunately, is not always recognized, and investigators not uncommonly assume the "plain meaning" of the present form of a legal rule or aggadic narrative and merely allude to it, a procedure which takes too much for granted. The proper critical exegesis of rabbinic pericopae demands attention not only to the substance of a given saying or story, but also to the contexts provided for it both by the document in which it appears and the larger literary division, chapter or tractate, which surrounds it, as well as the formal, literary and redactional traits the passage now exhibits. The examination of these elements can show how a given saying or story was revised and thus may help to establish the circle(s) responsible for the formation and transmission of the tradition. Only after this is done is it possible to raise more conventional historical problems and adequately to assess the probabilities of solving them.

The papers collected in this volume consistently apply the considerations described above to the investigation of small corpora of tradition about early rabbinic figures and institutions, and the four articles on rabbinic personalities (excluding the paper of Ira Schiffer) are the first genuinely critical studies of the subjects they treat. All the papers competently demonstrate the significance of exegesis as a technique of research, and each provides important insights into the process of tradition in rabbinic Judaism. It is expected that subsequent volumes in this series will offer comparable studies of other figures and institutions.

The collections of traditions considered here are small, but that fact ought not to diminish either their importance or their interest to scholars. To the contrary, although small corpora of tradition reveal little about the actual causes of the events they describe or the scope of the activities of the characters they depict, the study of such materials can help to identify the group(s) which dominated early rabbinism and to highlight and clarify its agendum. In this respect, the studies of Robert Goldenberg, Jack Lightstone and Diane Levine are particularly interesting. The documents of early rabbinism, Mishnah-Tosefta and the so-called Tannaitic *midrashim*, combine and organize the teachings of several generations of rabbinic masters and thus portray rabbinic Judaism as a single, seamless, unfolding tradition in which all rabbinic figures participated together. From this perspective, the evidence in Talmudic sources of hostility between Joshua b. Hananiah and the Yavnean Patriarch, Gamaliel II (and the interests they represented), is hardly self-serving. It therefore is to be taken seriously. In a virtually definitive exegesis, Goldenberg convincingly argues that the present versions of the conflict are composites and have been framed and altered by circles favorable to Gamaliel to minimize the disagreement and thus to portray Gamaliel's deposition "in the best possible light." Against the background of Goldenberg's conclusions, the studies of Lightstone and Levine yield an important result: Ṣadoq and Eleazar Ḥisma, both minor figures, appear in special relationships with Joshua *and* Gamaliel. Lightstone's analysis of the form and content of many of Sadoq's traditions suggests that he was a member of the Patriarchal party. But other traditions of Ṣadoq explicitly associate his legal rules with Joshua, and Lightstone argues that some of Ṣadoq's traditions may have been preserved by Joshua's circle. Likewise, Eleazar Hisma is alleged to have been a disciple of Joshua, but other traditions assert that he studied in the academy of Gamaliel and was appointed by him to the Sanhedrin. The presence of traditions representing Ṣadoq and Eleazar as disciples of both masters is rather curious and deserves additional inquiry; but the effect is clear. The significance of any opposition between Joshua and Gamaliel is diminished. Since the attempt to weld the conflicting traditions of the rabbinic and Patriarchal groups into a single, unified "rabbinic history" is evident elsewhere in early rabbinic sources,[5] the results described above may be part of that same effort. What is important is that this phenomenon would not have been evident without careful exegesis along the lines suggested above.

David Goodblatt's excellent study of the Beruriah traditions offers a different sort of insight into the workings of rabbinic tradition. By taking seriously both the documentary context and the linguistic character of the various traditions which allegedly concern Beruriah, he plausibly suggests that the traditions which attribute formal rabbinic learning to her have a late Sasanian Babylonian, rather than an early Palestinian, provenance. His argument that the traditions which identify Beruriah as both the daughter of Ḥananyah b. Teradyon and the wife of R. Meir are the result of the conflation of sources which identify each as a separate individual is highly suggestive, if not altogether probative. What Goodblatt exposes and documents in his investigation is the tendency of later tradents, in this case Amoraic masters, to create new traditions, and sometimes to invent new persons, out of earlier, initially discrete and unrelated materials.

Finally, the paper of Ira Schiffer differs from the others in that its subject is not an individual figure, but a pre-rabbinic institution. The Men of the Great Assembly (or "Synagogue") occupy a pivotal position in the rabbis' reconstruction of their history. According to M. Avot 1:1, it is through the Men of the Great Assembly that Torah, once the sole possession of prophecy, is definitively transferred to the earliest Pharisees. That much scholarly effort has been expended to reconstruct the activities of that institution is not too surprising. Schiffer's work helps place all that research into perspective simply by collecting all the source-material on the Men of the Great Assembly and subjecting it to sensible investigation. Although his comments are principally descriptive, he shows that the great bulk of material on this institution is non-legal and occurs mainly in post-Mishnaic literature. His conclusion, that the accounts of the work of this institution are largely the products of rabbinic imagination, is compelling and adds support to those scholars who regard the institution as essentially fictional. Schiffer's bibliographical study summarizes and criticizes some views on this matter.

All five of these papers, especially the biographical studies, demonstrate the extraordinary richness of rabbinic materials. Although the traditions considered here are small, each corpus offers a number of important and interesting exegetical and historical problems, and each constructs its own intriguing set of issues and concerns. Few groups from antiquity have bequeathed such an engaging legacy.

NOTES

INTRODUCTION

[1]Gershom Scholem, *The Messianic Idea in Judaism* (New York, 1971) pp. 285-86 [italics supplied].

[2]Jacob Neusner, *The Academic Study of Judaism* (New York, 1975) p. 77.

[3]For critical evaluations of various scholarly views on these matters, see Jacob Neusner, ed., *The Formation of the Babylonian Talmud* (Leiden, 1970) and *The Modern Study of the Mishnah* (Leiden, 1973). For *midrash*, see Gary G. Porton's forthcoming "Midrash: The Jews and the Hebrew Bible in the Greco-Roman Period," in *Aufstieg und Nedergang der römischen Welt* (Berlin-New York, 1977).

[4]This latter view is explicit in E. E. Urbach, *The Sages* (Hebrew) (Jerusalem, 1969).

[5]See Jacob Neusner, *The Rabbinic Traditions about the Pharisees before 70*, Vol. I (Leiden, 1971) pp. 15-23.

THE DEPOSITION OF RABBAN GAMALIEL II: AN EXAMINATION OF THE SOURCES

Robert Goldenberg
Wichita State University

During the time that Rabban Gamaliel II presided at Yavneh, an insurgency among the Rabbis there unseated him, and he was temporarily replaced by the young priest R. Eleazar b. Azariah. No other even briefly successful uprising of this kind is mentioned in surviving records,[1] although an abortive attempt was directed against Gamaliel's son and eventual successor Simeon.[2]

Gamaliel's deposition is reported in both Talmudim. The purpose of this paper is to evaluate the two reports as historical sources.

I

The Palestinian Talmud

The following, y. Ber. 4:1 7c-d, has a parallel in y. Ta. 4:1 67d; variants will be indicated in the footnotes. Italics represent passages in Aramaic.

A. And[3] it once happened that a certain student came and asked R. Joshua, "How is the law about the evening prayer?" He said to him, "Optional."

[The student] came[4] and asked R. Gamaliel, "How is the law about the evening prayer?" He said to him, "Compulsory."

[The student] said to him, "But R. Joshua said 'Optional'!"[5] [R. Gamaliel] said to him, "Tomorrow, when I come into the meeting-house (בית הועד), get up and ask about this law."

The next day[6] that same student got up and asked R. Gamaliel, "How is the law about the evening prayer?" He said to him, "Compulsory." He said, "But R. Joshua said[7] 'Optional.'"

R. Gamaliel said to R. Joshua, "Is it you who says 'Optional'?" He said, "No."

[R. Gamaliel] said to him, "Stand on your feet, and let them bear witness against you." And R. Gamaliel sat and taught, and R. Joshua remained standing, until the whole assembly shouted[8] and said to R. Ḥuṣpit the Meturgeman,[9] "Dismiss the assembly!"

B. They said to R. Zenon the Hazzan, "Say..."[10] He began to speak; the whole assembly began, and they rose to their feet and said[11] to [R. Gamaliel], "For upon whom has not come your unceasing evil?"[12]

C.1. They went[13] and appointed (מינו) R. Eleazar b. Azariah to the Academy (בישיבה).

C.2. (He was sixteen years old, and all his hair turned gray.)

D.1. R. ʿAqiva was sitting sorrowfully and saying, "Not that he is more learned (בן תורה) than I,[14] but he is of more illustrious parentage (בן גדולים) than I.[14] Happy is the man whose fathers have gained him merit! Happy is the man who has a peg on which[15] to hang![16]

D.2. (And what was R. Eleazar b. Azariah's peg? He was[6] the tenth generation[6] in descent from Ezra.)

E. (And[6] how many benches were there? R. Jacob b. Sisi said, "There were 80 benches there of students,[17] besides those standing behind the fence." R. Yosi b. R. Abun[18] said, "There were 300, besides those standing behind the fence.")

H.[19] [This is the reference of] *what we learn elsewhere*: "On the day they seated (הושיבו) R. Eleazar b. Azariah in the Academy."[20]

I. (*We learn elsewhere*: "This is a *midrash* which R. Eleazar b. Azariah expounded before the Sages at the Vineyard in Yavneh."[21] But was there a vineyard there?! Rather, those are the students who were arranged in rows, as in a vineyard.)

J.1. R. Gamaliel immediately went to the home of each person to appease him.

J.2. *He went*[22] *to R. Joshua; he found him sitting making needles. He said to him, "Is this how you make a living?"*[23] *He said, "And are you just now trying to find out?* Woe to the generation of which you are the steward (פרנס)."

K. [R. Gamaliel] said to him, "I submit to you."

L.1. *And*[6] *they sent a certain laundry-worker* (קצר) *to R. Eleazar b. Azariah.*

L.2. *(but some say it was R. 'Aqiva).*

O. [The messenger] said to him, "The sprinkler, son of a sprinkler,[25] should sprinkle; shall he who is neither a sprinkler nor the son of a sprinkler say to the sprinkler, son of a sprinkler, "Your water comes from a cave, and your ashes from roasting'?"[26]

P. [R. Eleazar b. Azariah] said to them, "Are you satisfied? You and I shall wait at R. Gamaliel's door."

Q. Nonetheless they did not depose [R. Eleazar b. Azariah] from his high dignity, but rather appointed him *Av Bet Din.*

The text as we now have it is clearly composite. I would break it down as follows:

Main story--A, B, C.1, J, K, L, O, P, Q

Elaborations of the main story--C.2, D, J.2, L.2(?)

Interpolations--E, H, I

If later accretions are disregarded, the story can be summarized as follows: An anonymous student became aware of a disagreement between Joshua and Gamaliel. He made the dispute known to the latter, who took the opportunity to humilate Joshua before the assembled Rabbis. Outraged, they broke up the meeting, and R. Eleazar b. Azariah was brought into the Academy. It is not stated, but we infer that Eleazar became its new head. R. Gamaliel thereupon made amends to each of the offended Rabbis, and had a message sent to Eleazar, expressing his claim to an inherited right to the presidency. Eleazar voluntarily resigned, and was rewarded with the second place in the hierarchy.

The relationship between the Eleazar-story and the Joshua-story presents a problem. There is no section in the narrative in which both men play a role. Their two stories can be told without reference to each other, although admittedly each would then be somewhat episodic. Since the references to ʿAqiva (sections D.1, L.2) are both insertions, dating from a later stage in the development of the narrative, the question arises whether there was also a still earlier stage in which the Joshua-scenes and the Eleazar-scenes constituted separate traditions.[27] The present text has obviously been pieced together.[28] The narrative progression is not always smooth;[29] such flaws often indicate the interweaving of two different traditions. On the other hand, the Palestinian narrators were evidently rather unconcerned with such esthetic considerations; we should not, therefore, be too ready to see different "sources" wherever the narrative structure fails to meet our literary standards.[30] All we can say with assurance is that the Eleazar-Joshua story is the backbone of the present narrative. At a later date, references to ʿAqiva were inserted, the most important being in section D. Still later, a number of miscellaneous interpolations were added as well (sections E, H, I).

The text of section B is unclear, and apparently corrupt. The two extant versions differ concerning the speakers' identity; it is not explained what anyone actually says and at one point there is a lacuna. We have here, it seems, an alternative description of the disruption of the Academy.[31] It was presumably added to a story drawn primarily from other traditions because it offered a clearer statement of the Rabbis' motivation.[32] But even if this passage was part of the "original" story, it has by now become so obscure that there is little hope of determining its meaning, or even of restoring its text.

Section E is a very late addition designed to emphasize the large number of men who collaborated in the overthrow.[33]

In three places in the Mishnah,[34] Simeon b. ʿAzzai cites a tradition which he heard "from seventy-two elders on the day they seated R. Eleazar b. Azariah in the Academy." The phrase was apparently used to date certain traditions. Its insertion into our story (section H) seems to have two purposes; to explain the phrase itself, which by Amoraic times was apparently no longer understood, and also to indicate why that day was important enough to become a point of reference.

The fanciful interpretation of "Vineyard in Yavneh," found in section I, recurs in Song of Songs R. 8:11. In that place it has no connection with R. Eleazar b. Azariah, nor is this exegesis there or anywhere else associated with M. Ket. 4:6. The reason for its insertion into our story and the identity of the interpolator are unknown. The name of R. Eleazar b. Azariah provides the only possible link. It is not even hinted, however, that Eleazar expounded the *midrash* in question on the occasion of his installation.

Section D, the most important elaboration, takes careful note of ʿAqiva's own availability to succeed Gamaliel, and purports to explain why he was in fact bypassed. At a later time, ʿAqiva was so universally admired that any hearer of the story would have wondered why he had not been chosen.

The central interest of the account is political. It revolves around the presidency over the Rabbinic gathering and the question of who might legitimately exercise it. There is no tendency to turn the original incident into a pretext for moral instruction, concerning the manner in which persons in authority ought to treat their subjects. Nor is the story used as a legal precedent; the halakhic dispute between Gamaliel and Joshua appears in both Talmudim as a separate datum prior to the narrative. From the time of R. Judah the Patriarch, the hold of the Hillelite dynasty on the Patriarchate was secure. Political interest would thereafter have naturally shifted to other issues. The main story therefore seems to antedate the ascendancy of Judah the Patriarch, ca. 185 C.E. Once formed, the composite continued to grow until fairly late in the Amoraic period. The reference to R. Yosi b. R. Abun points to the second half of the fourth century.

The story is told in Hebrew. Only the following passages are in Aramaic:

1. The introductory formulae in sections H and I. Since these sections were added by some Amoraic redactor, it need not surprise us that standard redactional language was used.

2. The indicated portions of J, and all of L. This presents a problem. In J in particular the transition from Aramaic back to Hebrew occurs in the middle of R. Joshua's retort. I doubt that a single narrator would have composed such a short statement in two languages. The final sentence ("Woe...") appears verbatim in the BT, and may have been associated with this story from an early date, but these Aramaic passages suggest some later revision. We shall return to this question below, in part III.

II

The Babylonian Talmud

The following is from b. Ber. 27b-28a. Section A has a parallel in b. Bekh. 36a; this parallel will be introduced in an additional note to part II. As before, all Aramaic portions will be in italics.

A. *Our Rabbis taught*: It once happened that a certain student came before R. Joshua. He said to him, "Is the evening prayer optional or compulsory?" He said to him, "Optional."

[The student] came before R. Gamaliel. He said to him, "Is the evening prayer optional or compulsory?" He said to him, "Compulsory."

[The student] said to him, "But did not R. Joshua say 'Optional'?!" [R. Gamaliel] said to him, "Wait until the Shield-Bearers enter the study-house (בית המדרש)."

When the Shield-Bearers entered, the inquirer rose and asked, "Is the evening prayer optional or compulsory?" R. Gamaliel said to him, "Compulsory."

R. Gamaliel said to the Sages, "Is there anyone who disagrees in this matter?" R. Joshua said to him, "No."

[R. Gamaliel] said to him, "But did they not tell me 'Optional' in your name?!" He said to him, "Joshua, stand on your feet, and let them bear witness against you."

R. Joshua rose to his feet and said, "If I were alive and [the witness] dead--the living can contradict the dead. But now that I am alive and he is alive--how can the living contradict the living?"

And R. Gamaliel sat and taught, and R. Joshua remained standing, until the whole assembly shouted and said to Ḥuṣpit the Turgeman, "Stop!" So he stopped.

C.1.[35] *They said, "How long will he go on insulting him? Last year he insulted him* (in Rosh Hashanah),[36] *he insulted him in the incident of R. Sadoq* (in Bekhorot),[36] *and now he has insulted him again. Let us remove him! Whom shall we appoint* (נוקים)*? Shall we appoint R.*

Joshua? He is a party to the dispute.[37] *Shall we appoint R. ʿAqiva? He might be punished, since he has no* ancestral merit.[37] *Let us rather appoint R. Eleazar b. Azariah, since* he is wise, and he is rich, and he is tenth in descent from Ezra."

C.2. (He is wise, [that is], *if questioned, he can answer;* he is rich, [that is], *if* [R. Gamaliel] *has to go pay honor to Caesar,* [R. Eleazar b. Azariah] too *can go pay honor;* he is tenth in descent from Ezra, [that is], *he has* ancestral merit,[37] *and he cannot be punished.*)

C.3. *They came and said to him, "Would the Master consent to become head of the Academy?"*

C.4. *He said to them, "Let me go consult my household." He went and consulted his wife.*

She said to him, "They may remove you." He answered, "Let a man use a valuable cup one day, and let it be broken the next."

She said to him, "You have no white hair." That day he was eighteen years old; a miracle occurred to him, and eighteen rows of his hair turned white.

C.5. (*That is* [why] *R. Eleazar b. Azariah said,* "Behold I am about seventy years old," *and not* "seventy years old.")[38]

E.1.[39] It was taught: That day (אותו היום) they removed the doorkeeper, and the students were given permission to enter. For R. Gamaliel had used to proclaim: "Any student whose outside is not like his inside shall not enter the study-house."

E.2. (*On that day* (ההוא יומא) *a number of benches were added. R. Yoḥanan said, "The matter is disputed by Abba Joseph b. Dostai and the Rabbis; one* [view] *holds 400 benches were added, and one, 700.*")

E.3. *R. Gamaliel was greatly disturbed, and said,* "Perhaps, God forbid, I have withheld Torah from Israel." *In a dream, he was shown white casks filled with ashes.*[40] But that was not [the case]; *he was shown that just to calm his mind.*

F.1. *It was taught:* 'Eduyot was under review (נשנית) on that day (בו ביום).

F.2. (*and wherever it says* "on that day" *the reference is to that day*).

F.3. and there was no law which had been left pending in the study-house which was not decided.

G. And even R. Gamaliel did not absent himself from the study-house for as much as one hour, *as we learn:* On that day (בו ביום) Judah, an Ammonite proselyte, came before them in the study-house. He said to them, "Am I permitted to enter the congregation?" R. Gamaliel said to him, "You are forbidden to enter the congregation." R. Joshua said to him, "You are permitted to enter the congregation."

R. Gamaliel said to [R. Joshua], "But has it not already been said, 'An Ammonite or a Moabite shall not enter the congregation of the Lord'?"[41]

R. Joshua said to him, "Then do Ammon and Moab dwell in their own places? Sennacherib, King of Assyria, has already come up and mixed together all the nations, as it is said, 'And I have removed the boundaries of peoples, and have plundered their treasures; like a bull I have brought down those who sat on thrones'[42]--*and anything which comes out* [of a composite mass is assumed to have] *come from its largest element.*"[43,44]

R. Gamaliel said to him, "But has it not already been said, 'And afterwards I shall bring back the captivity of the children of Ammon, says the Lord'[45]--so they have returned?"

R. Joshua said to him, "But has it not already been said, 'And I shall return the captivity of my people Israel'?[46] And they have not yet returned!"

They immediately permitted [Judah] to enter the congregation.[47]

J.1.[48] *R. Gamaliel said, "Such being the case,*[49] *I shall go and appease R. Joshua."*

J.2. *When he got to his house, he saw that its walls were black.* He said to him, "From the walls of your house, one can tell that you are a charcoal-maker."[50] He said to him, "Woe to the generation of which you are the steward (פרנס). You do not know of the troubles of the scholars and of how they support and sustain themselves."

K. [R. Gamaliel] said to him, "I submit to you; forgive me." [R. Joshua] *paid him no attention.*

[R. Gamaliel said further,] "Do it out of respect for my father." [R. Joshua] *was appeased.*

L. *They said, "Who will go and inform the Rabbis?" A certain washerman* (כובס) *said, "I shall go."*

M. *So R. Joshua sent* [a message] *to the study-house: "Let him who wears the garment wear the garment; should he who does not wear the garment say to him who wears it, 'Take off your garment and let me wear it'?"*

N. *R. ʿAqiva said to the Rabbis, "Shut the doors, so that R. Gamaliel's servants not come and disturb the Rabbis." R. Joshua said, "I had better go to them myself."*

O. *He came and knocked on the door, and said to them,* "The sprinkler, son of a sprinkler, should sprinkle; shall he who is neither a sprinkler nor the son of a sprinkler say to the sprinkler, son of a sprinkler, 'Your water comes from a cave and your ashes from roasting'?"[51]

P. R. ʿAqiva said to him, "R. Joshua, have you been appeased? We have done nothing except for your honor. Tomorrow you and I shall wait at [R. Gamaliel's] door."

Q. *They said, "How shall we act? Shall we remove* [R. Eleazar b. Azariah]? *Tradition holds that* one may increase the sanctity of an object, but not decrease it.[52] *Should each Master expound one Sabbath* [at a time]? *That will lead to jealousy. Rather let R. Gamaliel expound three Sabbaths*[53] *and R. Eleazar b. Azariah one Sabbath."*

R. (*That is what the Master meant when he said,* "Whose Sabbath was it? R. Eleazar b. Azariah's.")

S. (And that student [who started the whole episode] was R. Simeon b. Yoḥai.)

If we begin with the tripartite division which we used in part I, the results are as follows:

Main story--A, C.1.3, J.1, K, L, O, P, Q

Elaborations--E.1.3, J.2, M, N[54]

Interpolations--C.2.4.5, E.2, F, G, R, S

The central narrative is broadly similar to the Palestinian version. There is, however, one major difference. Here, the Rabbis are described as acting exclusively in Joshua's interests. They cite no offenses against other members of the group. Gamaliel need offer only one apology, to Joshua himself. ʿAqiva even says (section P) that Joshua's honor was their sole motivation for removing

Gamaliel.[55] This change reduces the political aspect of the narrative, and turns it into a story about a personal dispute.

The elements concerning Eleazar and Joshua have been somewhat more closely integrated. The question, "Who will go and inform the Rabbis," referring to the reconciliation between Joshua and Gamaliel, means "Who will inform Eleazar and his supporters." In section P, ʿAqiva, addressing Joshua, alludes to the deposition of Gamaliel and (presumably) Eleazar's promotion. This tightening-up of the narrative is not surprising, since we shall see (in part III) there is abundant evidence that the Babylonian story is a later development of the Palestinian.

Most of the later interpolations come at the same point in this story as in the PT, but the two sets have almost nothing in common.[56] The only shared item is the dispute about the benches,[57] and even it plays strikingly different roles in the two stories. In the PT, the reference indicates the wide backing for Gamaliel's removal. Here, it demonstrates the result of reversing one of his specific policies, the policy of limiting access to the Academy.

In general, the additions to the Babylonian story concern what might be called the Rabbinic life-style. Two of them (sections C and Q) take what was originally a political problem and use it for a display of Rabbinic dialectics. Section E, as noted, concerns the question of who was worthy to study Torah at all. In keeping with this same theme, section F provides a bit of literary history.[58] Section G, which returns to R. Gamaliel's concern for Torah, was included because it is the only Mishnah[59] beginning "on that day" which actually mentions R. Gamaliel.

These additions change the tone of the whole narrative. Political interest, as mentioned above, has faded from view. The story, considerably "improved," has been made more interesting and more edifying for later audiences. This Babylonian version cannot be dated. It mentions no names which might be useful, except for that of R. Yoḥanan, a Palestinian who died ca. 279. The story certainly continued to develop in Babylonia after his time. The reference to R. Simeon b. Yoḥai is clearly late, added by someone with no knowledge of Tannaitic chronology.

The Babylonian version contains much more Aramaic than the Palestinian. Apparently, the narrative "improvements" were made in the vernacular, often displacing older Hebrew material. Section E, in particular, shows a curious shifting back and forth between Hebrew and Aramaic. The first part, here called a *beraita*, centers around R. Gamaliel's proclamation; this may well have been a proverbial expression in certain Babylonian circles--the same expression, again in Hebrew, is attributed to Rava on b. Yoma 72b. Perhaps the same explanation could be applied to R. Gamaliel's exclamation in section E.3.

Additional Note

The following appears on b. Bekh. 36a. Italics denote Aramaic, as before.

> *R. Ṣadoq had a firstling. He fed it with barley* in wicker baskets of peeled willow-branches.[60] *As it was eating, its lip became split.*
>
> *He came before R. Joshua. He said to him,* "Do we distinguish at all between a *ḥaver* and an *'am ha'areṣ*?"[61] R. Joshua said, "Yes."
>
> *He came before R. Gamaliel. He said to him,* "Do we distinguish between a *ḥaver* and an *'am ha'areṣ*?" R. Gamaliel said, "No."
>
> *He said to him,* "But (והא) R. Joshua said, 'Yes'!" He said to him, "Wait until the Shield-Bearers come up to the study-house."
>
> When they entered the study-house, the inquirer rose and asked, "Do we at all distinguish between a *ḥaver* and an *'am ha'areṣ*?" R. Joshua said, "No."

R. Gamaliel said to him, "But did they not (והלא) say 'Yes' in your name?! Joshua, stand on your feet and let them bear witness against you."

R. Joshua rose to his feet and said, "How can I act? If I were alive and he dead--the living can contradict the dead. Now that I am alive and he is alive, how can the living contradict the living?"

And R. Gamaliel stood[62] and taught, while R. Joshua remained on his feet, until the whole assembly shouted and said to Ḥuṣpit the Meturgeman, "Stop!" So he stopped.

It is impossible that two stories should develop independently, and become so similar to one another as this one and the story in Ber. One has obviously become assimilated to the other. Since the Bekh. version begins in Aramaic and then abruptly shifts to Hebrew, it seems likely that Ber. has the earlier setting for the present narrative.[63] A number of traditions recounting disputes between Gamaliel and Joshua were in circulation; another has survived in M. R.H. 2:8-9. One of these, concerning R. Ṣadoq's firstling, eventually became an echo of the story about the evening prayer. This may have occurred because the story about the evening prayer culminated in Gamaliel's removal and thus became better known. In the end the story about the firstling was forgotten, and there remained only a tradition that *something* concerning a firstling had happened. The present narrative was supplied.[64]

The story in Bekh. has no sequel. If the narrator had known more of the story in Ber., he would have had no reason to omit it.[65] It seems safe to infer that he knew only this part; we thus have an indication that parts of the whole story at some point circulated separately.

III

Synopses

Where a section appears in both Talmudim, the two versions are set side by side for detailed comparison. When a phrase used in one version is found unchanged in the other, I show this with (" " "). If a phrase is entirely absent, I use (- - -). Aramaic passages appear in italics, as before. Synopses either quote or paraphrase the text, as circumstances require.

A. The Disgrace of R. Joshua

y. Ber. 4:1	*b. Ber. 27b*	*b. Bekh. 36a*
1. And it once happened that	1. *Our Rabbis taught:* It once happened that	1. *R. Ṣadoq had a firstling...Its lip became split.*
2. a certain student came and asked R. Joshua	2. a certain student came before R. Joshua. He said to him,	2. *He came before R. Joshua. He said to him,*
3. "How is the law about the evening prayer?"	3. "Is the evening prayer optional or compulsory?"	3. "Do we at all distinguish between a *ḥaver* and an *ʿam ha'areṣ*?"
4. He said, "Optional."	4. " " "	4. R. Joshua said, "Yes."
5. He came and asked R. Gamaliel,	5. He came before R. Gamaliel. He said to him,	5. *He came before R. Gamaliel. He said to him,*
6. [= 3 above]	6. [= 3 above]	6. [= 3 above, omitting "at all"]
7. He said, "Compulsory."	7. " " "	7. R. Gamaliel said, "No."
8. He said to him, "But (והא) R. Joshua said 'Optional.'"	8. He said to him, "But did not (והלא) R. Joshua say 'Optional'?"	8. He said to him, "But (והא) R. Joshua said 'Yes.'"
9. He said to him, "Tomorrow, when I come into the meeting-house, get up and ask about this law."	9. He said to him, "Wait until the Shield-Bearers enter the study-house."	9. He said to him, "Wait until the Shield-Bearers come up to the study-house."

	y. Ber. 4:1	*b. Ber. 27b*	*b. Bekh. 36a*
10.	The next day that same student got up and asked R. Gamaliel,	When the Shield-Bearers entered, the inquirer got up and asked,	When they entered the study-house, the inquirer got up and asked,
11.	"How is the law about the evening prayer?" He said, "Compulsory."	"Is the evening prayer optional or compulsory?" R. Gamaliel told him, "Compulsory."	"Do we at all distinguish between a *ḥaver* and an *ʿam ha'areṣ*?" R. Joshua said, "No."
12a.	He said, "But (והא) R. Joshua said 'Optional.'"	- - - [see 12d]	- - - [see 12d]
12b.	R. Gamaliel said to R. Joshua, "Is it you who say 'Optional'?"	R. Gamaliel said to the Sages, "Is there anyone who disagrees in this matter?"	- - -
12c.	He said, "No."	R. Joshua said to him, "No."	- - -
12d.	- - - see 12a	He said to him, "But did they not (והלא) say 'Optional' in your name?"	R. Gamaliel said to him, "But did they not (והלא) say 'Yes' in your name?"
13.	He said to him, "Stand on your feet, and let them bear witness against you."	He said to him, "Joshua, stand on your feet..."	Joshua, stand on your feet..."
14.	- - -	R. Joshua rose to his feet and said, "If I were alive and he dead--the living can contradict the dead. But now that I am alive and he is alive--how can the living contradict the living?"	" " " [adds "How shall I act?"; deletes "But"]
15.	And R. Gamaliel sat and taught, and R. Joshua remained standing, until the whole assembly shouted,	" " "	" " " [printed text has "R. Gamaliel stood..."]
16.	and they said to R. Ḥuṣpit the Meturgeman,	" " " [Ḥuṣpit the Turgeman]	" " " [Ḥuṣpit the Meturgeman]

y. Ber. 4:1	*b. Ber. 27b*	*b. Bekh. 36a*
17. "Dismiss the assembly!"	17. "Stop!"	17. "Stop!"
18. - - -	18. So he stopped.	18. " " "

These tables leave no doubt as to how the three stories are related. In only one case (#10) is it even remotely possible that the PT is an expansion of the BT. In that case, the name of R. Gamaliel may have been added, but the different narrative schemes in #11-12 make this evidence very weak. On the other hand, the BT expands the PT in a number of cases: #1, 2=5, 3=6=11 (11 twice), and 13.[66] In #3=6=11, the question has been elaborated in an obviously secondary way. The word "before" in #2=5 is also a later addition. In #11, the name of the respondent is supplied, as is R. Joshua's name in #13. In all these cases, the direct literary dependence of the BT on the PT is beyond question.

The close relationship of the two Babylonian stories, and the dependence of Bekh. on Ber., are also demonstrable. In every case where y. Ber. and b. Ber. differ, b. Bekh. agrees with the latter, with the single trivial exception of #8. Bekh., furthermore, has expanded Ber. in #4, 7, 10, and 14. Finally, in #2=5, Bekh. has translated Ber. into Aramaic, presumably under the influence of the Aramaic narrative (#1) which introduces its story. The three narratives differ in sequence only once, in #12. In y. Ber., Joshua's disagreement with Gamaliel is revealed before he is forced to lie publicly, while in b. Ber. the revelation follows the confrontation.[67] Since #12b-c has no intrinsic connection with #12a=12d (Bekh. omits #12b-c entirely), the reversal is not important.

The language of the Babylonian version has been adapted to its surroundings. The term for "evening prayer" is consistently and characteristically תפילת ערבית. The version in y. Ber. uses the Palestinian תפילת הערב, as does the Mishnah itself.[68] Similarly, the distinctively

Palestinian בית הועד (meeting-house) has been changed in b. Ber. to the more common בית המדרש.[69]

It has been suggested that the "Shield-Bearers" were actually armed guards at R. Gamaliel's disposal.[70] Although b. Ber. does refer (section N) to "R. Gamaliel's servants," we have no idea who these were; for all we know, the reference is altogether anachronistic. To draw any inference from the Gothic soldiers whom the Patriarch over a century later could command[71] would be most unwise. The more common, and preferable, interpretation is that the "Shield-Bearers" were the Rabbis themselves, the epithet being metaphorical.

The story in Bekh. ends abruptly with the order to Ḥuṣpit the Meturgeman. Ginzberg thought there was an "original *baraita*" which carried the story through to its conclusion,[72] but it is difficult, as I have said, to imagine why the narrator would have omitted the rest, had he known it.

C. The Appointment of R. Eleazar B. Azariah

PT	*BT*
1. - - -	1. *They said, "How long will he go on...Let us remove him!"*
2. - - -	2. *Whom shall we appoint* (נוקים)? *R. Joshua?...R. ʿAqiva?...*
3. They went and appointed (מינו) R. Eleazar b. Azariah into the Academy.	3. *Let us rather appoint R. Eleazar b. Azariah, since...*
4. - - -	4. (He is wise, that is,...)
5. - - -	5. *They came and said to him, "Would the Master consent...?"*
6. - - -	6. *He said to them, "Let me go consult..." He went and consulted his wife.*
7. - - -	7. *She said, "They may remove you." He said, "Let a man..."*
8. (He was sixteen years old, and all his hair turned gray.)	8. *She said to him, "You have no white hair." That day he was eighteen years old; a miracle occurred to him and eighteen rows of his hair turned white.*

PT	*BT*
9. - - -	9. (*That is* [*why*] *R. Eleazar b. Azariah said, "Behold,..."*)

Two simple declarative sentences, one probably added later than the other, constitute the entire Palestinian report of Eleazar's entrance into the Academy. The elaborate story in the BT can hardly be considered merely an expansion of the Palestinian version. It is an original creation. It may, to be sure, have roots in older narratives, but these can no longer be traced. Much of the story in any case derives from the Babylonian storyteller.

The two versions have three items in common. One of these is the report of Eleazar's prematurely gray (or white) hair. This was probably an independent tradition, attached only at a later time to Eleazar's statement in M. Ber. 1:5. If the story had been invented to explain that statement (as the BT might lead us to suppose), we could not account for the PT's failure to cite it. The two Talmudim disagree concerning how old Eleazar was "on that day." Variant readings in the PT report still other figures.[73] These presumably reflect different guesses at Eleazar's previously unspecified age.[74]

The second shared element is the account of Eleazar's introduction to the Academy. The accounts differ. According to PT, Eleazar was appointed to the Academy, while BT asserts that he was openly invited to become its leader. Since most of BT is obviously fictional we cannot automatically assume that it here reflects an older and more authoritative source. PT, however, may well mean the same thing. Unless Eleazar had become not merely a member, but the Academy's new president, it would be hard to account for Gamaliel's great concern or his emphasis on hereditary legitimacy. PT further implies that Eleazar's eventual appointment as *Av Bet Din* represented a demotion, since that office was the second in the standard rabbinic hierarchy.[75] It seems reasonable, therefore, to accept

BT's report on this matter.[76] Because of PT's obscurity on this important point, it was subsequently thought necessary to specify[77] that the day of Eleazar's installation was indeed the day of the events here recounted.

The final common element in the two stories is Eleazar's alleged descent from Ezra (see section D). Since section D.2 may well be a later insertion, the presence of this claim in the BT possibly offers evidence that some Babylonian additions reflect older, independent traditions.[78] The reference to Eleazar's descent also appears in y. Yev. 1:6 3a. Apparently it was a commonly accepted belief. At a time when Davidic ancestry was claimed by any politically ambitious person, descent from Ezra was an appropriate priestly counterclaim.

E. The Benches

PT	*BT*
1. - - -	1. *It was taught*:
2. - - -	2. That day (אותו היום) they removed the doorkeeper...
3. - - -	3. For R. Gamaliel had used to proclaim...
4. And how many benches were there?	4. *On that day* (ההוא יומא) *a number of benches was added.*
5. - - -	5. *R. Yoḥanan said, "The matter is disputed by Abba Joseph b. Dostai and the Rabbis;*
6. R. Jacob b. Sisi said, "There were 80 benches of students there, besides those standing behind the fence."	6. *one* [view] *holds 400 benches were added,*
7. R. Yosi b. R. Abun said, "There were 300, besides those standing behind the fence."	7. *and one, 700."*
8. - - -	8. *R. Gamaliel was greatly disturbed...*
9. - - -	9. *In a dream, he was shown...*
10. - - -	10. But that was not the case...

The PT reports that the dispute concerns the number of benches (of men) *present*; the BT, the number of benches *added*. Since the two reports contain neither the same numbers nor the same names, it is possible that they are unrelated, despite their apparent connection. If the two were found in isolation, there would be no way to determine their relationship. The rest of the material in the BT permits at least a guess.

The BT offers #1-3 as a *baraita*. This is the only portion of the episode in Hebrew. The story of the doorkeeper may have been in independent circulation--perhaps, like the story of R. Eleazar's hair, always told in connection with R. Gamaliel's ouster. When it was combined with the dispute about the benches, the change in the latter was a natural consequence. This hypothesis is strengthened by the fact that #4 is in Aramaic. In our story, this generally seems a sign of a later reworking. The *baraita* itself is possibly Babylonian; we have already seen that Rava shared R. Gamaliel's concern that a student's motivation and behavior correspond.

This episode replaces the earlier hostility towards R. Gamaliel with patronizing condescension. True, Gamaliel was harsh, and true, he was wrong to be so, but still he meant well, and after all no permanent harm was done. This shift probably indicates that the episode was constructed of elements which had already taken shape before their inclusion. Whoever inserted it was unable to achieve complete consistency in the story's characterization.

F. "On that Day"[79]

Epstein's demonstration relative to the sense of "on that day" has already been referred to.[80] Tradition took the claim at face value; we can no longer trace how this understanding developed.

Epstein also rejected the tradition about ʿEduyot, but he apparently interpreted it as referring to the Mishnaic tractate. The beginning of Tosefta ʿEduyot records that the men of Yavneh set themselves the task of collecting and arranging older traditions. At the time of the uprising against Gamaliel, they may well have been at work on that project. It is in fact possible that the word עדיות here refers simply to the mass of "testimonies" which the Yavneans were trying to organize, not to the particular literary unit which later received that name. The suggested translation of the verb נשנית ("was under review") is designed to preserve that possibility, while the alternative reading תקנום, cited by Epstein,[81] lends it still greater credence. The report that no pending dispute was left unresolved is fully consistent with the kind of activity we have just postulated but there is no way to determine if it is historical.

J. R. Gamaliel Makes Amends

PT	*BT*
1. R. Gamaliel immediately went to each person, to appease him in his home.	1. - - -
2. - - -	2. *R. Gamaliel said, "Such being the case, I shall go and appease R. Joshua."*
3. *He went to R. Joshua;*	3. *When he came to his house,*
4. *he found him sitting making needles.*	4. - - -
5. - - -	5. *he saw that its walls were black.*
6. *He said to him, "Is this how you make a living?"*	6. - - -
7. - - -	7. He said to him, "From the walls of your house, one can tell that you are a charcoal-maker."
8. *He said to him, "And are you just now trying to find out?*	8. - - -
9. Woe to the generation of which you are the steward."	9. He said to him,
10. - - -	10. "You do not know of the troubles of scholars and how they support and sustain themselves."

The relationship between the Talmudim is more complicated in this section than elsewhere. Each version has four items which are missing from the other #1, 4, 6, 8 in PT, #2, 5, 7, 10 in BT). Each has an Aramaic portion using its own characteristic Aramaic dialect,[82] and the contents of the two in no way coincide (cf. #3-8 in PT, #2-5 in BT). Finally, each also has Hebrew passages missing from the other (#1 in PT, #7, 10 in BT). Only once, in #9, do the two versions significantly agree, and then--aside from BT's introduction--they are identical.

These are the first Aramaic passages which we have encountered in PT. Earlier narratives probably contained no exchange between Gamaliel and Joshua. A Palestinian narrator must have felt the need for some discussion between them, and inserted the present one. A similar situation produced the Babylonian version of the conversation; BT, however, has already shown a number of similar cases.

The cause of this parallel development is the strong rebuke to R. Gamaliel which both Talmudim have preserved (#9). Its presence in both versions makes it likely that this remark early attained the status of a proverb, or a stock rejoinder. So striking an expression attracted the attention of those who heard and repeated this story. It is not surprising that even the Palestinian narrators were tempted to supply the setting in which it appeared.

Although part of a later expansion, #7 is in Hebrew. Presumably, #10 is an expansion of #9, of the kind which has already become familiar. It is in Hebrew because #9 is in Hebrew. #7, however, is an anomaly; the narrator apparently used Hebrew for dialogue, here and in the sequel.

L. The Messenger

PT	*BT*
1. - - - [see #3]	1. *They said, "Who will go and inform the Rabbis?"*
2. *So they sent a certain laundry-worker* (קצר)	2. *A certain washerman* (כובס) *said, "I shall go."*

PT	*BT*
3. *to R. Eleazar b. Azariah.*	3. - - - [see #1]
4. *but some say it was R. ʿAqiva.*	4. - - -

In both the story of the excommunication of R. Eliezer b. Hyrcanus[83] and the other recorded public dispute between Gamaliel and Joshua,[84] ʿAqiva plays the messenger. There must have been circles which considered this his characteristic role in Rabbinic politics during his youth. The reference here, however, contradicts other statements in the story, which describe ʿAqiva either as himself a candidate for the presidency (above, sections C and D), or as the ringleader of the rebellious Rabbis (below in BT, sections N and P). It has already been suggested[85] that at least part of the latter is an artificial construction, of negligible historical value, but the former presents a real problem.

G. Alon has observed that Joshua, in his dealings with the Patriarch Gamaliel, can be seen as the heir to Yoḥanan b. Zakkai.[86] When R. Meir, in the next generation, joined a conspiracy against Gamaliel's son,[87] he may well have carried a similar heritage from his own teacher ʿAqiva. In any event, ʿAqiva was no doubt deeply involved in political activity; it need not, therefore, surprise us that various groups, in ʿAqiva's and the following generation, represented him in a manner corresponding to their own political tendencies.[88] If in the eyes of his own supporters ʿAqiva appeared as a disappointed candidate, frustrated by factors beyond his control, Gamaliel's party could well picture him as a disgruntled ringleader trying to hinder reconciliation. How these different perspectives all came into one story is difficult to explain. We must note, however, that all the references to ʿAqiva the peacemaker or to ʿAqiva the recalcitrant (that is, *not* to ʿAqiva the candidate) are in Aramaic; in these texts, this has generally suggested a later, secondary addition to the story.

Both versions of this section are in Aramaic. Probably they are later inventions, designed to integrate better the metaphors of the garment and of the sprinkler into the story as a whole. What the washerman represents, or how he got into both versions, seems a matter for conjecture.[89]

The two versions of the central narrative have differed most significantly in their portrayal of the mass of the Rabbis (see above, pp. 19-20). We find striking evidence of this in the present section. In the PT, R. Gamaliel had to win over all the Rabbis. We therefore now read that "they" (referring back to section J.1) sent the messenger specifically to R. Eleazar b. Azariah, the others having already rejoined Gamaliel. In the BT, however, only Joshua had to be appeased, and only "they" (the two men, Gamaliel and Joshua; cf. section K) sent the messenger; the latter had merely to "inform the Rabbis." Further elaborations of this change appear below, in section P.

M. The Garment

The metaphor of the garment is in Aramaic. It was probably added simply as an artistic "improvement" on an older version of the story. Unlike the image of the sprinkler, this one lays no stress on Gamaliel's parentage. It merely implies that the job was originally Gamaliel's, and that the others had no right to take it away.

N. "Shut the Doors"

This section is inconsistent with the rest of the story. ʿAqiva appears here for the first time as a leader of the other Rabbis. More importantly, this is the only place in the BT where the Rabbis exhibit distrust of Gamaliel beyond that which their zeal for Joshua would seem to demand. Their suspicion that his "servants" may come to enforce his will hints at tyrannical behavior extending beyond the three disputes with Joshua reported in section C.

This section was evidently added to justify the presence of two messages in defense of R. Gamaliel's legitimacy when either of the two would apparently have been sufficient. The easiest way to accomplish this task was to explain why the first had not succeeded. In section M, Joshua sends a message to the study-house. Section N reports its failure, so in section O Joshua personally delivers a second. Section N thus turns redundancy into progression.

O. The Sprinkler

PT	*BT*
1. - - -	1. *R. Joshua said, "I had better go to them myself."*
2. - - -	2. *He came and knocked on the door;*
3. He said to them, "The sprinkler,..."	3. " " "

The text of message is precisely the same in both versions. The BT has merely added an Aramaic introduction to complete the transition from the first message, while the second is itself retained in Hebrew. This confirms the analysis offered above.

P. "Have You Been Appeased?"

PT	*BT*
1. He said to them, "Are you satisfied?	1. R. ʿAqiva said to him, "R. Joshua, have you been appeased?
2. - - -	2. We have done nothing except for your honor.
3. You and I shall wait at R. Gamaliel's door."	3. Tomorrow you and I shall wait at his door."

In addition to the familiar expansions, we see here final evidence for the systematic Babylonian change of structure. In #1, the speaker in PT is Eleazar b. Azariah. He asks the Rabbis, in the *plural*, if they have been satisfied. In the BT, ʿAqiva, acting as spokesman, asks Joshua, in the *singular*, if he has been appeased.

Q. The Settlement

The PT here tells us Eleazar's new title, while the BT instead supplies one detail of the new working arrangement. Either of these details, or both, might be authentic. This text alone, however, permits no firm conclusion. For further discussion, see below, part IV.

J. N. Epstein[90] took the reference to "Sabbaths" in the BT as referring to weeks, not Sabbaths. He claims that the question "Whose Sabbath was it?" means "Which student was on duty that week to serve the Rabbis?" He cites in support b. Pes. 36a, where R. ʿAqiva, alluding to such an arrangement, recalls, "It was my Sabbath."[91] Since the whole exchange in the BT is in any case artificial, it was probably inspired by the question repeated in section R.

R. "Whose Sabbath was It?"

The citation in our text is from the following story in b. Ḥag. 3a:

> Our Rabbis taught: It once happened that R. Yohanan b. Beroqa and R. Eleazar Ḥisma went to call on R. Joshua at Peqiʿin. He said to them, "What novelty did you learn at the study-house today?" They said to him, "We are your disciples, and we drink your water." He said to them, "Just the same, one cannot have a study-house without some novelty. Whose Sabbath was it?"[92]--"It was R. Eleazar b. Azariah's."

This story, with only irrelevant changes, also appears in Tos. Soṭah 7:9 (ed. Zuckermandel, p. 307), and ARN 18:2 (ed. Schechter, p. 67). On the other hand, in three other locations (Mekhilta Pisḥa 16, ed. Horowitz-Rabin, pp. 58-59; y. Ḥag. 1:1 75d; Yalquṭ Jer. #295), we find the following variant:

> Once the disciples spent the Sabbath at Yavneh, while R. Joshua did not. When his disciples came

> to him, he said to them, "What did you do at Yavneh?" They said to him, "After you, Rabbi."[93] He said to them, "And who spent the Sabbath there?"[94] They said to him, "R. Eleazar b. Azariah." He said to them, "Is it possible that R. Eleazar b. Azariah spent the Sabbath there, and he taught you nothing new?"

Again, the three versions are not identical,[95] but they all agree on the crucial detail that the root שבת appears in a verbal, not a nominal form. Now unlike its use as a noun, the *verbal* use of שבת is limited in its reference to the Sabbath day.[96]

IV

Conclusions

In reporting the deposition of R. Gamaliel, neither Talmud offers a simple coherent narrative. Both versions are composite; they expand what may be presumed were earlier versions, and insert, at undetermined moments, entirely extraneous interpolations. Yet the two versions are not independent of one another. The Babylonian recension is clearly based on the Palestinian; cf. especially Joshua's humiliation, Gamaliel's apology, and the materials surrounding the metaphor of the sprinkler.

In parts I and II we discussed the development of each narrative. It was then observed that the Babylonian and the Palestinian interpolations break in at the same point. The basic story can be divided into a "rising" action (dispute-humiliation-deposition) and a "falling" action (apologies-appeal to heredity-reinstatement). The interpolations separate these two. If we now examine the two parts separately we see that the earlier is harsher to R. Gamaliel than the latter. To a great extent, of course, this distinction is inherent in the logic of the narrative as a whole, but we also recall that the initial episode of the story was told separately from the rest. This raises the possibility that circles favorable to R. Gamaliel took over an already circulating story of his deposition, and gave it a conclusion putting the whole incident into the best possible light. If several versions of the deposition-story existed, these same circles may have decided which particular version would thus be taken as the basis for the "complete" story. This hypothesis explains the striking triviality of the dispute over the evening prayer which reportedly led to Gamaliel's removal. It would have been in the interests of Gamaliel's followers to divert attention from whatever more serious matters were involved (see below). Apparently, however, they would not or could not wilfully alter traditions which had already received fixed form, so they chose the least damaging version, and gave it a relatively favorable conclusion.

These narratives show a long history of development. They were not contemporary archival records. They may well have begun from some historical "event," but as we have them now they are full of anachronism (the "Academy," R. Gamaliel's "servants"), legend (R. Eleazar b. Azariah's hair), and inconsistency. Just what role did R. ʿAqiva play? Precisely whom had R. Gamaliel offended?

Earlier scholars, while acknowledging the fragmentary nature of surviving documents, did not question their essential reliability. Their method therefore consisted of gathering as many details as they could, and then synthesizing the data thus collected. L. Ginzberg, for example, thought it useful for determining the duration of the episode to cite the opinion of medical experts stating that a man's hair cannot turn gray in less than several months.[98] In the *Jewish Encyclopedia*, Wilhelm Bacher described the events as follows:[99]

> But Gamaliel manifested the excellence of his character most plainly upon the day on which he harshly attacked Joshua b. Hananiah, in consequence of a new dispute between them, and thereby so aroused the displeasure of the assembly that he was deprived of his position. Instead of retiring in anger, he continued to take part, as a member of the assembly, in the deliberations conducted by the new president, Eleazar b. Azariah.

> He was soon reinstated in office, however, after asking pardon of Joshua, who himself brought about Gamaliel's restoration in the form of a joint presidency, in which Gamaliel and Eleazar shared the honors. (Ber. 27b-28a; y. Ber. 7c,d)

Bacher names the PT, but pays it no attention. The PT does not refer to a "joint presidency" at all. The apology to Joshua is there only one of many. Joshua has no particular part in Gamaliel's reinstatement. All Bacher offers here is a summary of b. Ber., accepted as historically reliable on every point (except, apparently, Eleazar's hair). The problem of the passage in b. Bekh. is not even mentioned.

Taking the whole evidence into consideration, we may conclude that some serious disturbance interrupted the period of Gamaliel's leadership. This conclusion is supported by the fact that the three central characters--the Hillelite Gamaliel, the priest Eleazar, and Yoḥanan b. Zakkai's disciple Joshua--represent three of the major political factions of the early post-Destruction period. It is highly plausible that an intense power-struggle should have revolved around these three men.[100]

It is impossible to identify from these stories the range of issues separating these groups, or specific developments in their relations. Several observations, however, are germane. The Patriarchal regime was just beginning to consolidate its power. The Rabbinic conclave in general must have resented this. At least two rival groups, the priests and Yoḥanan's circle, are likely to have had aspirations of their own. The stakes in the struggle--control over the remnant of Jewish autonomy in Palestine--were large. Gamaliel's ouster must have involved more basic concerns than the trivial events which surviving records report. The men who created the Talmud forgot as much of their own past as they remembered. In consequence, beyond the basic data thus outlined, their stories may not be relied on as historical records.

Nevertheless, the sources do reveal a great deal though not necessarily that which they purport to convey. Much can be learned from them about the men who formed and transmitted them--especially in places such as this where their conscious attention was diverted from themselves--and about the way in which Talmudic narratives developed. The constant appearance of Rabbinic dialectics and folk-wisdom (e.g., the exchange between Eleazar and his wife) no doubt reflects a living ideal of the narrator and his circle. This is how the ideal Rabbi was expected to make a decision. R. Gamaliel's refusal to be deterred from Torah study, and his worry that he might have deterred others, are also certainly offered as examples. There is even an insertion-within-an-insertion, lest Gamaliel's repudiation of hypocrisy seem discredited. Finally, the triad of wealth, wisdom, and ancestry is noteworthy. In a world where a learned *mamzer* could take precedence even over a high priest, should the latter be an ignoramus, a rich Rabbi was still better than a poor one.

NOTES

THE DEPOSITION OF RABBAN GAMALIEL II

[1]There has been some debate over whether Gamaliel's predecessor, R. Yoḥanan b. Zakkai, died in office, retired, or was forced to resign. Cf. J. Neusner, *A Life of R. Yoḥanan b. Zakkai* (2nd ed., Leiden, 1970) p. 225, and the literature cited there, n. 1, chiefly G. Alon, *Meḥqarim beToledot Yisra'el* I [Studies in Jewish History] (Tel Aviv, 1967) 253-73, esp. p. 271.

[2]b. Hor. 13b; cf. J. Neusner, *History of the Jews in Babylonia* I (2nd ed., Leiden, 1969) pp. 79-85.

[3]Lacking in Ta. The connection is with an earlier mention of the halakhic dispute between Gamaliel and Joshua.

[4]Ta.--And he came.

[5]Ta.--But did not (והלא) R. Joshua say.

[6]Lacking in Ta.

[7]Ta.--says.

[8]Ta.--shouted at him.

[9]Ta.--Turgeman.

[10]Text apparently defective.

[11]Ta.--"Say..." They began to speak, and the whole assembly began to rise to their feet. They said...

Alternatively: "Say 'Begin'!" But they said "Begin," and the whole assembly rose to their feet. They said...

The latter alternative makes less sense, but the former, as well as the translation in the text, requires rendering the expression התחיל ל- as "began to..."

[12]Nahum 3:19.

[13]Ta.--They immediately went.

[14]Ta.--than he. Used twice, the phrase is probably a euphemism for "than I."

[15]Lit., on whom.

[16]Ta.--a peg to hang from them.

[17]Ta.--benches of students there.

[18]Ta.--R. Yosi b. R. Bun.

[19]Sections F and G lacking in the PT (= Palestinian Talmud).

[20]M. Zev. 1:3; M. Yad. 3:5, 4:2.

[21]M. Ket. 4:6.

[22]Ta.--came.

[23]Ta.--Do you make your living from these?

[24]Sections M and N lacking in the PT.

[25]Phrase lacking in Ta.

[26]The imagery refers to the ritual of the red heifer, ordained in Numbers 19.

[27]This possibility was first suggested to me by Professor Jacob Neusner in whose graduate seminar this paper was originally read.

[28]We shall see below (part II--Additional Note) that the first scene (section A) apparently circulated independently.

[29]The choice of R. Eleazar b. Azariah is nowhere explained; he just appears. In section J, the Rabbis have not yet come back together, while in section P Eleazar can address them collectively. The PT never explicitly reports that R. Joshua "was appeased," as does the BT (= Babylonian Talmud).

[30]It is of course possible that crucial links were lost in the process of putting things together. But if the redactors were so insensitive as to let them fall out, it may also just not have occurred to a narrator to put them in.

[31]I owe this suggestion to Professor Neusner.

[32]L. Ginzberg hypothesized that there were two steps in adjourning any meeting. After the Meturgeman ended the session, he suggested, the Ḥazzan would pronounce some formula of benediction. See his *Commentary on the Palestinian Talmud* III (New York, 1941) pp. 176-77. This interpretation does explain the presence of both fragments in our text, but there is no evidence to support it. It also assumes the non-existent reading, "He (i.e., Ḥuṣpit) said to R. Zenon..."

[33]Cf. ibid., p. 188.

[34]See above, n. 20.

[35]Section B lacking in the BT.

[36]The citation of the tractate is a later gloss.

[37]These Hebrew phrases had been absorbed into the Aramaic vernacular.

[38]Cf. M. Ber. 1:5.

[39]Section D lacking in the BT.

[40]I.e., to indicate that he had acted correctly.

[41]Deut. 23:4.

[42]Is. 10:13, RSV translation. In the Bible these words are attributed to an unnamed King of Assyria.

[43]Thus Judah is presumably a descendant of one of the other sixty-eight gentile nations.

[44]This Aramaic insertion is a common legal principle in the BT. It is not found in the parallel in M. Yad.

[45]Jer. 49:6.

[46]Amos 9:14.

[47]Cf. M. Yad. 4:4.

[48]Sections H and I lacking in the BT.

[49]Referring to his deposition.

[50]Or "smith." Cf. PT--he was making needles.

[51]See n. 26 above.

[52]The Hebrew phrase is a common legal dictum.

[53]MS. Munich reads "two" Sabbaths, which makes more sense in the present context, but could be a learned correction.

[54]See synopsis below, part III.

[55]'Aqiva's other reported comment, in section N, is not consistent with this new point of view. Since the change is otherwise carried through, it is likely that section N is a later addition, part of an attempt to explain the presence of two different metaphors--in sections

M and O--where either would be sufficient. See synopsis below, part III.

[56]See part IV.

[57]One edition of the PT contained the reference to ʿEduyot (section F.1). Cf. B. Ratner, *Ahawath Zion We-Jeruscholaim* I (Vilna, 1901) p. 104 bottom.

[58]J. N. Epstein has already shown that the interpretation given the expression "on that day" cannot possibly be taken at face value. Cf. his *Prolegomena ad Litteras Tannaiticas* (Jerusalem, 1957) pp. 424-25.

[59]Yad. 4:4.

[60]The Hebrew phrase is a gloss inserted to explain a corrupt Aramaic reading. I have followed the reading suggested in *Shiṭṭah Mequbbeṣet*, as indicated in the margin of the standard Vilna edition (n. 5).

[61]I.e., do we assume that a *ḥaver* would not intentionally cause such an injury, and may now therefore use the animal for his own purposes? The two expressions are italicized because they are technical Hebrew terms; they are not Aramaic.

[62]The translation follows the standard text. It is corrected in the margin to "sat."

[63]This will be corroborated by the synopsis in part III.

[64]It is possible that these were once separate versions of the story of Gamaliel's deposition and that R. Judah the Patriarch adapted for his Mishnah a version stressing Joshua's eventual reconciliation, rather than his earlier defiance. This suggestion, however, requires that we suppose that all such traditions, although mutually contradictory, emerged very soon after the events they purported to recount. Such a hypothesis, furthermore, receives less support from the sources than does our first, and has no greater intrinsic historical probability.

[65]The context in Bekh. concerns a litigant who is forced to tell the truth because independent witnesses would reveal his lie. This is precisely R. Joshua's predicament. If, however, someone had inserted, on the basis of this connection, what he knew to be an excerpt from a longer narrative, he would have included less. The disruption of the Academy is irrelevant to such an interpolator's point.

[66]Of these, #1 represents the standard Babylonian formula תנו רבנן, while #8 reflects merely a textual variant which could accidentally have crept in.

[67]Bekh. has only the revelation, but, as we would expect, its version agrees in all relevant details with b. Ber. as against the PT.

[68]Cf. Ginzberg, *Commentary* III, p. 175. This change occurs even in passages found in both texts. Ours is one such; cf. as well the *aggadah* that the three Patriarchs instituted the three statutory prayers--b. Ber. 26b, y. Ber. 7a-b.

[69]Ibid.

[70]The idea is found in the *'Arukh*. It was adopted by R. Samuel Edels; cf. his commentary, in the standard editions, *ad* Bekh., ad loc. In modern times, the interpretation was accepted by N. I. Weinstein, *Zur Genesis der Agada* (Göttingen, 1901) pp. 168-70, and rejected by W. Bacher in his review of Weinstein in *Revue des Études Juives* 43 (1901) p. 152.

[71]Cf. y. Hor. 3:1 47a.

[72]*Commentary* III, p. 176.

[73]Cf. Ratner, *Ahawath* I, pp. 104-5.

[74]Ginzberg observed (*Commentary* III, p. 180) that all the numbers have the same initial letters in Hebrew. He therefore suggested that they reflect different interpretations of the same acronym. But this presupposes that the story received written form very early, and also fails to explain why all the variant readings are in the PT tradition. The interpretation suggested here seems much simpler.

[75]Cf. b. Hor. 13b.

[76]J. N. Epstein held that Eleazar's elevation took place after his entrance into the Academy (*Prolegomena*, pp. 424-25). His argument seems based primarily on technical distinctions between the terms מנה and הושיב, but such distinctions may well be anachronistic; Ginzberg (*Commentary* III, pp. 190-95) though there was no difference at all between the two terms.

[77]Section H.

[78]That is, the Babylonian insertion may have been made independently of the Palestinian text, and not merely adapted from it.

[79]In the interests of brevity I have omitted texts whenever no synopsis was possible. The reader may find them above, in parts I and II.

[80]Section F.2, n. 58 above.

[81]*Prolegomena*, p. 422, n. 7. Cf. especially the plural suffix ום--. After עדיות was taken to refer to the tractate, the feminine singular נשנית was a natural development. We must otherwise take the form תקנום simply as an inexplicable anomaly.

[82]Cf. the use of חזי in the BT (the PT would more likely have חמי), and כדון and איליך in the PT, both characteristic Palestinian expressions.

[83]y. M.Q. 3:1 81c-d; b. B.M. 58b-59a.

[84]M. R.H. 2:8-9.

[85]Above, n. 55.

[86]Cf. Alon, *Meḥqarim* I, pp. 271-72.

[87]See above, n. 2.

[88]It is worth noting incidentally that a fuller knowledge of these different factions would provide a powerful tool for the *literary* analysis of Talmudic sources.

[89]Note the equally puzzling mention of a laundry-worker in connection with the funeral of R. Judah the Patriarch. Each Talmud uses there the same word which appears here. Cf. y. Kil. 9:4 43b; b. Ket. 103b.

[90]*Prolegomena*, p. 427.

[91]Cf. ibid., n. 62, where Epstein cites as well Tos. Neg. 8:2 and its parallels.

[92]שבת של מי היתה.

[93]Either, "we do not discuss Torah unless you begin," or, "we are your disciples," as in b. Ḥag.

[94]ומי שבת שם.

[95]The translation follows the Mekhilta.

[96]Cf. the dictionaries of Levy and Jastrow, s.v. שבת. Levy inexplicably makes no reference even to the noun שבת = week.

[97]Epstein refers to the version in Mekhilta, but writes as if the noun and verb שבת have the same ranges of meaning. He also says that y. Ḥag. "used" the Tosefta; on at least this point, however, that was apparently not the case.

Further, Mekhilta reads כבר שבתו תלמידים ביבנה ולא שבת שם ר׳ יהושע. But if the weekly shifts were specifically the *disciples'* duty, as Epstein holds, the reference to R. Joshua is altogether inappropriate.

[98] *Commentary* III, p. 181, n. 200.

[99] S.v. Gamaliel II, in vol. 5, p. 560.

[100] Alon already recognized the importance for our story of the fact that Eleazar was a priest. Cf. *Toledot haYehudim be'Ereṣ Yisra'el biTequfat haMishnah vehaTalmud* I [The History of the Jews in Palestine in the Period of the Mishnah and the Talmud] (1967) p. 200.

ṢADOQ THE YAVNEAN

Jack Nathan Lightstone
Concordia University

PART ONE: THE TRADITION

I. Introduction

Ṣadoq may be said to be a minor rabbinic figure in the same sense that the minor prophets have been so designated. The body of traditions about him is extremely small compared to the corpora of traditions of other Yavnean masters, such as Eliezer b. Hyrcanus. There are over two hundred legal traditions of Eliezer b. Hyrcanus;[1] Ṣadoq's legal corpus numbers a little over a dozen traditions. That this represents the sum total of legal issues with which Ṣadoq dealt is highly improbable. Moreover, the criteria for selection which determined the preservation and transmission of the extant traditions are unclear. Hence, for reasons of scarcity of data alone, it is impossible to formulate a complete picture of the man behind the traditions, his attitudes and his concerns.

But these negative factors can be a starting point for other questions. Why is there such a paucity of material about Ṣadoq? Was he peripheral to the circle of tradents representing the "mainstream"? If so, with what circle can we associate the formulation and preservation of his tradition, and what is its relationship to the mainstream? In short, studies of the traditions of such "minor" figures as Ṣadoq are important because they lend themselves to the exploration of a set of questions relevant to our further understanding of the redactional circles responsible for the transmission, formulation, and compilation of the traditions of the *Tannaim*.

In the analysis of the traditions we shall examine the source material from which Ṣadoq's biographical "facts" derive to assess their historical value.[2] For example, notions about his piety are based on an Amoraic tradition in b. Qid. 40a and on a similar story in ARNa 16. Likewise, claims that he was an ascetic and fasted for many years to avert the destruction of Jerusalem are based on b. Giṭ. 56, another late, Amoraic pericope. That he was a priest rests on implications such as those of an Amoraic passage in b. Bek. 36a and on one explicit claim to the effect in ARNa 16. That he must have been an older contemporary of Yoḥanan b. Zakkai arises from details provided by the Amoraic passage in b. Giṭ. 56 and from information offered by a still later midrash in Lam. R. 1:31. Our claims are more modest; it is likely that Ṣadoq was a Pharisee at Yavneh, a contemporary of Joshua, Eliezer and Gamaliel II, and he may have been aligned with the patriarchate of the latter. We can adduce reasons for suggesting that the redactional circle of Gamaliel II was the major locus for the formulation and preservation of Ṣadoq material.

Our study covers all traditions, legal and non-legal, in Mishnah, Tosefta, Tannaitic Midrashim and the Palestinian and Babylonian Talmuds in which the term "R. Ṣadoq" appears. This also includes most of the sources in later midrashic compilations as well as references by Eleazar b. R. Ṣadoq to his "father." Where the reference to "R. Ṣadoq" is suspect on the basis of manuscript evidence or for other reasons, the source has not been included. For example, there are instances where manuscript evidence supports a reading of "R. Eleazar b. R. Ṣadoq" or "R. Isaac" rather than "R. Ṣadoq." As we shall see, a scribal error in which Isaac is rendered Ṣadoq is easily made.

A. Hyman has attached the corpus of traditions about "R. Ṣadoq" to four figures so named.[3] The *Encyclopaedia Judaica* holds that the body of traditions refers to two figures.[4] I can see no reason to so divide the corpus. Such attempts merely are an endeavor to harmonize sources.[5] As we shall see, the evidence does not force the hypothesis (or fabrication) of several Ṣadoqs.

The methods used in this analysis of the traditions concerning Ṣadoq are literary-critical and form-critical. Each source will be examined according to the following agendum: (1) the explication of the issue dealt with in the pericope; (2) the use of literary-critical techniques and the identification of the form in which a tradition has been cast, enabling, where possible, the identification of the units of tradition comprising a source concerning Ṣadoq and a discussion of the way in which the passage took shape; (3) the role of Ṣadoq in the pericope. Relevant parallel versions of a tradition will be compared in an attempt to ascertain the earlier. Since we are dealing with sources which appear in "compilations," I do not automatically assume that the version appearing in the earlier compilation is the earlier version. That conclusion can come only as the result of critical analysis. Such is our task in Part One.

In Part Two we shall be in position to view the corpus of traditions as a whole. Its distribution both over the various compilations and, more importantly, over the various forms will be discussed and interpreted. The legal agendum of the traditions of Ṣadoq will be examined in order to establish what claims concerning the "man behind the traditions" may or may not be put forward.

The order of our sources follows that of the tractates in the Mishnah, as we move through the pericope in Mishnah-Tosefta, the *beraitot* of the Babylonian and Palestinian Talmuds, and the Amoraic materials of the Talmuds respectively. Finally, we shall deal with several sources appearing in later midrashic compilations. Our sources in the Tannaitic Midrashim all appear as parallel versions of material in Mishnah-Tosefta or in *beraitot*; they are not presented as a separate section.

II. Mishnah-Tosefta

(1)

A. Unclean locusts which have been pickled with clean locusts do not render their brine unfit.

B. Testified R. Ṣadoq concerning (ʿL) brine [made] from unclean locusts that (Š) it is clean.

M. Ter. 10:9

Comment: For several reasons, our pericope seems out of place in M. Ter. 10. First, the chapter deals with cases in which *terumah* has in some way flavored common produce, rendering the latter "forbidden" (ʾSWR) to Israelites. M. Ter. 10:8 and 10:9A, on the other hand, deal with brine made from both clean and unclean produce. Second, the use of a "testimony" formulary (B) is found nowhere else either in this tractate or in Seder *Zeraʿim* of Mishnah.

The language of this pericope may explain its appearance in M. Ter. In general, unfit (PSWL) and clean (ṬHWR) are not used as matched opposites in Mishnah-Tosefta. However, when the terms ṬMʾ/ṬHWR and PSWL are used together, *terumah* usually is the object of discussion (see M. Toh. 1:5, 6, 9; 2:3, 4, 6, 7, 8). Perhaps our redactor assumed that A discussed brine intended as *terumah*, and, hence, found a place for it in our tractate. B, on the other hand, betrays no allusion to *terumah*. It appears, then, that A and B reached our redactor as a unit.

However, even if the pericope has reached its present position as a unit, it is in itself not unitary. Ṣadoq's testimony does not attest to A, nor does it depend upon A for a meaningful context. In fact, underlying A and B are contrary opinions. A presents a ruling on an intermediate case in which clean and unclean locusts have been pickled together. It must be assumed that the authors of A's ruling held that brine made entirely of clean locusts is clean. However, what inference may be made concerning their opinion of brine made entirely of unclean locusts? If they shared Ṣadoq's view that such brine is clean, then no motive can be given for their concern with the intermediate case. The need for a ruling in such a situation is understandable only if the authors of A held, contrary to Ṣadoq, that brine made entirely of unclean locusts *was* unclean.

Ṣadoq's opinion seems to have been rather insensitively appended by a previous redactor to an opinion whose authors are in disagreement with Ṣadoq. The relation between the two independent opinions is merely thematic.

A. Testified R. Ṣadoq concerning (ʿL) brine [made] from unclean locusts that (Š) it is clean,

B. for the first mishnah (ŠMŠNH R'ŠWNH) [taught that] unclean locusts which have been pickled with clean locusts do not render their brine unfit.

M. ʿEd. 7:2

Comment: In this pericope the sections of M. Ter. 10:9 have been reversed and joined by what is a unique redactional phrase for Mishnah-Tosefta, ŠMŠNH R'ŠWNH. The phrase MŠNH R'ŠWNH (without the initial Š), although uncommon, is used in a consistent manner where it appears. First, it always separates contradictory opinions. Second, it attests to the authority of the "later" mishnah; it is not a value-free presentation of contrary opinions. In several cases, the redactors represent the "later" mishnah as a deliberate revision of the "first" by a court decision (see M. Ket. 5:3; M. Giṭ. 5:6). Bartinoro (see M. Sanh. 3:4) states that the law is never in accordance with the "first" mishnah. The first mishnah is traditionally held to be the chronologically earlier (see Albeck, *Nashim*, p. 210; *Nezikin*, p. 177).

The effect of the initial Š ("for"), on the other hand, is to claim that the sages' opinion provides support for Ṣadoq's testimony. That this is the redactor's intent is indicated by M. ʿEd. 7:1, 3 and 4 in which Ṣadoq's ruling is in each case supported by the sages' opinions; indeed, in M. ʿEd. 7:1 the redactor used an Š for just this purpose.

In using MŠNH R'ŠWNH, then, our redactor seems to hold that Sadoq's testimony and the sages' opinion are not simply tantamount to one another and that some underlying difference is involved. However, in using Š, he also appears to hold that Ṣadoq's testimony is the logical consequence of the sages' lenient position that the mixed brine of both clean and unclean locusts is clean; hence, the sages' ruling may be called upon to legitimate what to the redactor is Ṣadoq's authoritative reinterpretation of that ruling. Ṣadoq is here represented as standing in the mainstream of tradition and as an authoritative interpreter of that tradition.

What, if any, may be the relationship between M. Ter. 10:9 and M. ʿEd. 7:2? It is unlikely that the redactor of M. Ter. 10:9 could have been familiar with M. ʿEd. 7:2 and still presented A and B as independent, unrelated opinions. Even if this were the case, there does not seem to be any reason for the redactor of M. Ter. 10:9 to reverse the order of the rulings as found in M. ʿEd. 7:2. A reversal of the order of opinions by the redactor of M. ʿEd. is, however, quite reasonable. First, the use of ŠMŠNH R'ŠWNH seems syntactically to require that the "first" mishnah follow the "later" in the order of presentation. Second, since the redactor of M. ʿEd. 7:2 holds that Ṣadoq's view is the authoritative opinion, it is understandable that he would give it the preferential position, placing it first. Lastly, the use of Š would require that the legitimating opinion follow the legitimated ruling. In all probability, then, M. ʿEd. 7:2 is a later formulation of the pericope found in M. Ter. 10:9.

The redactor of M. ʿEd. has chosen to place his collection of Ṣadoq's testimonies with those of other Yavnean figures, notably with those of Joshua and Eliezer. In fact, in M. ʿEd. 7:1, Joshua and Ṣadoq give joint testimony. As we shall have occasion to point out several times, the redactor appears to consider Ṣadoq contemporary with Joshua and Eliezer.

A. Testified R. Ṣadoq concerning (ʿL) brine [made] from unclean locusts that (Š) it is clean,
B. and is permissible for eaters of *terumah*.

Tos. ʿEd. 3:1, ed. Zuckermandel, p. 459, line #11

Comment: Ṣadoq's testimony stands at the beginning of a series of thematically unrelated testimonies given by various figures. However, those testimonies which immediately follow Ṣadoq's are all attributed to Yavnean figures.

B. does not appear with A in M. Ter. 10:9, M. ʿEd. 7:2 or Sifra Shemini 5:10; it is a gloss. "And is permissible for eater of *terumah*" does more than merely provide emphasis for A; it is a substantive addition to the tradition. Without the gloss, one may hold that although the brine of unclean locusts is clean for purposes of normal consumption, it is unclean for eaters of *terumah*. In this pericope, the level of uncleanness of unclean locusts has been fixed at "third-degree" uncleanness.

A. Rabbi says, "*Every winged swarming thing which has four feet is unclean for you* [Lev. 11:23: ŠQṢ]. If it has five [feet], it is clean."
B. *It is detestible* (Lev. 11:23) except for mixtures of it.
C. From here said the sages, "Unclean locusts which have been pickled with clean locusts do not render their brine unfit."
D. Testified R. Ṣadoq concerning (ʿL) brine [made] from unclean locusts that (Š) it is clean.

Sifra Shemini 5:10, ed.
I. H. Weiss, p. 50b

Comment: This pericope terminates a series of discussions concerning those species (locusts among them) *within* the category of winged swarming things which move on four feet, exegeses on Lev. 11:20-23. Rabbi's exegesis of Lev. 11:23 (A) does not deal with distinctions of cleanness within this category. The opinion of the sages (C), however, returns to matters within this first category and in this sense is unrelated to A. The exegesis of Lev. 11:23 (B) in support of the sages' opinion was either known or invented by the redactor and provides the only unifying bond between A and C. However, B fulfills no such function for Ṣadoq's testimony; it provides no support for it. C and D (M. Ter. 10:9) have reached this pericope as a unit. "It is from here that the sages said" glosses C and was added by the author of B.

What, then, is the relationship of the four presentations of Ṣadoq's testimony? It appears that Sifra Shemini 5:10 is later than M. Ter. 10:9 and is dependent upon it. Tos. ʿEd. 3:1 either expanded with its gloss on Ṣadoq's testimony or is based on a different version of it. Since no other attestation to such a variant version has survived, the former is probably the case. It is unlikely that the redactors of either pericope in Mishnah would have eliminated "and is permissible for eaters of *terumah*" had they known of such a version. It is impossible to assert whether Tos. ʿEd. 3:1 is dependent upon any one of the pericopae. The substance of the gloss, the concern with *terumah*, would lead one to suspect that the glossator may have been familiar with at least M. Ter. 10:9.

The major problem is the relationship of M. ʿEd. 7:2 to M. Ter. 10:9 and to Sifra Shemini 5:10. The redactor of the latter, in providing exegetical support for the sages' opinion, appears to present that opinion as the more important. Ṣadoq's testimony is an incidental appendage in this pericope, as it is in M. Ter. 10:9. It is unlikely, therefore, that the redactor was aware of M. ʿEd. 7:2 or of any other tradition which claimed that the sages' opinion had been superseded by Ṣadoq's. Furthermore, as was discussed above, it is equally unlikely that the redactor of M. Ter. 10:9 knew of M. ʿEd. 7:2. It appears, then, that M. ʿEd. 7:2 too is a later reformulation of the pericope in M. Ter. 10.

(2)

A. They pour water over wine-dregs to dilute them; they strain wine through a napkin or Egyptian basket; they put an egg in a mustard strainer;

and (W) they prepare honied wine on the Sabbath.

B. R. Judah says, "[One prepares it] on the Sabbath in a cup, on a Festival-day in a flagon, and during mid-festival in a jar."

C. R. Ṣadoq says, "All depends on the [number of] guests."

M. Shab. 20:2

Comment: The pericope begins with a list of simple statements of law enumerating several operations which may be carried out on the Sabbath in preparing food and drink. The general statements do not indicate whether the preparation must be regulated in any way. Judah's lemma deals with the quantity in which beverages may be prepared on the various kinds of holy days. On the Sabbath, drink may be prepared only a cup at a time as it is required. On days less holy in status, beverages may be prepared in greater quantities without strict regard to preparing exactly what is needed. Ṣadoq's opinion is represented as in dispute with that of Judah. Ṣadoq does not hold that the operative principle is that drink may be prepared a given quantity at a time, the quantity varying with the type of holy day. According to Ṣadoq, only enough for one's needs may be prepared on any holy day. It is a more strict opinion.

B does not depend upon A, although it relies upon A for a meaningful context. In addition, Judah's lemma is not applicable to all the cases of A; his ruling appears to refer only to the preparation of liquids or beverages. It does not seem relevant to the straining of an egg. Lastly, the context of B exceeds that of A; while A concerns itself merely with certain operations permitted on the Sabbath, B introduces the issue of Festivals and mid-festivals above and beyond the issue of the Sabbath. Judah's lemma is not original to this setting. If so, the redactor has imported the lemma in an attempt to deal with more detailed issues about which the general law is silent.

C needs a context for intelligibility, and B supplies an adequate one. There is, however, no internal evidence in C which necessitates its dependence upon B. Furthermore, Judah b. Ilai lived in the middle of the 2nd century, two generations after Ṣadoq. Perhaps B or C has been mistakenly attributed. In any case, it appears that their relationship in this pericope, and hence the dispute, is artificial and the work of the redactor.

(3)

A. They roast the Passover-offering neither on a [metal] spit nor on a grill.

B. Said R. Ṣadoq, "(M'ŚH B) Rabban Gamaliel once said to his slave Ṭabi, 'Go and roast for us the Passover-offering on the grill.'"

C. If it [the Passover-offering] touched the earthenware of the oven, that part must be pared away [from the offering].

D. If some of its [the Passover-offering's] juice dripped on to the earthenware and dripped again on part of the carcass, that part must be removed [from the offering].

E. If some of its [the Passover-offering's] juice dripped on to the flour, a handful [of flour] must be taken from that place.

M. Pes. 7:2

Comment: In accordance with the Biblical injunction of Ex. 12:8, the Passover-offering must be roasted by fire and may not be prepared in any other manner. The opening statement of law (A) maintains that one has not fulfilled the injunction if a metal spit or grill is used, for in this case some of the roasting is done by the hot metal. Ṣadoq cites the behavior of Rabban Gamaliel to legitimize the opposite opinion. C and D are a composite. They follow the opinion of A and extrapolate further, more detailed laws based on the same principle. If a portion of the carcass touches the earthenware of the oven, that portion is considered roasted by the heat of the earthenware and not of the fire. D is a similar extrapolation. Although E replicates the literary form of C and D, it deals with a different issue. In E, the juice of an offering has been rendered unfit by mixture with other produce; it cannot be eaten and must be burnt. It is not integral to the composite.

Since the roasting of the Passover-offering was not carried out after the destruction of the Temple in 70 (Albeck, *Moʿed*, p. 451), the attribution of B to Ṣadoq represents him as a transmitter of pre-70 traditions. The Tannaitic sources are, as we shall see, consistent in representing Ṣadoq both as contemporaneous with Joshua b. Ḥananiah (see M. ʿEd. 7:1) and Eliezer b. Hyrcanus (see M. Ned. 9:1), and as having close ties with the patriarch Gamaliel II (see y. Sanh. 1:4; b. Qid. 32b). Hence, assuming the reliability of the attribution, Gamaliel II probably is the figure referred to in the pericope.

It is noteworthy that the incident (B) has not generated a legal lemma either in Ṣadoq's or Gamaliel's name, as is the case in M. Ber. 1:1. It could have been as follows:

> R. Ṣadoq (or Gamaliel) says, "They roast on a grill."

Why such a generative process does or does not take place as yet cannot be asserted.

It remains to point out that B does not depend upon A. It is quite intelligible on its own, and has been appended to A by a redactor.

(4)

A. (MʿŚH B) Two priests were running neck-and-neck, and ascending the slope [of the altar]. One of them pushed his fellow to within four cubits [of the altar]. He lifted a knife, and drove [it] into his heart.

B. R. Sadoq came, and stood on the stairs of the entrance [Erfurt, First Printing, London: H'WLM; Vienna: H'YLYM], and said, "Hear me our brethren, the house of Israel.

"Behold it says, *If anyone is found slain ...then your elders and judges shall come forth, and they shall measure...* (Deut. 21:1, 2).

"Come and we shall measure. Upon whom is it incumbent to bring the calf--upon the Temple, or upon the [Temple] courts?" They all burst forth after him in weeping.

C. And afterwards, the father of the boy (TYNWQ) came. He said to them, "Our brethren, may I be your atonement ('NY KPRTKM). My son [Erfurt, First Printing, London: BNY; Vienna: BNW] still writhes, and the knife has not been rendered unclean."

D. [This suffices] to teach you that the uncleanness of a knife is more serious to Israel than the shedding of blood.

E. Thus He says, *Moreover Manasheh shed very much innocent blood, till he had filled Jerusalem from one end to the other* (II Kings 21:17).

F. From here they said, "For the iniquity of the shedding of blood the *Shekinah* ascended (N'LYT) [from the Temple], and the Temple was rendered unclean."

Tos. Kip. 1:12, ed. Lieberman, p. 224, lines #55-64 (Tos. Shevu. 1:4; b. Yoma 23a; y. Yoma 2:2)

Comment: The pericope is not unitary. The central event (A) is a scuffle and the resulting murder of one priest by his fellow during a footrace to the altar. Such footraces were the means by which the honor of cleaning the ashes from the altar was allocated (M. Yoma 2:1).

B tells of Ṣadoq who takes up position on the stairway of the Temple entrance and addresses those present.

The content of his sermon is curious given its position following A. The ritual of ʿGLH ʿRWPH (Deut. 21:1, 2), to which he refers, applies only to those cases in which a slain victim has been found in a rural area and the identity of the murderer is unknown. First, in A the identity of the culprit is known. Second, the Temple and Temple courts could never be alternative choices in any case of ʿGLH ʿRWPH (see M. Soṭah 9:2). There is nothing in the content of B which unifies it with A (see Lieberman, *Tos. Kif.: Moʿed*, p. 736; b. Yoma 23b).

The substance of the father's words, in C, are meant to be comforting to whomever he is addressing. The theme is not the murder, but the unclean knife. The father does not address the populace of B; his words would constitute no comfort for them. C refers directly back to A, and the presence of B between them only serves to interrupt an otherwise coherent story.

D is a pithy, concise polemic, and makes a powerful ending to the story of A + C. The criticism of over-concern with the minutia of the cult and ritual coupled with moral laxity is a standard motif in sectarian disputes. The motif appears not only in rabbinic literature, but also in the prophetic condemnation of the cult (see Is. 1:10-17; Amos 5:21-27; Jer. 7:3-15), and the reproof of the Pharisees in the Gospels (see Mt. 15:11; Mk. 7:15; Lk. 11:37-41).

Neither E nor F is integral to the rest of the pericope. They are probably the last additions to the piece. For F, the pericope confronts the enigma of the destruction of God's Temple.

The problem of the pericope, then, is the interpolation of B in the unitary account of A + C + D. It appears that what lies behind the pericope as we have it are two stories, one of which a redactor has eliminated. As a result, B has been left without a context which would render Ṣadoq's words intelligible.

Lieberman (ibid., p. 736) suggests that the Ṣadoq of B is Ṣadoq the Pharisee whom Josephus mentioned

(Antiquities, XVIII:4) as an anti-Roman agitator in league with Judas the Galilean. Ṣadoq's words cannot be construed as an anti-Roman address unless assertion of the moral decadence of the Temple is tantamount to criticism of Roman rule. The motif of the pre-70 masters' admonishing of the priesthood and the superiority of the former over the latter is a typical theme of rabbinic literature dealing with the period prior to the destruction (see Neusner, *Development*, pp. 105, 121, 153). The content of B certainly cannot form a basis for the acceptance of Lieberman's guess, which has nothing to recommend it.

Finally, we may simply remark that this pericope is often included among the evidence adduced for the claim that Ṣadoq was of priestly descent (Lieberman, *Tos. Kif.; Mo'ed*, p. 735).

(5)

A. They eat as a snack both food and drink ('WKLYN WŠWTYN 'R'Y) outside the *sukkah*.

B. (M'ŚH W) They brought cooked food to Rabban Yoḥanan b. Zakkai to taste, and two dates, and a pail of water to Rabban Gamaliel, and they said, "Bring them up to the *sukkah*."

C. And when they gave R. Ṣadoq less than an egg's bulk of food, he took it in a towel and ate it outside the *sukkah* and did not say the Benediction after it.

M. Suk. 2:4d, 5

Comment: In accordance with the Biblical injunction of Lev. 23:42, during the Feast of Tabernacles, one is obliged to "dwell" in the *sukkah*, a temporary booth. This requirement is interpreted as demanding that one sleep and eat one's meals there. Our pericope begins with a simple statement of law that mere snacks are not eaten in the *sukkah*.

Yoḥanan and Gamaliel are represented in B as holding a more strict opinion. According to their behavior, even food which does not constitute a proper meal is eaten in the *sukkah*. Ṣadoq's behavior in C supports the general law of A, the mainline tradition. The details of C stress that the food was not intended as a meal.

B and C are quite independent of A. Furthermore, although B and C are presented by the redactor as one incident, C is neither dependent upon B nor in need of B for an intelligible context. The redactor appears to have joined two narratives. Perhaps he intended that the Ṣadoq incident offset the overly strict view represented in B by Yohanan and Gamaliel.

(6)

A. Said R. Leazar b. R. Ṣadoq, "When I was studying with Yoḥanan b. Haḥoranit, I saw that he ate a dry piece of bread, for they were years of dearth (b. Yev. 15b: BṢWRT).

"I came and told my father; he said to me, 'Bring olives to him.'

"I brought him olives; he took them and looked at them and saw that they were moist. He said, 'I don't eat olives.'

"I came and told my father; he said to me, 'Go say to him: [The jar in which the olives were kept] was broached in accordance with the words of the House of Hillel, but the lees stopped it up [not allowing the liquid to drain].'"

B. [This story serves] to inform you that he ate unconsecrated food in [a state of] purity.

C. For even though he was among the disciples of the House of Shammai, he used to behave only in accordance with the words of the House of Hillel.

Tos. Suk. 2:3, ed. Lieberman, pp. 261-62, lines #16-26 (Tos. ʿEd. 2:2; b. Yev. 15b)

Comment: The issue behind the pericope involves rendering foodstuff susceptible to uncleanness by means of contact with liquid. According to Mishnah's interpretation of Lev. 11:38 (M. Maksh. 1:1), liquids render foodstuffs susceptible to uncleanness only if liquid is intentionally applied to the foodstuff, or, if the liquid has naturally exuded from the food, the presence of the liquid on the food is desired. This latter case concerns us.

According to the House of Hillel (M. ʿEd. 4:6), a jar in which olives are kept must be perforated so as to allow drainage of any liquid; hence one indicates by one's action that any liquid which may exude from the olives is undesired and, therefore, does not render the olives susceptible to uncleanness. The House of Shammai, on the other hand, hold that the jar need not be perforated; no visible indication of one's intentions is required. If the jar had been perforated and subsequently the perforations became clogged, stopping drainage, the House of Hillel hold that the remaining liquid does not render the olives susceptible to uncleanness; because the jar was originally perforated, one's intentions are manifestly clear.

Both Ṣadoq and Yoḥanan, then, behave here in accordance with Hillelite law. Yoḥanan, however, is often represented by the sources as having been a disciple of the House of Shammai (e.g., M. Suk. 2:7; see Neusner, *Pharisees* II, pp. 151-53). Hence, the subscription, C, explicates the obvious inference for anyone familiar with the Houses' dispute on this matter, and with the Shammaite leanings of Yoḥanan; good Shammaites, although in disagreement with the Hillelites, follow the latter's law. It is a "stock" phrase of the Houses' material (ibid., p. 156).

As Neusner points out, B glosses A explicating yet another inference to be made from Eleazar's narrative.

What the pericope leads us to question, however, is Ṣadoq's leanings. Is he represented by the redactor as a second Shammaite in the pericope who acts "in accordance with the words of the House of Hillel"? Eleazar b. R. Ṣadoq is here represented as having studied under a Shammaite; he did so, according to the pericope, with Ṣadoq's knowledge. A, therefore, appears to hold that Ṣadoq *is* a Shammaite. This is the only source in which such a notion surfaces (see Lieberman, *Tos. Kif.: Moʿed*, p. 855).

One last point of note concerns the phrase "in accordance with the words of the House of Hillel" toward the end of A. It states the obvious for anyone familiar with the Houses' dispute of M. ʿEd. 4:6 and is probably a later interpolation into A.

(7)

A. R. Eliezer says, "They open [the way] for a man [to be released from a vow] in regard to (B) the honor due to his father and mother."

B. And the sages forbid it.

C. Said R. Ṣadoq, "Before (ʿD) they open [the way] for him [to be released from a vow] in regard to the honor due to his father and mother, let them open [the way] for him in regard to the honor due to Heaven; if so, there are no [binding] vows."

D. But the sages agree with R. Eliezer as regards a (B) matter between him and his father and mother, that (Š) they open [the way] for him [to be released from a vow] in regard to the honor due to his father and mother.

M. Ned. 9:1

Comment: A sage may release one from a vow provided he is assured that the vow was made under a false presupposition (Albeck, *Nashim*, p. 141). Eliezer (A) presents a rather lenient view of what may constitute such a false presupposition. Albeck (ibid., p. 174) explains that, according to Eliezer, all the sage need ask is whether one would have vowed so rashly had one known that by such behavior one brings discredit upon, and hence dishonors, one's parents. All the sage need receive is a negative answer in order to nullify the vow. The sages dispute the general application of Eliezer's principle, but are represented in D as accepting Eliezer's view if the substance of the vow specifically pertains to one's parents. D, then, compromises the sages' opinion in B. Ṣadoq's remarks constitute a *reductio ad absurdum* of Eliezer's ruling, lending support to B.

As Neusner points out (*Eliezer* I, pp. 185-86), C interrupts the "balance" of the pericope, and is not integral to it. Without Ṣadoq's lemma, we have a common variation of the dispute form (A, B), followed by a compromise on the part of one of the disputants (D). Although Ṣadoq's lemma appears to refer directly to Eliezer's lemma, we may point out that, if a noun were supplied to replace the pronoun "him," C would be as intelligible on its own as A. Alternatively, C glosses A, and perhaps the redactor has meshed two sources, one approximately A, B, D, the other A, C.

In either case, in his *reductio ad absurdum* of Eliezer's ruling, Ṣadoq again is represented by the redactor as in alignment with the sages. Furthermore, Ṣadoq appears contemporaneous with Eliezer. Finally, we may point out that the preoccupation with vows at early Yavneh is strongly attested to both by the Tannaitic sources and by the Gospels, in which precisely this issue of the status of a vow concerning one's relations to one's parents is utilized in the anti-Pharisaic polemic (see Mt. 15:1-6; Mk. 7:5-13). Ṣadoq's involvement with the same issue is an attestation to his strong ties with early Yavneh.

(8)

A. The [seating of the] Sanhedrin was [arranged] like half of a round threshing-floor, so that they would all see each other. The Patriarch would sit in the center, and the elders would sit to his left and right.

B. Said R. Eleazar b. R. Ṣadoq, "When R. Gamaliel was sitting in Yavneh, my father and another (W'ḤR) [sat] at his right, and the elders at his left.

C. "And why did one ('ḤD) sit to the right of the elder [R. Ṣadoq]? Because of the honor of the elder."

Tos. Sanh. 8:1, ed. Zuckermandel, p. 427, lines #9-12

Comment: A redactor has used Eleazar's narrative as a precedent for the anonymous law in A. The story, which is independent of the foregoing, hardly serves the redactor's purposes. B-C makes no mention of the Sanhedrin, and the seating arrangement in the narrative does not locate Gamaliel in the center (Kanter, *Gamaliel*). C spells out the import of one of the details in the story and is not integral to Eleazar's report.

Although we have seen examples of Ṣadoq's ties with Gamaliel, this is the only Tannaitic tradition which actually locates him in Yavneh during Gamaliel's patriarchate. As we shall see, Tos. Nid. 4:3, 4 places Ṣadoq not in Yavneh, but in Ṭib'in in the Galilee, from where he made inquiries of persons at Yavneh. According to the pericope before us, Ṣadoq and a group of "elders" form some official body at Yavneh with Gamaliel as its center figure. In several sources Gamaliel is accompanied by such an entourage of "elders." While B does not explicitly designate Ṣadoq as a member of this group, the question in C does. This is the only instance in which the term is used of Ṣadoq; the question, moreover, is missing in y. Since "elder" is probably a title and not a description of age, the reference provides no information concerning Ṣadoq's age at the time of Gamaliel's patriarchate.

A. The Sanhedrin was like half of a circular threshing-floor. The Patriarch would sit in the middle, so that they would [both] see and hear him.

B. Said R. Leazar b. R. Ṣadoq, "When R. Gamaliel was sitting in Yavneh, my father and his brothers (ʾḤYW) sat on his right, and the elders on his left,

C. "because of the honor of the elder."

y. Sanh. 1:4

Comment: y's parallel is almost identical to the Toseftan version. The introductory question in C of Tosefta does not appear here and is probably an interpolation into the tradition. In y., however, it is not "another" person (ʾḤR) who sits beside Ṣadoq, but Ṣadoq's "brothers" (ʾḤYW). This is the only mention of such a group in the corpus of traditions. Kanter suggests that text in y. is probably faulty.

(9)

A. Three things R. Ṣadoq declares capable of becoming unclean,

B. and the sages declare incapable of becoming unclean.

C. A nail of a money-changer, and a chest of a grist-dealer, and a nail of a sundial--

D. R. Ṣadoq declares [them] capable of becoming unclean,

E. and the sages declare [them] incapable of becoming unclean.

M. ʿEd. 3:8

Comment: Only a metal object which "has a name unto itself" (M. Kel. 11:2), that is which is recognized as serving a specific function of its own, is susceptible to uncleanness. This is the operative issue behind the disagreement concerning the two types of "nails" in the pericope. Ṣadoq holds that the nails do conform to the above specifications and, hence, are susceptible to uncleanness; the sages hold the contrary opinion.

The issue behind the disagreement concerning the grist-dealer's chest is less clear. Rabad, in his commentary suggests that here too we may be dealing with a nail. The object in question is a nail used to secure the chest on a wagon. The issue, then, is comparable to that discussed above. If it is the chest itself with which we are concerned, as the plain sense of C would seem to indicate, Rabad holds the issue is "completion of work." A vessel or utensil is not susceptible to uncleanness until the fashioning of the article is complete. Rabad informs us that such chests usually are placed on wagons so as to be mobile. The sages apparently hold that until the wagon is constructed the work related to the already fashioned chest is incomplete; hence, it is as yet not susceptible to uncleanness (see Tos. Kel. B.M. 5:12). Ṣadoq, then, seems to hold that even without the wagon the chest is complete and, therefore, susceptible to uncleanness. On the other hand, Bertinoro holds that the issue is whether the chest is movable or not, for only movable vessels are susceptible to uncleanness. Regardless of the confusion concerning exactly what issues are involved regarding the chest, it is at least clear that in all three cases Ṣadoq, in contrast to M. Ter. 10:9, holds the more stringent view and the sages the more lenient position.

We may note that A-B and D-E provide the same information. Either A-B or D-E, then, is a later addition to the pericope. If it is A-B which is integral, there appears to be no reasonable motive for the addition of D-E. On the other hand, the addition of A-B to C-E is understandable. M. ʿEd. 3:8 is the second among six pericopae introduced by the formulary "n things Rabbi x...." The addition by the redactor of A-B to an already existing C-E would serve to integrate the pericope into the series of pericopae within which it appears. Furthermore, C-E is in the standard dispute form. C is a superscription followed by two, balanced, opposed rulings (D and E). C-E, then, is a carefully redacted pericope in itself, and probably forms the basic pericope to which a second superscription (A, B), appropriate to the format of M. ʿEd. 3, has been added. If so, the language of A, B has been borrowed from D, E.

As was mentioned above, M. ʿEd. 3:8 is the second in a series of six, similarly introduced pericopae. Dosa b. Harkinas, Joshua, Gamaliel and Eleazar b. Azariah, all Yavneans, are the other prominent figures in the chapter. The redactor appears to consider Ṣadoq their contemporary.

A. The nail of a blood-letter can become unclean.
B. and [the nail] of a sundial cannot become unclean.
C. R. Ṣadoq declares [that it] can become unclean.
D. The nail of a weaver can become unclean,
E. and a chest of a grist-dealer--
F. R. Ṣadoq declares [that it] can become unclean,
G. and the sages declare [that it] cannot become unclean.
H. [If] its [the chest's] wagon was metal, [the wagon] can become unclean.
I. A nail which was adapted to open or shut a lock can become unclean.
J. That [a nail] which was fashioned as a safeguard cannot become unclean.
K. A nail which was adapted to open a jar--
L. R. ʿAqiva declares [that it] can become unclean,
M. and the sages declare [that it] cannot become unclean
N. until it was smelted [anew].
O. A nail of a money-changer cannot become unclean.
P. R. Ṣadoq declares [that it] can become unclean.
Q. Three things R. Ṣadoq declares capable of becoming unclean,
R. and the sages declare incapable of becoming unclean.
S. A nail of a money-changer, and a chest of a grist-dealer, and a nail of a sundial--

T. R. Sadoq declares [them] capable of becoming unclean,

U. and the sages declare [them] incapable of becoming unclean.

M. Kel. 12:4, 5

Comment: With the exception of the grist-dealer's chest and its wagon (E-H), we have in A-P rulings on a list of different types of nails. The issue involved in the susceptibility of such metal objects to uncleanness has been explained above. As in M. ʿEd. 3:8, the reasons for the different rulings are not supplied. The confusion as to what issues are involved regarding the chest also was discussed above. The reason for the uncleanness of the metal wagon in H is rather more obvious (and one may well wonder why it has been explicitly dealt with). Unlike objects of other materials such as wood or leather, even flat, metal vessels or utensils are susceptible to uncleanness (see M. Kel. 11:1).

Three formulary patterns appear in A-P. The first is the designation of the object in question plus "clean" or "unclean" (A, D, I, J). The other two are variations of the dispute form. The first is the designation of the object plus "clean" or "unclean" followed by what appears a gloss giving the contrary view (B-C, O-P). The second is a standard dispute followed by a gloss which compromises, or, in the case of the wagon (H), gives a semblance of compromising the sages' opinion (E-H, K-N).

Q-U is identical to M. ʿEd. 3:8, and reviews those disputes between the sages and Ṣadoq. It is followed both in M. Kel. 12 and in M. ʿEd. 3 by a similar review of four of Gamaliel's disputes with the sages. However, in M. ʿEd. 3, both reviews are preceded and followed by pericopae which are similarly introduced by the formulary "n things Rabbi x...." In fact, it was earlier argued that M. ʿEd. 3:8 had had a second superscription added to it so as to have it conform to the form of the other pericopae in the chapter. Furthermore, unlike Q-U, only one of the disputes between Gamaliel and the sages listed in M. Kel. 12:6 (= M. ʿEd. 3:9) is presented elsewhere in M. Kel. 12. The present formulation of Q-U of M. Kel. 12:5 and M. Kel. 12:6 appears to have been borrowed from M. ʿEd. 3:8, 9 (see Albeck, *Ṭohorot*, p. 60, and Epstein, *Tan.*, pp. 434, 465).

What, then, might be the relation of M. Kel. 12:4, 5 A-P to S-U (= M. ʿEd. 3:8 C-E)? It is noteworthy that the order of the objects listed in S is exactly the reverse of that found in A-P. The probability of such a coincidence of order merely by chance is quite low.

S-U may have provided the basis from which a redactor glossed, or interpolated material into, a "nail-list" which lies behind A-P. The same pericope was known and used by the redactor of M. ʿEd. 3. The revised review of M. ʿEd. 3:8 (with the additional superscription) was then borrowed by some later redactor of M. Kel. 12. This would serve to explain why a grist-dealer's chest and its related wagon came to appear in the middle of a "nail-list." However, the explanation does leave us with one curious question. Why would a single redactor on expanding on a pericope before him use two different variations of the dispute form?

Alternatively, perhaps S-U had originally been abstracted from A-P and subsequently was adapted for M. ʿEd. 3. The review as we have it now in M. Kel. 12 was then "corrected" according to the version in M. ʿEd. 3 by some later hand. However, this leaves the presence of the chest and wagon in the middle of a "nail-list" quite inexplicable. The former solution seems a little less problematic.

(10)

A. Testified R. Joshua and R. Sadoq concerning the redemption [lamb] for the firstling of an ass that died that there is nothing here [Kaufmann, Parma, Lowe: K'N; Naples: BW] for the priest,

B. for (Š) R. Eliezer says, "They are accountable for it (ḤYBYN B'ḤRYWTW) as [in the case of] the five *selas* of a [first-born] son,"

C. and the sages say, "They are not accountable for it [Kaufmann, Parma, Lowe omit 'L'; Naples: 'L'] as [in the case of] the redemption [money] of second tithe."

M. ʿEd. 7:1

Comment: According to the Biblical injunction (see Ex. 13:11-13), all firstborn males of both humans and livestock are "holy." The firstlings of clean animals, if unblemished, were given to the priest to be sacrificed; if the firstling was blemished, the priest could do with the animal as he saw fit. The firstling of an ass was redeemed with a lamb which was then given to the priest; firstborn sons were ransomed with money which likewise was given to the priest. After the destruction of the Temple, animals which before 70 had to be sacrificed were kept until a blemish was contracted (see M. Bek. 4:1ff).

Our pericope discusses a case in which the lamb designated to replace the firstling of an ass has died. We have here, then, a middle case in which only part of the normally required act has been completed. Joshua and Ṣadoq give joint testimony (A) that in such a case the owner's obligation ceases. Eliezer (B) expresses the opposite opinion, holding that the case is analogous to that in which the money for a firstborn son has been lost. The five *selas* must be replaced (see M. Bek. 8:8). Likewise, with the death of the redemption lamb, the owner's obligation is not abrogated. The sages' view supports A, holding that the case in question is similar to that in which the redemption money for second tithe has been lost; no restitution need be made.

The use of "for" (Š) at the outset of B indicates that what is to follow lends support to A. Although C does supply such support, B does not. B-C constitutes a fairly standard dispute, but it lacks a standard superscription. A supplies a context for the dispute, hence, fulfilling the function of such a superscription. Furthermore, as Neusner points out (*Eliezer* I, p. 248), the operative language of A differs from that of B-C. A rules that "there is nothing here for the priest"; B-C disputes whether the owner "is accountable for it." B and C, therefore, appear to be unitary, and distinct from A.

Our pericope presents Ṣadoq as a Yavnean with close ties to Joshua, and as one whose opinions conform to those of the sages, the mainstream of the tradition.

One last point worth mentioning concerns the form of the testimony. The verb (Hʿ YD) is singular, but it is followed by two subjects. Of the seven times this "joint testimony-form" appears in the Mishnah, five involve Joshua as one of the testifiers.

A. He who sets apart the redemption [lamb] for the firstling of an ass and it [the lamb] died--

B. R. Eliezer says, "They are accountable for it as [in the case of] the five *selas* of a [firstborn] son,"

C. and the sages say, "They are not accountable for it as [in the case of] the redemption [money] of Second Tithe."

D. Testified R. Joshua and R. Ṣadoq concerning the redemption [lamb] for the firstling of an ass that died that there is nothing here for the priest.

E. The firstling of an ass died--

F. R. Eliezer says, "It must be buried and [the owner] is permitted the benefit of the lamb [set aside to redeem the firstling],"

G. and the sages say, "It need not be buried and the lamb [set aside to redeem it belongs] to the priest."

M. Bek. 1:6

Comment: In this pericope, A-C form a dispute introduced by a standard superscription. The testimony of Joshua and Ṣadoq lend support to the sages opinion rather than vice versa as in M. ʿEd. 7:1. The dispute between Eliezer and the sages in E-G deals with an issue related to the dispute of A-C. In E-G the lamb has been set aside for the firstling of an ass, but the firstling rather than the lamb has died. As Neusner explains (*Eliezer* I, p. 248), the opinions of Eliezer and the sages in F and G are congruent to their respective opinions in B and C. According to Eliezer, the setting aside of the redemption lamb does not fulfill one's obligation to redeem the firstling. Hence, if the firstling dies before the lamb is given to the priest its carcass is holy; the lamb is not. The opposite view of the sages presented in G also is consistent with their ruling in the first dispute.

The dispute of A-C and the testimony of D are independent. The differences in their operative language have been pointed out in the discussion of M. ʿEd. 7:1. The relationship between A-C and D is entirely thematic. As Neusner claims (ibid.), it appears that D has been interpolated into the pericope.

What, then, may be the relationship between M. ʿEd. 7:1 and this pericope? B and C of M. ʿEd. 7:1 appear dependent upon the dispute of A-C in M. Bek. 1:6. Whether D has been interpolated by some later redactor of M. Bek. 1:6 from M. ʿEd. 7:1, or whether M. ʿEd. 7:1 is dependent upon M. Bek. 1:6 both for the dispute between Eliezer and the sages, and for the joint testimony of Joshua and Ṣadoq cannot be ascertained. The former process has been seen before with regard to the relationship between M. Kel. 12:4, 5 and M. ʿEd. 3:8 (see Epstein, *Tan.*, p. 439).

(11)

A. Testified R. Ṣadoq concerning flowing [water] which exceeded [the amount of] dripping [water] which had mingled with it] that it is fit [as flowing water].

B. [Such] an incident occurred in Birat Hapilya' and the incident came before the sages, and they declared it fit.

M. ʿEd. 7:3

Comment: In many instances the removal of uncleanness involves the immersion of the unclean object or person in water. In the majority of cases immersion in a *miqveh* suffices (see Lev. 11:31, 32). In other instances, such as that of a male who has had a flux, a well or spring (MʿYN) of "living water" is required (see Lev. 15:13). A well or spring effects removal of impurity regardless of the amount of water; a *miqveh*, however, must contain forty *se'ahs* of naturally accumulated water. Flowing water, such as the water of rivers and streams, is regarded as a "living" well or spring; dripping water, such as rain, is considered identical to the water of a *miqveh*, and pools of such water must conform to the specifications of a *miqveh*.

Ṣadoq testifies that the status of flowing water is not affected by dripping water which was mixed with it so long as the amount of the former exceeds that of the latter. B supports Ṣadoq's view, informing us that in just such a case the sages ruled in accordance with A. B does not present the incident itself, but totally relies upon A for a meaningful context.

As in M. ʿEd. 7:1, Ṣadoq's view is legitimated by reference to the sages' opinion.

A. Flowing [water] is like a spring; dripping [water] is like an immersion-pool.

B. Testified R. Ṣadoq concerning flowing [water] which exceeded [the amount of] dripping [water which had mingled with it] that it is fit [as flowing water].

M. Miq. 5:5

Comment: The pericope begins with the general statement of law mentioned in the foregoing comments. B concerns itself with an intermediate case, and has already been discussed.

The testimony is entirely intelligible in itself; the relationship between A and B merely is thematic. Whether Ṣadoq's testimony has been borrowed from M. ʿEd. 7:3 or vice versa cannot be ascertained.

(12)

A. Testified R. Ṣadoq concerning flowing [water] which one made gush forth (QLḤN) through leaves of nuts that it is fit [as flowing water].

B. [Such] an incident occurred in ʾAhalyaʾ, and the incident came before [the sages of] the Chamber of Hewn Stone, and they declared it fit.

M. ʿEd. 7:4

Comment: As above, the concern of this pericope is water which is to be used for purposes of purification where "living" spring-water is required. The specific issue, however, differs from that of M. ʿEd. 7:3. According to Ṣadoq's testimony, the status of flowing water remains unchanged if the flow has been diverted or directed through the foliage of nuts. It is unclear, however, whether the problematic issue is the possibility of the foliage rendering the water unclean (see M. Par. 6:4 and M. Miq. 5:5), or the possibility, by redirecting or interrupting the flow, of changing the status of the water to that of standing or drawn water (see M. Miq. 5:1, 2).

As in M. ʿEd. 7:3, we are informed of a precedent case in which the sages' decision accords with Ṣadoq's view. In this pericope, however, the legitimation is based on a ruling of those who sat in the Chamber of Hewn Stone in the Temple, the "Great Sanhedrin" of pre-70 times. As in M. ʿEd. 7:3, the case itself is not described; without A, B would be unintelligible. In this pericope, as in the three pericopae which precede it in M. ʿEd. 7, accord of Ṣadoq's traditions with those of the authoritative sages is stressed.

(13)

A. R. Ṣadoq says, "Do not make them [the words of Torah] a crown with which to magnify yourself; neither [make them] an axe with which to feed [Kaufmann, Parma, Lowe: L'KL; Naples: LḤPWR] [yourself]."

B. And so Hillel used to say, "*And he who makes* [worldly] *use of the crown* [of Torah] *shall whither away*."

C. Hence [Parma, Lowe: H'; Naples: H' LMDT; Kaufmann missing both] [it may be inferred that] anyone who derives [worldly] benefit from the words of Torah removes his life from the world.

M. Avot 4:5

Comment: As Neusner points out, Hillel's Aramaic lemma of M. Avot 1:13 here appears in the semblance of a gloss of a lemma of Ṣadoq. C serves as a commentary on 3 (Neusner, *Pharisees* I, p. 227). There is, however, no necessary dependence of A, B and C upon one another. C could well be an anonymous lemma in itself. If Ṣadoq's lemma is his own restatement of Hillel's crown-saying, the lemma would probably have been given in the latter's name by Ṣadoq (ibid.). The redactor seems to have brought together three thematically related lemmas, and supplied joining language (see ibid.).

(14)

A. A block [of wood]--the part which is not a handbreadth high cannot become unclean.

B. And the part which is a handbreadth high--

C. R. Meir and R. Simeon declare [that it] can become unclean.

D. R. Yosé and R. Eleazar b. R. Ṣadoq declare [that it] cannot become unclean.

E. Said R. Meir, "(M'ŚH B) A person cut two blocks of date-palm in order to sit on them, and the matter came before the sages, and they declared them capable of becoming unclean."

F. Said R. Simeon, "(M'ŚH B) A person brought a stump (GRWPYT) of olive-wood, which was planed (MŠWPH) like a cupboard, before R. 'Aqiva, and [the person] said to him, 'On this I was sitting.' And he declared it capable of becoming unclean for him. He saw his students astonished. He said to them, 'Why are you astonished? Something more inappropriate [for sitting] (K'WRH) than this did R. Joshua declare capable of becoming unclean.'"

G. Said R. Joshua [should read: R. Yosé?], "(M'ŚH B) Four elders were sitting at R. Eliezer b. Azariah's, the craftsman (ḤRŠ), in Sepphoris: R. Ḥuṣpit and R. Yeshebav and R. Ḥalafta and R. Yoḥanan b. Nuri. And a person brought (pl.) before them the head of a post which was removed with a chisel (RHYṬNY). He said, 'On this I was sitting.' And they declared it incapable of becoming unclean for him."

H. Said R. Eleazar b. R. Ṣadoq, "Heads of posts were on the Temple Mount on which craftsmen would sit and polish stones, and the sages did not suspect them in respect to any uncleanness."

I. And so R. Eleazar b. R. Ṣadoq used to say, "Two blocks were in the house of my father, one capable of becoming unclean, and the other incapable of becoming unclean. I said before my father, On what account is this capable of becoming unclean and the other incapable of becoming unclean?' He said to me, 'This one which is hollowed out is capable of becoming unclean, and the other which is not hollowed out is incapable of becoming unclean. And on it sat Haggai the prophet.'"

J. And all of them, if one did not hollow them out intentionally, are incapable of becoming unclean.

K. If one found them hollowed out and gave thought to them, they receive uncleanness from then on.

L. If a deaf-mute, an insane person or a minor, or a man to whom they do not belong gave thought to them, they cannot become unclean.

Tos. Kel. B.B. 2:1-3, ed. Zuckermandel, pp. 591-92, lines #30-39 and 1-5

Comment: Only objects made in order to serve man, such as benches, chairs and utensils, can be rendered unclean. At issue in the pericope before us is whether or not a flat block of wood which is high enough to serve as a seat (i.e., one handbreadth) may be said to be a bench and, hence, susceptible to *midras*-uncleanness (Neusner, *A History of the Mishnaic Law of Purities*: *Kelim*, Part Two, pp. 208-10). The authorities of C hold that it is. In the opinion of Yosé and Eleazar, however, the block is not a sufficiently processed object (ibid.), even though it may serve the desired function.

In I Eleazar supports his view with a reminiscence of Ṣadoq's opinion. Only after the block has been hollowed will it be susceptible to *midras*-uncleanness. The last clause of the narrative lends support to Ṣadoq's ruling. Haggai had no reason to suspect that the flat block might be unclean. This improbable historical claim could be a gloss.

The fact that only Eleazar cites two precedents in support of his view suggests that either H or I is not integral to the pericope. Since the attributive language at the outset of I differs from that of E-H, I am inclined to hold that it is this second narrative of Eleazar which is the later addition. I provides the occasion for the clarifications of J-L. But "them" of these concluding sections cannot merely refer to the single, hollowed block in I. I-J appear to assume the entire construction before us.

The literary character of Eleazar's reminiscence of Ṣadoq is similar to that of Tos. Suk. 2:3. In both narratives Eleazar recounts dialogues he had with his father. Furthermore, in both Ṣadoq exhibits a similar attitude to intention. In Tos. Suk., Ṣadoq holds that simply not desiring the presence of a liquid on food will not prevent that liquid from rendering the food susceptible to uncleanness. Some action is also required (e.g., the perforation of the container of the food in order to facilitate drainage). In the pericope before us, it is Ṣadoq's view that intention alone will not make a flat block of wood into an object processed for a specific function and, hence, make the block susceptible to *midras*-uncleanness.

(15)

A. Said R. Eleazar b. R. Ṣadoq, "Two cases (M'ŚYM) my father brought from Ṭib'in to Yavneh."

B. (M'ŚH B) A woman was discharging (MPLT) [what looked] like red scales, and they came and inquired of R. Ṣadoq, and R. Ṣadoq went and inquired of the sages, and the sages sent and called for the physicians, and [the physicians] said, "There is a wound within her; therefore she discharges [what looks] like red scales."

C. (ŠWB M'SH B) [Another] woman was discharging [what looked] like red hairs, and they came and inquired of R. Ṣadoq, and R. Ṣadoq went

> and inquired of the sages, and the sages sent and called for the physicians, and [the physicians] said, "There is a mole in her belly; therefore she discharges red hairs."
>
> Tos. Nid. 4:3, 4, ed. Zuckermandel, p. 644, lines #16-22

Comment: A woman who has an issue of menstrual blood from her womb, whether during her regular menstrual period or not, is unclean (see M. Nid. 8:2, 3). In addition, a woman who gives birth, or miscarries a foetus with human features, becomes unclean, the duration of her uncleanness depending upon the sex of the child or foetus. Cases which present a problem are those in which something appears to have been miscarried, but the object bears no resemblance to a foetus (see M. Nid. 3:1ff). The woman is not considered to have given birth. However, if the object can be shown to be coagulated menses, she is unclean. Otherwise she remains clean.

The two incidents involving Ṣadoq each deal with a problem case of the aforementioned type. It appears that the incidents' purpose is to show, on the strength of the opinion of the physicians, that objects which resemble red scales or red hairs which issue from a woman's genitals can be quite unrelated either to the miscarriage of a foetus or to menstrual blood. We are not informed of the legal significance of the incidents.

B and C are not dependent upon A. In A, Eleazar simply states that Ṣadoq twice consulted the Yavneans concerning cases in Ṭib'in. No indication as to the issues involved is provided. B and C are the same story; only the differences in detail (which are quite minor) make B and C two separate cases. Neither case, however, mentions that Ṣadoq or the women involved were from Ṭib'in, or that the sages or physicians involved were from Yavneh. No attempt has been made to make B and C appear as part of Eleazar's lemma. In all probability B and C are primary while A is a later addition.

In both B and C Ṣadoq is represented as recognizing the authority of the sages, who in turn base their opinions on sound professional advice when their own scientific knowledge is inadequate. Eleazar's lemma likewise appears to claim that Ṣadoq recognized the Yavneans' authority.

In A, we have the first mention of a geographical location with which Ṣadoq had some relation. Ṭibʿin is a Galilean town west of Sepphoris.

A. WHTNYH: Said R. Eleazar b. Ṣadoq, "Two cases (MʿŚYM) my father brought from Ṭibʿin up to Yavneh.

B. "(MʿŚH B) A woman was discharging (MPLṬ) [what looked] like red scales, and they came and inquired of my father, and my father inquired of the sages, and the sages inquired of the physicians, and [the physicians] said to them, 'This woman has a wound within her belly from which she discharges [what looks] like red scales. Throw [the scales] into water; if they dissolve, [she is] unclean.'

C. "(WŠWB MʿŚH B) [Another] woman was discharging [what looked] like red hairs, and she came and inquired of my father, and my father inquired of the sages, and the sages of the physicians, and [the physicians] said to them, 'She has a mole within her belly from which she discharges [what looks] like red hairs. Throw [the hairs] into water; if they dissolve, [she is] unclean.'"

b. Nid. 22b

Comment: In b. Nid. 22b the entire pericope appears as the words of Eleazar b. R. Ṣadoq. However, A, B and C are no more unitary here than in Tos. Nid. 4:3, 4. The effect is only achieved by reading "my father" for "R. Ṣadoq."

The physicians' words in both B and C have been supplemented. There is, however, an incongruity between their diagnosis and their legal ruling. According to their diagnosis, the scale-like and hair-like objects are neither coagulated menstrual blood nor miscarried foeti, but the result of other internal conditions. The physicians then rule that the objects are to be put in water in order to see if they dissolve. If they do, the woman is unclean. According to M. Nid. 3:2, this is the sages' method of determining whether such objects are coagulated blood. The addition to the physicians' words not only turns them into legal authorities, but also decisively changes the law; an issue of blood known to be blood other than menses now renders unclean. The language of the addition in B and C is identical to that of the ruling in M. Nid. 3:2, and has probably been interpolated from there.

The Toseftan version of the pericope forms the basis for that of b. Nid. 22b. It is unlikely that the redactor of Tos. Nid. 4:3, 4 knowing a version of the pericope in which A, B and C were all attributed directly to Eleazar b. R. Sadoq would then only attribute A to Eleazar.

III. Other Traditions

A. Tannaitic Traditions in the *Gemarot*

(1)

A. MYTYBY: (M'ŚH B) R. Eliezer and R. Joshua and R. Ṣadoq were reclining at the wedding-feast of the son of R. Gamaliel, and R. Gamaliel *Beribbi* [BRBY: Munich] was standing and serving drink to them. He gave the cup to R. Eliezer and [R. Eliezer] did not take it. He gave it to R. Joshua and [R. Joshua] accepted it.

B. Said to him R. Eliezer, "What is this Joshua? We sit and R. Gamaliel *Beribbi* [BRBY: Munich] stands and serves drink to us?"

C. [R. Joshua] said to him, "We have found [one] greater than he who waited [ʾBRHM GDWL MMNW WŠMŠ: missing in Munich] Abraham was the greatest of the generation, and it is written concerning him: *And he stood over them* (Gen. 18:8). And lest you say, 'As ministering angels they appeared to him,' they appeared to him only as Arabs. And [as regards] ourselves should not R. Gamaliel *Beribbi* [BRBY: Munich] be standing and serving drink to us?"

D. Said to them R. Ṣadoq, "How long [will] you ignore the honor of Heaven while (W) you deal with the honor of creatures. The Holy One blessed be He causes the winds to blow, and clouds [ʿNNYM: Sifré Deut. 38] to ascend, and rain to descend, and the earth to blossom, and prepares a table before every single one. And [as regards] ourselves, should not R. Gamaliel *Beribbi* [BRBY: Munich] be standing and serving drink to us?"

b. Qid. 32b (Sifré Deut. 38; M. T. Deut. 11:10)

Comment: I have noted in the above text a variant (and preferable) reading from Sifré Deut. 38 (ed. Finkelstein).

The pericope presents two homilies on hospitality serving to interpret and legitimate Gamaliel's behavior toward the rabbis. Joshua (C) compares Gamaliel's behavior to that of Abraham. Abraham saw it his obligation to wait upon what appeared to him to be Arabs. Given Abraham's example, it is certainly fitting if not obligatory that Gamaliel, lesser than Abraham, serve distinguished sages, far greater than Arabs.

Ṣadoq (D) criticizes Joshua for his lack of piety, and appears the more saintly of the two. He holds that the wrong paradigm has been chosen to interpret Gamaliel's behavior. The analogy for Ṣadoq is God who out of grace sees to the needs of his creatures. For Ṣadoq, the

Patriarch's behavior toward the rabbis is comparable to God's grace. Such an identification would seem to aggrandize Gamaliel.

Eliezer in this pericope merely provides an occasion for the homilies of Ṣadoq and Joshua (*Eliezer* I, p. 407).

Were it not for the mention of Ṣadoq in A, the pericope could well end with C. Eliezer admonishes Joshua for permitting himself to be waited upon by the Patriarch, and Joshua proves that the behavior is quite fitting. To this limited end, justifying Gamaliel's behavior, Ṣadoq's additional homily adds little to Joshua's remarks. In all probability, D along with the interpolation of Ṣadoq's name into A are later additions to the pericope (ibid.).

Nevertheless, as we have argued, Ṣadoq's homily is not entirely redundant; it conveys a distinct shift in emphasis. The *obligation* of hospitality appears the theme of Joshua's homily; the Patriarch is not so far above the sages in status that hospitality toward the latter is not incumbent upon Gamaliel. The theme of D is grace. The Patriarch is to the rabbis as God is to the creatures. C's attitude to Gamaliel at best is neutral; D's is rather positive. I would suggest that some pro-patriarchate redactor thought that C presented Joshua in too positive a light while leaving the status of Gamaliel, the Patriarch, somewhat in doubt; corrective measures were then taken.

Assuming the above is correct, we may ask: Why was Ṣadoq chosen to support the Patriarch thus? Ṣadoq appears a figure to which both ʿAqivan and patriarchal redactional circles lay claim. On one hand, we have seen sources which represent Ṣadoq as having close ties with Joshua (M. ʿEd. 7:1; M. Bek. 1:6) and the circle of sages (M. ʿEd. 7:1, 2, 3, 4). Other sources have related him to Gamaliel (M. Suk. 2:5; M. Pes. 7:2). He is, therefore, a likely candidate for a pericope where both factions appear. Moreover, we shall see traditions which represent Ṣadoq as a strong supporter of Gamaliel's patriarchate (b. Bek. 36a; y. Sanh. 1:4). An aggrandizement of Gamaliel would, therefore, not seem atypical of him.

The tension, then, between the patriarchate faction (here represented by Ṣadoq) and the circle of the sages (for which Joshua speaks) is redactional; therefore, this is only an instance of a rather pervading tension between these factions on a redactional level in Tannaitic materials (primarily in the Mishnah). It is not a phenomenon unique to Ṣadoq's traditions. Hence, the historical value of the details of this pericope to a biography of Ṣadoq is rather slight. Nevertheless, the choosing of Ṣadoq by the redactor of the pericope suggests a strong tie between Ṣadoq and pro-Gamaliel redactional circles. On the other hand, it implicitly admits to a relation of Ṣadoq traditions with redactors of Joshua's material as well. Perhaps some type of historical alignment of Ṣadoq with the patriarchate of Gamaliel II explains, in part, the paucity of Ṣadoq's traditions preserved in the literature deriving from the ʿAqivan redactors.

Our last point concerns the term *Beribbi*. That it is honorific appears clear. However, as D. Goodblatt points out to Neusner (ibid., p. 409), there is a disagreement as to the actual meaning of the term. Jastrow (*Dict.*, p. 189) remarks that the term is usually applied to disciples of Judah the Patriarch, but is sometimes extended to his predecessors. It might, therefore, be a third century interpolation into the pericope.

A. This matter expounded R. Isaac and said:

B. When R. Gamaliel made a banquet for the sages, all the sages of Israel were reclining by him. R. Gamaliel stood and waited upon them.

C. Said the sages, "It is not right [ʾYNW BDYN: Oxford, Munich, Wien] that he wait upon us."

D. Said to them R. Joshua, "Leave him that he may wait [upon us], for we have found that [one] greater than R. Gamaliel waited upon the creatures.

E. They said to him, "Who is it?"

F. He said to them, "[It is] Abraham our father the greatest of the world who waited upon the ministering angels, and thought regarding them that they were Arabian men [and] worshipers of idols. [Concerning] R. Gamaliel who will wait upon sages, sons [BNY: Wien] of Torah, how much the more so [is such behavior fitting]."

G. Said to them R. Ṣadoq, "Leave him that he may wait [upon us]. We have found [one] greater than R. Gamaliel and [greater] than Abraham who waited upon the creatures."

H. They said to him, "Who is it?"

I. He said to them, "The Holy One blessed be He [foregoing according to Oxford]. He gives to every single one [according to] his needs, and to every single creature according to its lack [foregoing according to Oxford, Munich]--and not to fit men and [to] the righteous only, but even [to] the wicked, worshippers of idols. [Concerning] R. Gamaliel, how much the more so [it is fitting] that he will wait upon sages, and sons of Torah."

Mekh. Ish.: Amaleq, eds., Horovitz, Rabin, pp. 195, 196

Comment: Essentially we have in this pericope the same homilies and story as in b. Qid. 32b. Here the entire story is attributed to R. Isaac, an Ushan *Tanna* originally from Babylonia. There are, however, a few noteworthy differences between this pericope and the *beraita*. The feast is now for the sages, and the major issue is whether it is proper that Gamaliel serve "the sages, sons of Torah." Joshua's apparently disrespectful behavior is not mentioned. It is the sages, not Eliezer, who provide the occasion for the homilies and additional leading questions (E, H). Finally, the homilies of Joshua and Sadoq serve a rather different end than that in b. Qid. 32b. Here they are not only homilies on hospitality, but also, and primarily, homilies arguing that the "sages, the sons of Torah," are the most worthy of men. If any group or person emerges in favorable light in this pericope, it is the circle of the sages.

Although on the whole this pericope seems to be an expansion and adaptation of a pericope very much like b. Qid. 32b, it does not appear directly dependent upon the latter. The sages' leading questions, as we have noted, expand the pericope; the statement "Leave him...wait" has been added to both Joshua's and Ṣadoq's sayings (D, G). In Joshua's homily the detail concerning the idolatry of the Arabs has been added, and in Ṣadoq's homily God's grace to men has been drawn out. On the other hand, Joshua's quotation of scripture in the *beraita* is missing in this pericope, and Ṣadoq's remarks concerning the "honor of Heaven" are also absent. What is particularly noteworthy, then, is that we have a skeletal theme, Gamaliel's hospitality at a banquet, which has produced two stories making essentially different points.

If the attribution to R. Isaac is accurate, both pericopae may depend upon some common source dating at least from Ushan times.

A. This matter expounded R. Ṣadoq:

B. When R. Gamaliel was standing and waiting [upon the sages],

C. they said, "Is it right that we are reclining and R. Gamaliel stands and waits upon us?"

D. Said to them R. Joshua, "We found [one] greater than R. Gamaliel who stood and waited [upon others]."

E. They said to him, "And who is it?"

F. [R. Joshua] said to them, "Abraham (ʾBRHM BPYNH) the greatest of the generation, as it is said: *and he stood over them* (Gen 18:8).

And [they were] not fit men, but men who worship idols and provoke Heaven to anger (MK'YSYN LPNY HMQWM). How much the more so [is such behavior fitting] for R. Gamaliel who stands and waits before men [who are] fit and engage in Torah."

G. Said to them R. Ṣadoq, "We found [one] greater than Abraham and [greater] than R. Gamaliel who stands and waits [upon others].

H. They said to him, "Who is it?"

I. [R. Ṣadoq] said to them, "The God of Heaven blessed be He who gives to every single one [according to] his needs, and to every single creature according to its lack, as it is said: *He gives food to all flesh* (Ps. 136:25). And [Scripture] says: *He gives to the animal its food* (Ps. 146:9). And [thus He acts toward] not [only] fit men, but men [who] worship idols and provoke His anger (MK'YSYN LPNYW). How much the more so [is such behavior fitting] for R. Gamaliel who stands and waits before men [who are] fit and engage in Torah."

Mekh. Sim.: Yitro, ed., Epstein, pp. 131, 132

Comment: The formal structure of this pericope is identical to that of Mekh. Ish. The story is now attributed directly to Ṣadoq. It seems rather odd to attribute a story to one of the persons quoted within it by name and in the third person. Since in a manuscript the dropping of the initial Y in "Isaac" would make the name look very much like "Ṣadoq," it appears that the attribution of the story to Ṣadoq is a scribal error.

B seems to be an elliptic version of B in the previous pericope. The opening remarks of Joshua and Ṣadoq in Mekh. Ish. ("Leave...wait") are absent here. The homilies themselves, however, have been expanded upon, and have been provided with scriptural verses. This pericope, then, appears to be a later development of that in Mekh. Ish.

(2)

A. TNW RBNN: At first (BR'ŠWNH) they used to say, "[If] the woman reaches orgasm (MZR'T) first, she gives birth to a male. [If] the man reaches orgasm first, she gives birth to a female."

B. And the sages did not explain the matter [from scripture] until R. Ṣadoq came and explained it.

C. *These are the sons of Leah whom she bore to Jacob in Paddan Aram, with Dinah his daughter* (Gen 46:15).

D. [Scripture] assigned the males to the females, and the females to the males.

b. Nid. 31a

Comment: Here Ṣadoq's talent as an exegete is stressed. Ṣadoq manages to find scriptural support for some contemporary medical "knowledge" (A); the sages, on the other hand, had been unable to do so. The exegesis is based on the observation that the verse represents Jacob's sons as belonging to Leah, while Dinah is "his daughter." This is taken to mean that males were born when she had her orgasm first, females when his preceded hers.

The lemma in A could well be a folk maxim which predates the pericope. It is noteworthy that C and D are not represented as the direct words of Ṣadoq. If the redactor knew them to be so, he would probably have presented them as a lemma in his name. Perhaps C and D are later additions, the original exegesis of Ṣadoq having been forgotten. Furthermore, D only explicates the message of the verse. It could be a gloss in itself.

B. Amoraic Traditions in the *Gemarot* and Some Other Traditions in Later Compilations

(1)

A. [During the siege of Jerusalem, Martha the daughter of Boethius, among the richest women in the city, sent her man-servant to buy flour; he was, however, unable to buy her even the coarsest grain.]

B. She removed [her] shoes, [but] she said, "I will go out and see if I can find anything to eat."

C. Dung stuck to her foot, and she died.

D. R. Yoḥanan b. Zakkai applied to her (QRY ʿLH) [this verse]: *The most tender and delicate woman among you who would not venture* [*to set*] *the sole of her foot* [*upon the ground*...] (Deut. 28:56).

E. Some say [that] she ate a dried fig of R. Ṣadoq, and she took sick and died,

F. 1. for (D) R. Ṣadoq sat forty years in fast that Jerusalem might not be destroyed. [He became so thin that] when he used to eat anything, [the food] could be seen from the outside [as it passed down his throat]

2. When they wished to refresh him (HWH BRYH), they used to bring him dried figs. He sucked the juice from them and threw them away.

G. When [Martha] was about to die (NYḤH NPŠH), she brought out all her gold and silver [and] threw it in the marketplace. She said, "What need have I of this?..."

H. [Yoḥanan b. Zakkai escapes from the sieged city of Jerusalem and wins Vespasian's favor by predicting his appointment to the throne.]

I. [Vespasian] said to him, "I am about to go, and I will send another man [to take my place], but ask something of me that I may give [it] to you."

J. 1. [R. Yoḥanan b. Zakkai] said to him, "*Give me Yavneh and its sages,*

2. "and the chain of R. Gamaliel,

3. "and physicians to heal R. Ṣadoq."

K. R. Joseph applied [this verse] to him [i.e., Yoḥanan], and some say [that it was] R. ʿAqiva: [God] *turneth wise men backward and maketh their knowledge foolish* (Is. 44:25).

L. [Yoḥanan] should have told him [i.e., Vespasian] to leave them this time,

M. but [Yoḥanan] thought [that] perhaps all this [Vespasian] would not do, and [as a result] even this little amount of relief (HṢLH) he would not possess.

N. Physicians to heal R. Ṣadoq--How was it accomplished (M'Y HY')?

O. The first day they gave him water with bran [in it] to drink; the next day, water with meal [in it]; the next day, water with flour [in it]; until his belly expanded little by little.

b. Giṭ. 56a, b

Comment: The above is excerpted from a collection of loosely redacted materials dealing with the events preceding the siege of Jerusalem, the affects of the siege, Yoḥanan b. Zakkai's escape from the city, and the subsequent fall of Jerusalem to the Romans. Our excerpt is in Aramaic with the exception of those sections in italics which are in Hebrew. Ṣadoq is mentioned or dealt with only in E, F, J3, N and O.

F informs us of Ṣadoq's forty-year fast and of the method by which Ṣadoq was fed when he had to be revived. The section represents a marked digression in what is otherwise a collection of Martha-traditions, and is an interpolation. Only E provides a link between F and its setting. However, E itself appears appended to the preceding story. In fact, E begins with rather typical Amoraic joining language. Perhaps E has provided the occasion for the interpolation of F. More likely, E comes from the interpolator himself, and is part of his attempt to insert Ṣadoq material into the collection.

O offers information very much like that of F2. It relates how Ṣadoq was fed. Only the context makes O the method by which Ṣadoq was treated by the Roman physicians. O and F2 *may* be different versions of the same tradition, each version having been used in a different context.

The context for O is provided by N, which commences with what seems a direct quotation of J3, and then asks the question, M'Y HY'. N, like the beginning of E, is rather typical Amoraic joining language, and again could be part of a redactor's attempt at slipping Ṣadoq's material into the larger collection.

The only remaining section in which Ṣadoq is mentioned is J3. However, Yoḥanan's lemma (J) begins in Hebrew (J1) and then abruptly switches to Aramaic (J2, J3). It seems unlikely that a unitary lemma would exhibit such a trait. In my opinion, J1, 2 and 3 have been joined by a redactor; Yoḥanan's reference to Ṣadoq, then, most likely is not integral to the lemma at all.

To summarize our comments to this point, we see that a stratum of Ṣadoq material has been "woven into" this collection of Jerusalem stories by some redactor or group of redactors. We have as yet proposed no date either for the addition of Ṣadoq materials or for the larger collection.

In regard to the latter concern, it is unlikely that K (whether attributable to Joseph or ʿAqiva), L and M are of much value in dating J in its entirety, or in dating *any* of its component parts. K is not dependent upon J or any of its components; furthermore, in substance it need not refer to J at all. L and M, on the other hand, substantively do refer to J. However, L and M are not integral to K and, therefore, cannot be attributed to Joseph or ʿAqiva. In fact, K appears elsewhere (top of b. Giṭ. 56b), in a different context and followed by a different explication of the meaning of the verse. L and M, therefore, have been generated by K's placement in this particular context. In short, I do not think we can postulate a date earlier than the fourth century for the pericope.

Finally, the image of Ṣadoq presented throughout the pericope is that of a "holy man" and ascetic. The detail of "forty years" in F is, however, worthy of note. Taken at face value this detail would make Ṣadoq a contemporary (or older contemporary) of Yoḥanan b. Zakkai. One would surmise that he was between sixty and seventy years of age at the time of the destruction, and that he must have died soon thereafter. The pericopae which we have seen to this point are rather consistent in representing Ṣadoq as having strong ties with the patriarchate of Gamaliel II, and as being a contemporary of Joshua and Eliezer. In fact, he appears to have survived Yohanan b. Zakkai. Only this detail in F represents him as possibly being much older. Finally, we may attribute the use of the number forty to its mythic significance both in the biblical and Rabbinic traditions. Among other things, it appears to represent the notion of "a generation's time" or simply "a significant part of one's life." Good kings reign for forty years (e.g., I Kings 1:11), and exceptional figures live for three times forty years, involved in a different state of affairs in each of the forty-year-periods (e.g., Sifré Deut. #357, ed. Finkelstein, p. 429). In short, F appears a late tradition of little or no biographical significance.

A. When Vespasian was about ('T') to conquer the city [of Jerusalem], he said to R. Yoḥanan b. Zakkai, "Make a request, and I will perform [it]."

B. [Yoḥanan] said to him, "I demand of you--spare the city and leave."

C. [Vespasian] said to him, "*All the sons of Rome themselves made me king only by reason of the dealings with this city*, and you say to me, 'Spare the city,' and I will leave?"

D. [Yoḥanan] said to him, "And if that be so, I demand of you--leave the western gate which leads to Lydda open for three hours. Whatsoever passes through [the gate] and emerges from it do not kill."

E. When Vespasian was about to ('T') conquer it [i.e., Jerusalem], [Vespasian] said to him [i.e., Yoḥanan], "If you have any relative [in Jerusalem], send and bring [him] out."

F. [Yohanan] sent and brought out all the rabbis.

G. He searched for R. Ṣadoq and his son, and he did not find them. He sent for R. Eliezer and R. Joshua to bring out R. Ṣadoq and his son. They labored and toiled in the city for three days, and they did not find them. After the third day, they found him at one of the gates of the city.

H. They brought him before R. Yoḥanan b. Zakkai. As soon as [Yoḥanan] saw him he stood on his feet. Said to him Vespasian, "Before this emaciated man you stand on your feet?"

I. [Yoḥanan] said to him, "Had there been in the city another like him, you would not have ever been able to capture it."

J. [Vespasian] said to him, "What is his strength?"

K. [Yoḥanan] said to him, "For he eats a bean-size piece of bread (PT PWL) and on it he teaches one hundred lessons."

L. [Vespasian] said to him, "Why is he so thin?"

M. [Yoḥanan] said to him, "From his fasts and abstinences."

N. [Vespasian] sent and brought physicians. He said to them, "Restore his health (GWPYH) to him." And they fed him little by little until his strength (NŠMTW) returned to him.

O. *Said to him* [i.e., Ṣadoq] *R. Eliezer his son, "Father, give the physicians their reward so that they may not have a portion in the world to come."*

P. And he gave them weigh-scales, and that calculation by fingers.

Q. *Said R. Eleazar b. R. Ṣadoq, "May I see comfort--Although father lived all those years after the Temple was destroyed, he did not regain the health of those former years* (L' ḤZR GWPW 'LYW KMWT 'WTM HŠNYM ŠHYH).

R. [This is] *to fulfill that which is said* [in Scripture]: *Their skin has shriveled upon their bones; it has become dry as wood* (Lam. 4:8).

Lam. R. 1:31, ed. Buber,
pp. 68, 69

Comment: As was the case with b. Giṭ. 56, this pericope is excerpted from a collection of materials dealing with the siege of Jerusalem, the escape of Yoḥanan b. Zakkai and Vespasian. Our pericope is mostly in Aramaic with the exception of the sections in italics and the quotation of scripture (R) which are in Hebrew.

The pericope appears to present two versions of Vespasian's granting of a request to Yoḥanan (A-D and E-N). In the first, the substance of the criticism of K, L and M of b. Giṭ. 56 has been incorporated into the story. However, the language of the request in B of Lam. R. differs from that of J in b. Giṭ. 56. Moreover, Lam. R. knows nothing of Yoḥanan's requests regarding Yavneh, the "chain of R. Gamaliel," or Ṣadoq. Thus, although the adjustment of Lam. R. in accordance with the criticism suggests that this story is later than that of b. Giṭ. 56 (Neusner,

Development, p. 232), the dependency of Lam. R. (A-D) on b. Giṭ. 56 cannot be demonstrated.

As was mentioned, in E-N we seem to have another version of Yoḥanan's request. We may note that F of Lam. R. concerns itself with the saving of "rabbis" and not "sages" as is the case with b. Giṭ. 56.

From G on, Ṣadoq becomes the central figure of the story. In G, Lam. R. supplies a long and involved story of the rescue of Ṣadoq which does not appear in the b. Giṭ. 56 account. H-I is consistent with b. Giṭ. in representing Ṣadoq as a "holy man" and ascetic, but knows nothing of a forty-year fast. There is, however, an added theme in the portrayal of Ṣadoq in Lam. R. Not only is Ṣadoq a "holy man," but he is also, and primarily, a teacher of Torah (K). At several points, then, we see the presence of an underlying "rabbinic myth" in Lam. R. and its absence in the b. Giṭ. accounts.

O and P are an odd twist in the story. Until this point, the Romans, and particularly Vespasian, are pictured in relatively favorable light. It seems that O and P are an attempt to compensate. In P, the Romans are represented as so backward that before receiving their "reward" from Ṣadoq they did not possess weigh-scales. The meaning of "calculation by fingers" is unclear. According to the *Aruk Hashalem* (Vol. III, p. 513), it is a game. Jastrow (*Dict*., p. 441) suggests that it might refer to "Roman notation." In either case, or taken literally, it represents a rather patronizing attitude toward the Roman invaders. I do not know what can be made of the fact that O is in Hebrew. It does not appear elsewhere.

Q and R seem to have been appended to the story. They have no parallel in earlier sources and do not appear in the Vilna text at all. They are probably a late embellishment. Oddly enough, however, Q does offer information which our analysis of earlier sources has shown is quite correct, namely that Sadoq did in fact survive the destruction of the Temple in 70 by many years.

As we have noted, the evidence suggests a fairly late date for Lam. R. 1:31. On the basis of the criticism of the Arabs which surfaces in other sections of this collection of siege-stories, Neusner (*Development*, p. 232) suggests that Lam. R. as we have it dates from a time subsequent to the Arab conquest in the seventh century.

(2)

A. *You mighty ones who do his word, hearkening to the voice of his word* (Ps. 103:20)--for example, R. Ṣadoq and his companions.

B. R. Ṣadoq was summoned by a certain matron (MṬRWNYT') [for immoral purposes].

C. [R. Ṣadoq] said to her, "I am fainthearted and I am unable. Is there anything to eat?"

D. She said to him, "There is an unclean thing."

E. He said to her, "What does one learn from this? One who does this [immoral act] eats this [unclean food]."

F. She heated the oven and was placing it [the unclean food within when Ṣadoq] got up and sat in it [the oven].

G. She said to him, "What is this?"

H. He said to her, "He who does this [immoral act] falls into this [i.e., the fire of Gehenna]."

I. She said to him, "If I had known all this [was so despicable to you], I would not have tormented you."

b. Qid. 40a

Comment: Here Ṣadoq is represented as both saintly and somewhat shrewd. According to Jastrow (*Dict*., pp. 769, 770), the term "matron" (MṬRWNYT') usually refers to a Roman lady of high rank or status. Presumably for this reason Ṣadoq could not simply refuse her request. Perhaps she had the power to bring down sanctions upon him. Nevertheless, Ṣadoq manages to resist temptation under coercion, and communicate in a graphic manner his abhorrence of complying with her demands.

The pericope is entirely in Aramaic with the exception of the verse. B-I is a unitary story. A, however, does not seem to belong to this pericope. It cites a scriptural verse, and states that "R. Ṣadoq and his companions (ḤBYRYW)" exemplify the verse. One would now expect some story concerning "R. Ṣadoq and his companions." B-I, on the other hand, only talks of Ṣadoq. A, then, appears to be an introduction to some story other than the one we have before us. A's proper referent, however, has not survived; nor is there any indication in our sources of who Ṣadoq's "companions" may be.

(3)

A. And do not be astonished concerning Joseph the Righteous, for lo, R. Ṣadoq was the great one of the generation--

B. When he was taken captive to Rome, a certain matron (MṬRWNYT') took him and sent him a beautiful handmaid [to cohabit with]. As soon as he saw her he turned his eyes to the wall so that he would not see her, and he sat and repeated [words of Torah] all night.

C. At dawn [the handmaid] went and complained to her mistress. [The handmaid] said to her, "Death is preferable to me (ŠWH LY HMWT) than that you should give me to this man."

D. [The matron] sent and called for him, and said to him, "Why did you not do with this woman as men do?"

E. He said to her, "And what shall I do? I am [descended] from the High Priesthood; I am from a great family.

F. "I said, '[I fear] lest I cohabit ('B') with her and [thereby] multiplied bastards amongst Israel.'"

G. As soon as she heard his words she attended him and sent him off with great honor.

ARNa 16, ed. Schechter, p. 32a

Comment: We have here a second pericope involving R. Ṣadoq and a matron, a Roman lady of high rank. This story and that of b. Qid. 40a share the same basic theme: Sadoq, in both tempting and compelling circumstances, refuses to involve himself in sexual immorality. There are, however, significant differences in the details of the two. Most noteworthy is the method by which Ṣadoq resists temptation. It is the study of Torah which saves him from immorality. In addition, here reasons are given for his lack of compliance in terms of *halakah*; he does not wish to profane the priestly bloodline, nor does he wish to procreate bastards. In b. Qid. 40a, Ṣadoq's saintliness was reason enough. In short, in this pericope the details are rather more "rabbinic" in character than in b. Qid. 40a. Here Ṣadoq is a "rabbi" rather than a "holy man." It appears that some tradition concerning Ṣadoq's involvement with a Roman lady has generated several stories differing in detail.

Several of the details are noteworthy. In A, Ṣadoq is described as "the great one of the generation." This pericope, however, is the second of four pericopae dealing with the moral fortitude of rabbis (i.e., Joseph the Righteous, Ṣadoq, ʿAqiva and Eliezer) under tempting circumstances. Each figure is represented as being "greater" than the previous one. A, then, is merely a redactional device. This is also the first, and only, pericope which mentions that Ṣadoq ever went to Rome, or that he was ever taken captive by the Romans.

Lastly, this is the only source which *explicitly* ascribes priestly status to Ṣadoq (E). However, it should also be noted that two separate "reasons" are given in E and F. The detail of his priestly descent is irrelevant to his concern for procreating bastards. In all probability either E or F is integral to the pericope, but both are not. There seems no probative evidence upon which a choice can be based.

(4)

A. *R. Ṣadoq had a firstling. He set down for it barley* in wicker baskets of peeled willow-twigs [BSLY NSRYM ŠL ʿRBH QLWPH: corrected reading in Shiṭṭah Meqqubbeṣet of Aramaic text]. *During the time it was eating its lip was split.*

B. [R. Ṣadoq] *came before R. Joshua.* [R. Ṣadoq] *said to him,* "Have we distinguished between a *ḥaver* [of priestly descent] and an *ʿam ha-ʾareṣ* [of priestly descent]?" Said to him R. Joshua, "Yes."

C. [R. Ṣadoq] *came before R. Gamaliel.* [R. Ṣadoq] *said to him,* "Have we distinguished between a *ḥaver* [of priestly descent] and an *ʿam haʾareṣ* [of priestly descent]?" *Said to him* R. Gamaliel, "No."

D. [R. Ṣadoq] *said to him,* "But lo R. Joshua said to me, 'Yes'." [R. Gamaliel] said to him, "Wait until the Shield-Bearers ascend to the House of Study."

E. As soon as they entered the house of study, the inquirer stood and asked, "Have we distinguished at all between a *ḥaver* [of priestly descent] and an *ʿam haʾareṣ* [of priestly descent]?"

F. Said to him R. Joshua, "No."

G. Said to him R. Gamaliel, "But is it not in your name [that] they said to me, 'Yes'? Joshua, stand on your feet so that they may testify against you."

H. R. Joshua stood on his feet and said, "What shall I do? If indeed I were alive and he [the witness] dead, the living could contradict the dead. Now that I am alive and he is alive, how can the living contradict the living?"

I. And R. Gamaliel was standing and expounding, and R. Joshua was standing on his feet until all the people shouted and said to Ḥuṣpit the *meturgeman*, "Stop!" And he stopped.

b. Bek. 36a

Comment: In this pericope Ṣadoq appears a firm supporter of Gamaliel. It comes to Ṣadoq's attention that Joshua is publicly avowing a legal opinion with which Gamaliel disagrees. Ṣadoq then informs Gamaliel of this development, which may affect the latter's exercise of authority. Furthermore, Ṣadoq allows himself to become the occasion by which Joshua is to be disciplined. This representation of Ṣadoq's alignment with Gamaliel's patriarchate parallels that of b. Qid. 32b in which Ṣadoq's homily serves to admonish Joshua for his lack of piety, and aggrandizes the patriarch.

Of interest is the abrupt shift in whom the story favors, Joshua or Gamaliel. Without I, Joshua is caught attempting to lie to Gamaliel and the sages, but is unsuccessful and confesses in humiliation. With I, the rightful discipline of Joshua becomes a story of Gamaliel's overly disrespectful treatment of Joshua. Perhaps the humiliation story originated within pro-Gamaliel circles and was later taken into, and subtly adapted by, pro-Joshua redactors.

Also noteworthy is the shift from Aramaic (in italics) to Hebrew. With the exception of the actual query of Ṣadoq, A-C are Aramaic. From D on (excluding "said to him" in D) the pericope continues in Hebrew. This would suggest that the details of the story of the humiliation of Joshua by Gamaliel and the details of the case of Ṣadoq's firstling do not form a unitary pericope. Different sources may lie behind b. Bek. 36a. It appears that a tradition concerning the case of Ṣadoq's firstling has been assimilated to a story involving the discipline of Joshua by the patriarch.

Lastly, the substance of the case presented in b. Bek. 36a (A-C) is important for our purposes. As was explained above in reference to M. ʿEd. 7:1, an unblemished firstling of a clean animal was sacrificed. If blemished, the firstling was given to a priest, and he could do with it as he pleased. After the destruction of the Temple, the owner waited until the animal contracted a blemish and then gave it to a priest. No one, however, was permitted intentionally to blemish the animal, or allow any activity which could lead to the blemishing of the animal. When a blemish did appear, one had to testify, or provide a witness to testify, that the blemish arose by accident. According to M. Bek. 5:4, the testimony of an Israelite is *always* accepted, for he has nothing to gain by intentionally blemishing the animal. (Whether the Israelite is a *ḥaver* or an *ʿam haʾareṣ* is inconsequential.) The testimony of priests, however, is not accepted, for they could conceivably conspire with a firstling's owner by agreeing to perjure themselves in return for receiving the firstling, or two priests could decide to reciprocate. Lastly, a priest who himself was the owner of a firstling might blemish the animal and perjure himself in order to slaughter it for his own use.

In this pericope, Ṣadoq witnesses the accidental blemishing of his firstling. According to the law, he would now testify to the sages that the blemish was accidentally contracted. Ṣadoq may testify if he is not of priestly descent; if he is a priest, he must provide an Israelite witness or wait for another blemish to be contracted. Ṣadoq, however, inquires if any distinction is made between an *ʿam haʾareṣ* and a *ḥaver*. As we mentioned above, for purposes of such testimony, whether a witness is an *ʿam haʾareṣ* or a *ḥaver* is inconsequential, if the witness is an Israelite. If the context of Ṣadoq's question is testimony concerning a blemished firstling, then it appears that Ṣadoq may be inquiring whether, although of priestly descent, he may testify since he is a *ḥaver*, and *ḥaverim* would not be suspected of perjuring themselves in these matters. It seems that the redactor of this pericope may have known some tradition which ascribed priestly descent to Ṣadoq. This claim is made outright, only once, in ARNa 16.

A. TNW RBNN: (M'ŚH B) A certain disciple came before R. Joshua. [The disciple] said to him, "Is the evening prayer optional or compulsory?" [R. Joshua] said to him, "[It is] optional."

B. [The disciple] came before R. Gamaliel. [The disciple] said to him, "Is the evening prayer optional or compulsory?" [R. Gamaliel] said to him, "[It is] compulsory."

C. [The disciple] said to him, "But did not R. Joshua say to me [that it is] optional?" [R. Gamaliel] said to him, "Wait until the Shield-Bearers enter the house of study."

D. When the Shield-Bearers entered, the inquirer stood and asked, "Is the evening prayer optional or compulsory?" Said to him R. Gamaliel, "[It is] compulsory."

E. Said R. Gamaliel to the sages, "Is there any man who disputes this matter?" Said to him R. Joshua, "No."

F. [R. Gamaliel] said to him, "But is it not in your name they said to me [that it is] optional?"

G. R. Joshua stood on his feet and said, "If indeed I were alive and he [the witness] dead, the living could contradict the dead. But now that I am alive and he is alive, how can the living contradict the living?"

H. R. Gamaliel was sitting and expounding, and R. Joshua was standing on his feet until all the people shouted and said to Huspit the *turgeman*, "Stop!" And he stopped.

I. *They said, "How long will* [R. Gamaliel] *go on shaming him?*

J. "*On New Year last year he shamed him. With regard to firstlings in the incident of R. Ṣadoq* [R. Gamaliel] *shamed him. Here again he shamed him.*

L. "*Come let us remove him* [i.e., R. Gamaliel from his position as patriarch]."

M. [The narrative continues with a discussion of who will replace R. Gamaliel, and the offering of the position to R. Eleazar b. Azariah.]

b. Ber. 27b

Comment: A through H of this pericope presents a story of Gamaliel's humiliation of Joshua similar to that in b. Bek. 36a. Here, however, the question of an anonymous disciple provides the occasion for the incident. Furthermore, the case which gives rise to the humiliation is not that of b. Bek. 36a but a disagreement between Gamaliel and Joshua concerning the status of the evening prayer. That which has been said about the affect of I in b. Bek. 36a equally applies to H in this pericope. Lastly, here A-H is entirely in Hebrew.

From J onward, the pericope continues in Aramaic (in italics). The humiliation story (A-H) now becomes the occasion for the deposition of Gamaliel related in the Aramaic sequel. Ṣadoq is mentioned only in J which cross-references two other such humiliation-incidents. The reference to Ṣadoq appears to refer directly to the incident of b. Bek. 36a. Certainly no other motive for the inclusion of such an oblique reference to Ṣadoq seems apparent. However, J with its cross-references is not integral to the story. K would be quite intelligible immediately following I. The cross-references, then, could well be interpolations into the deposition story. (See Goldenberg's complete analysis above, pp. 9-48.)

Bracketing the cross-reference to the case of Sadoq's firstling in J, and turning our attention merely to A-H, the similarities between b. Ber. 27b and b. Bek. 36a are too striking for the humiliation-stories to have developed independent of one another. The following synoptic table will aid us in discussing which version is dependent and which independent.

b. Bek. 36a	b. Ber. 27b
1. *R. Ṣadoq had a firstling... its lip was split.*	1. -- -- --
2. *He came before R. Joshua. He said to him,*	2. A certain disciple came before R. Joshua. He said to him,
3. "Have we distinguished...?"	3. "Is the evening prayer...?"
4. Said to him R. Joshua, "Yes."	4. He said to him, "Optional."
5. *He came before R. Gamaliel He said to him,*	5. He came before R. Gamaliel. He said to him,
6. "Have we distinguished...?"	6. "Is the evening prayer...?"
7. *Said to him* R. Gamaliel, "No."	7. He said to him, "Compulsory."
8. *He said to him,* "But lo R. Joshua said to me, 'Yes'."	8. He said to him, "But did not R. Joshua say to me, 'Optional'?"
9. He said to him, "Wait until the Shield-bearers ascend to the house of study."	9. He said to him, "Wait until the Shield-bearers enter the house of study."
10. As soon as they entered the house of study, the inquirer stood and asked,	10. When the Shield-bearers entered, the inquirer stood and asked,
11. "Have we distinguished...?"	11. "Is the evening prayer...?"
12. Said to him R. Joshua, "No."	12. Said to him R. Gamaliel, "Compulsory."
13. -- -- --	13. Said R. Gamaliel to the sages, "Is there anyone who disputes this matter?"
14. -- -- --	14. Said to him R. Joshua, "No."
15. Said to him R. Gamaliel, "But is it not in your name they said to me, 'Yes'?"	15. He said to him, "But is it not in your name they said to me, 'Optional'?"
16. "Joshua stand on your feet and they will testify against you."	16. He said to him, " " "
17. R. Joshua stood on his feet and said,	17. " " "

b. Bek. 36a	b. Ber. 27b
18. "What shall I do?	18. -- -- --
19. "If indeed I were alive and he dead, the living could contradict the dead. Now that I am alive and he is alive, how can the living contradict the living?"	19. "If indeed...dead. But, now that I am alive...living?"
20. And R. Gamaliel was standing and expounding...Ḥuṣpit the *meturgeman*, "Stop!" And he stopped.	20. R. Gamaliel was sitting and expounding...Ḥuṣpit the *turgeman*, "Stop!" And he stopped.
21. -- -- --	21. *They said, "How long will he go on shaming him?*
22. -- -- --	22. *"On New Year last year he shamed him. With regard to firstlings in the incident of R. Ṣadoq he shamed him. Here again he shamed him.*
23. -- -- --	23. *"Come let us remove him."*

We may now point out the differences in the pericopae, ignoring those which are due to the different subject matter. As was mentioned, in 1-8 of b. Bek., Aramaic is used, in 9-20 only Hebrew. 1-20 of b. Ber. is entirely in Hebrew while the deposition story (21, 23) and the cross-references (22) are in Aramaic. In 4, 7 and 15, b. Bek. has expanded on b. Ber. by supplying the names of the figures. In 10 b. Bek. adds "house of study" (but deletes "Shield-bearers"). 18 is a significant addition to Joshua's statement and does not appear in b. Ber. 13 and 14, on the other hand, do not appear in b. Bek. Lastly, in 9 the Shield-bearers "ascend to the house of study" in b. Bek., while they merely "enter" in b. Ber.

If we ignore those parts of the story which are not parallel at all (13, 14, 21, 22 and 23), we see that b. Bek. appears to have expanded on b. Ber. in 4, 7, 10, 15 and 18. Only one deletion has been made by b. Bek. (10). Furthermore, since the use of the verb "ascend" serves to aggrandize the institution of the house of study while "enter" is a neutral term, it appears to me that the change from "enter" in b. Ber. to "ascend" in b. Bek. is more likely than vice versa.

It seems that b. Bekh., if not directly dependent on 1-20 of b. Ber., is at least dependent on a source which lies behind the latter. The only evidence to the contrary is the lack of 13 and 14 in b. Bek. It is my suggestion that several traditions concerning disputes which led to confrontations between Joshua and Gamaliel were circulating. One involved the case of Ṣadoq's firstling; however, the actual details of the confrontation between Joshua and Gamaliel in this case had been lost. Some Amoraic redactor then assimilated what he knew of the Ṣadoq-case to a known and complete story concerning a humiliation-incident precipitated by a disagreement over the status of the evening prayer (1-20 of b. Ber.). This explanation would account for the presentation of the firstling-case in Aramaic, followed by the abrupt shift to Hebrew for the details of the humiliation of Joshua. Some later redactor of b. Ber. turned the evening-prayer-incident into the immediate antecedent of the deposition story. Either he or some later interpolator then cross-referenced the other humiliation-stories, one of which was the reconstructed story of b. Bek., relegating these other incidents to the status of anterior events leading up to the evening-prayer-confrontation and the deposition.

(5)

To facilitate my discussion of the following tradition, I shall give both versions of the tradition side by side. The reliance of one tradition upon the other will then become manifestly clear.

A. (M'ŚH B) Miriam the daughter of Naqadimon was one awaiting the decision of a *levir* (ŠWMRT YBM) [her husband having died without offspring]. And she came to R. Ṣadoq, and he apportioned her twenty-five *liṭrot* of silver for perfumes	A. (M'ŚH B) The sages apportioned to the daughter of Naqadimon b. Gurion five hundred *dinars* of gold each day for perfumes, and she was merely [in the status of] one awaiting the decision of a *levir* (ŠWMRT YBM).

[and] for food, and two *se'ahs* of wine for her meals every week.

B. And she said to him, "So you (pl.) should apportion to your (pl.) daughters."

C. And when the famine came [during the siege of Jerusalem], her hair fell out due to the famine. And R. Ṣadoq saw her when she was going about with her father in the market-place. [Her father] said, "She is the very Miriam to whom you apportioned (sing.) such-and-such weekly (BŠBT), and she cursed you (pl.)."

D. Said R. Ṣadoq, "May [evil] come upon me if I did not see her gathering bran-flour from amongst the dung of cattle.

E. "And I applied to her (WQR'TY ʿLYH) this verse: *If you know not O fairest among women follow in the tracks of the sheep* (Song 1:8)."

Pesiqta Rabbati 29/30, ed. Friedmann, p. 140a

B. Yet she cursed them and said, "So you (pl.) should give to your (pl.) daughters."

C. -- -- --

D. Said R. Leazar b. R. Ṣadoq, "May I see comfort if I did not see her gathering barley from beneath the hooves of horses in Acco.

E. "I applied to her (QR'TY ʿLYH) this verse: *If you know not O fairest among women [follow in the tracks of the sheep]* (Song 1:8)."

Tos. Ket. 5:9-10, ed. Lieberman, p. 74, lines #44-48 (y. Ket. 5:11 = Lam. R. 1:48; b. Ket. 66b, 67a)

Comment: Pesiqta Rabbati clearly is dependent upon the Toseftan pericope (as stands to reason). The theme of the Tosefta version is the demise of the ungrateful. The daughter of Naqadimon who was treated most generously by the executors of her husband's estate nevertheless cursed her benefactors; her end was abject poverty. Ṣadoq does not appear at all in the original version, and the report (D) and application of the verse (E) with which the pericope ends is attributed to Eleazar b. R. Ṣadoq.

The redactor of the pericope in Pesiqta Rabbati has, with the interpolation of C, changed the entire theme of the story. The famine which resulted from the siege of Jerusalem was so widespread that even the most wealthy, such as Miriam, were unable to get anything to eat or preserve their health. It appears that the redactor, in order to facilitate the interpolation of the famine tradition, made Ṣadoq into the executor of the estate and attributed E and F to him. Further indication that Ṣadoq's presence in A is indeed pseudopigraphic is the use of the plural in C of Pesiqta Rabbati. C must refer not to Ṣadoq but to some group of executors, as it does in the Toseftan version.

In Pesiqta Rabbati, the redactor has represented Ṣadoq as a witness to the state of Jerusalem both before the siege and resulting famine (A), and during the said events (D, E). The Ṣadoq tradition in C has no demonstrable dependence on any earlier Ṣadoq tradition.

(6)

A. "They sprinkle on them [i.e., bones collected for secondary burial] wine and oil," the words of R. ʿAqiva.

B. R. Simeon b. Nanos says, "Oil but not wine, because wine deteriorates [the bones] [MṬRP: Oxford Mich. 175, Venice]."

C. But the sages say, "Neither oil nor wine, because they increase upon them worms;

D. "but they put on them dry herbs."

E. Said R. Eleazar b. R. Ṣadoq, "Thus said my father to me at the hour of his death, 'My son, first bury me in a trench, and later gather my bones and put them in an ossuary; but do not gather [them] yourself [ʾTH: Oxford Mich. 175, Adler; ʾWTK: Oxford Opp. 726] in your [own] hands.'

F. "And thus I did to him. Yoḥanan entered and gathered [them], and spread over them a sheet. [W: missing in Oxford Mich. 175, Adler, Venice] I entered and rent [my chothes] over them, and placed on them dry herbs.

G. "As he did to his father, so I did to him."

Sem. 12:9, ed. Higger
pp. 197, 198

Comment: Secondary burial was a common practice among the Jews of late antiquity from at least Herodian times on (E. R. Meyers, *Jewish Ossuaries: Reburial and Rebirth* (Rome, 1971) pp. 39-44). This pericope as well as the rest of Semaḥot 12 and y. M.Q. 1:5 gives evidence that it was also practiced in Rabbinic circles. According to Semaḥot 12 and y. M.Q. 1:5, the corpse was buried and left until the flesh had decayed. y. M.Q. 1:5 informs us that this temporary interment merely was in a mount of debris. Subsequently, the bones were collected and placed in an ossuary for their second and permanent burial. According to the opinion of Yoḥanan b. Nuri (Sem. 12:7), however, one could not himself collect the bones of his mother and father; no reason is given for the opinion.

A-D disputes what is spread upon the bones during ossilegium. The narrative (E-G), with which the pericope concludes, supports D of the sages opinion. In fact, only one detail in F is directly relevant to the dispute. Eleazar b. R. Ṣadoq's narrative is not, however, dependent upon the dispute. Furthermore, it is completely intelligible by itself;;the relationship between the narrative and dispute is redactional. One last point concerns G. According to G, not only are E and F merely the burial rites which Eleazar observed at the death of his father, but they are also those performed at the death of his grandfather. G gives the impression that the rites have always been thus. It provides, therefore, further legitimation for the practices presented in E and F. G could well be a later addition to Eleazar's narrative.

PART TWO: ANALYSIS OF THE TRADITION

IV. The Distribution of the Tradition

Thus far we have analyzed and discussed each tradition. We may now begin to address rather more general issues with the entire corpus of traditions at our disposal. The first issue at hand is the location of the pericopae within the body of rabbinic literature. Below is a summary listing of the Ṣadoq-corpus which will provide us with a point of departure. The order of traditions in the list roughly corresponds to the order in which the traditions were discussed in Part One. [See next page]

Item	I Mishnah- Tosefta	II Tannaitic Midrashim	III *Beraitot*	IV Amoraic Material	V Later Compilations
1. Brine of unclean locusts is clean.	M. Ter. 10:9 M. ʿEd. 7:2 Tos. ʿEd. 3:1	Sifra Shemini 5:10			
2. Amount of drink depends on the number of guests.	M. Shab. 20:2				
3. Gamaliel roasted the Passover-offering on a grill.	M. Pes. 7:2				
4. Who shall bring the calf (see Deut. 21: 1, 2)?	Tos. Kip. 1:12 Tos. Shevu. 1:4		b. Yoma 23a y. Yoma 2:2		
5. R. Ṣadoq ate less than an egg's bulk outside the *sukkah*.	M. Suk. 2:4d, 5				
6. Ṣadoq and Yoḥanan b. Haḥoraniṭ and the moist olives.	Tos. Suk. 2:3			b. Yev. 15b	
7. Ṣadoq's *reductio ad absurdum* of Eliezer's opinion on vows.	M. Ned. 9:1				
8. Ṣadoq sat on Gamaliel's right at Yavneh.	Tos. Sanh. 8:1		y. Sanh. 1:4		

Item	I	II	III	IV	III
9. A nail of a money-changer, a chest of a grist-dealer, and a nail of a sundial are unclean.	M. ʿEd. 3:8 M. Kel. 12:4, 5				
10. Concerning the redemption lamb for a firstling that died.	M. ʾEd. 7:1 M. Bek. 1:6				
11. Concerning flowing water which exceeded the amount of dripping water.	M. ʿEd. 7:3 M. Miq. 5:5				
12. Concerning flowing water made to gush through foliage of nuts.	M. ʿEd. 7:4				
13. Do not make them a crown...nor an axe.	M. Avot 4:5				
14. Hollowed blocks of wood are unclean.	Tos. Kel. B.B. 2:1-3				
15. Two cases of the discharges of women.	Tos. Nid. 4: 3, 4		b. Nid. 22b		
16. Ṣadoq on hospitality.	Mekh. Ish.: Amaleq Mekh. Sim.: Yitro Sifré Deut. 38	b. Qid. 32b			

Item	I	II	III	IV	V
17. Ṣadoq explains the procreation of male or female.			b. Nid. 31a		
18. Ṣadoq fasts to avert the destruction; he is treated by Roman physicians.				b. Giṭ. 56	Lam. R. 1:31
19. Ṣadoq and the Roman matron.				b. Qid. 40a	
20. Ṣadoq, the Roman matron and the beautiful handmaid.					ARNa 16
21. The case of Ṣadoq's firstling, and the humiliation of Joshua b. Ḥananiah.				b. Bek. 36a b. Ber. 27b	
22. Ṣadoq and Miriam the daughter of Naqadimon.					Pesiqta Rabbati 29/30
23. The burial of Sadoq.					Sem. 12:9

We may now divide our sources into legal and non-legal traditions and examine their relative distribution over the different strata (I-V). The following chart indicates in which stratum any one tradition *first* appears. The numbers in the chart correspond to those of the above summary listing of our sources.

	I	II	III	IV	V
Legal	1, 2, 3, 5, 6, 7, 8, 9, 10, 11, 12, 14, 15				23
Non-legal	4, 13	16	17	18, 19 21	20, 22

The chart aptly demonstrates that the traditions do not distribute randomly over the body of literature at all. By far the greater portion of the legal materials first appear in stratum I (Mishnah-Tosefta), while the general trend for the non-legal materials, such as biographical materials and non-legal, exegetical sources, is quite the opposite. Most of the latter do not make their first appearance until strata IV and V (Amoraic material and later compilations). More precisely, 93% of the legal traditions are accounted for by Mishnah-Tosefta. The one remaining legal tradition is that in Semahot 12:9 (number 23). Of the non-legal traditions, 56% do not appear until strata IV and V; 11% are found in *beraitot*; the same is true of the Tannaitic Midrashim; and 22% appear in Mishnah-Tosefta. One of the latter (i.e., 11% of the non-legal traditions), however, is M. Avot 4:5. A random distribution, on the other hand, should have produced figures of approximately 20% for each box in the chart.

In short, the trends in our distribution resemble those found by Neusner in his study of the corpus of the traditions of Eliezer b. Hyrcanus (*Eliezer* II, pp. 1-18). Thus while almost all of the legal traditions make their appearance in the literature in the earliest stratum, the greater part of the non-legal (historical and biographical) traditions do not surface until the late Amoraic strata and have no demonstrable connection with earlier Tannaitic traditions. All the non-legal sources found in these late strata are attested only by the documents in which they appear. Although there is no reason these late documents cannot contain early traditions, we have no evidence that such is in fact the case in regard to Ṣadoq's traditions. Finally, if one were to argue that the distribution can be accounted for by the strictly legal nature of the Mishnah-Tosefta corpus, we may point out that non-legal traditions *are* found in Mishnah-Tosefta. Neusner has pointed out that some of Eliezer's non-legal traditions do appear there, and we have seen that 22% of Ṣadoq's non-legal traditions make their appearance in this earliest stratum of rabbinic literature.

Our conclusions, therefore, must be very much like those of Neusner concerning Eliezer. On the whole, the biographical and historical materials appear to have been formulated later than the legal traditions, and, hence, the former are less likely to be representative of the man, his concerns, and his pursuits than the latter.

V. Forms

It has already been established[6] that the traditions of the *Tannaim* were cast and transmitted in a relatively small number of distinct forms. Our analysis of Ṣadoq's traditions has produced no new forms, but the relative distribution of Ṣadoq's material (and primarily of the legal material) over the various established forms differs considerably from that exhibited in the traditions of the Houses, Eliezer b. Hyrcanus, and Ishmael. The forms which shall concern us are (A) Disputes, (B) Independent Sayings, (C) Narratives and (D) Testimonies.

Neusner has shown that most of the traditions of the Houses[7] and of Eliezer[8] are cast in variations of a single form, the dispute. Similarly, Porton shows that fifty-six percent of the Ishmael's legal traditions exhibit the same form.[9] With our own materials, the case has been quite the opposite, for approximately 8.5% of all the traditions concerning Ṣadoq appear in dispute form. Even if we discount all non-legal traditions in our computations, the figure only rises to approximately 13.4%.

The 'testimony,' on the other hand, plays a rather more substantial role in our corpus. Neusner found the form occasionally used in traditions of several pre-70 figures.[10] The form did not appear, however, in either the Houses' or Eliezer's material. Likewise, only one tradition of the rather large Ishmael-corpus is cast in testimony-form. The frequency of the use of the testimony-form in the Ṣadoq traditions is about double that of the dispute form (approximately 16.5% of the entire corpus and 26.6% of the legal corpus). Furthermore, of the thirty-three uses of the testimony form in Mishnah-Tosefta, only Joshua appears more frequently than Ṣadoq, a fact which we shall discuss at greater length below.

Narratives account for the greatest proportion of the tradition. They make up 62.5% of the entire corpus, and 46.6% of the legal materials. The remainder of the traditions appear as independent sayings used for various purposes by the redactors in question. They comprise 12.5% of the whole and 13.4% of the legal traditions.

A. Disputes

As was mentioned above, only 8.5% of the Ṣadoq-corpus and 13.4% of the legal corpus are formulated in disputes. The standard version of the form is as follows:

Superscription
Authority x says ('WMR) "..."
Authority y says ('WMR) "..."[11]

Neusner has shown, however, that the form exists in several variations, two of which are relevant to the traditions of Sadoq. One such variation "is the exclusion of a second authority, leaving the first in dispute with an anonymous statement of law:

> Statement of law or legal problem
> Authority x + says + opinion ..."[12]

Finally, the direct discourse of the authorities in the standard dispute may be replaced by "intensive, transitive verbs (Piʿel, Hiphʿil), present tense, e.g., *declare liable*, declare clean, etc...."[13] We may now examine in detail the use of the dispute in our sources.

(1) *Standard Dispute Form*

M. Shab. 20:2

> They pour water over wine-dregs to dilute them; they strain wine through a napkin or Egyptian basket; they put an egg in a mustard strainer; and they prepare honied wine on the Sabbath.
>
> R. Judah says, "[One prepares it] on the Sabbath in a cup, on a Festival-day in a flagon, and during mid-festival in a jar."
>
> R. Ṣadoq says, "All depends on the [number] of guests."

As Porton points out, "In a true dispute, both comments should deal with the problem set forth in the superscription, and the two comments should respond to each other."[14] Our analysis of this pericope in Part One showed that Judah's lemma, although in need of the legal statement for a context, is not dependent upon the anonymous law, nor does it deal with an issue raised in the superscription. Furthermore, the lemma goes beyond the context established in the legal statement. Similarly, Ṣadoq's lemma is not dependent upon the superscription, or upon Judah's lemma. Rather than disputing with Judah, Ṣadoq introduces a completely different principle. Lastly, it was noted that two generations separated the disputants. The dispute, therefore, was deemed "artificial." In this pericope, then, the dispute form has been poorly used.

(2) *Superscription*
Authority x + intensive tr. vb.
Authority y + intensive tr. vb.

M. ʿEd. 3:8 (=M. Kel. 12:5)

A nail of a money-changer, and a chest of a grist-dealer, and a nail of a sundial--

R. Ṣadoq declares unclean;

And the sages declare clean.

By the criteria stated above, this is an "authentic" dispute. Both parties respond to the superscription and to each other, and the opinions are balanced. It will be remembered, however, that this is not quite the form in which the tradition is found in M. ʿEd. and M. Kel. Preceeding the list of objects was the introductory statement, "Three things R. Ṣadoq declares unclean and the sages declare clean." Only in arguing that the latter is an additional superscription were we able to hold that the above dispute is the primary element of the pericope. As we pointed out in our commentary, *if* the opposite is the case, and the "introduction" and "list" are primary, then we do not have a dispute at all.

M. Kel. 12:4

(W) A chest of a grist-dealer--

R. Ṣadoq declares unclean;

And the sages declare clean.

As it stands, this is a good dispute. We argued, however, that it is dependent upon, and hence later than, the tradition discussed immediately above (M. ʿEd. 3:8).

(3) *Statement of Law*
Authority x + intensive tr. vb.

M. Kel. 12:4, 5

(a) (W) [The nail] of a sundial--clean
R. Ṣadoq declares unclean.

(b) A nail of a money-changer--clean
R. Ṣadoq declares unclean.

Both of these disputes appear in the same pericope from which we excerpted the dispute of M. Kel. 12:4. Our remarks in regard to the latter apply equally well here.

In summary, only two of Ṣadoq's traditions appear in dispute-form. One of them (M. ʿEd. 3:8), however, has yielded three secondary formulations (M. Kel. 12:4, M. Kel. 12:4, 5 [a] and [b]). The other tradition (M. Shab. 20:2) is a poor example of the use of the form. Later we shall discuss the implications of the paucity of traditions which have been formulated in disputes, and of the poor use of the form in the case of one of the two traditions.

B. Independent Sayings

A saying of Ṣadoq may be deemed independent in that, although the saying appears within a pericope to which it is relevant and which may present the sayings of other authorities, Ṣadoq's saying is independent of the rest of the pericope and is intelligible on its own. The independent sayings of Eliezer[15] and Ishmael[16] usually assume the form, *authority x says*, "...". Only one of the three independent sayings of Ṣadoq takes this form. The other two use the perfect tense with the verb preceeding the subject: *Said R. Ṣadoq*, "...". In both of the latter two cases, the redactor has used the saying to bring evidence against the first *fully articulated* legal opinion which preceeded it.

(1) *R. Ṣadoq says*, "..."

M. Avot 4:5

> R. Ṣadoq says, "Do not make them [the words of Torah] a crown with which to magnify yourself; neither [make them] an axe with which to feed [yourself]."

The saying is followed by, and redactionally joined to, a similar "crown saying" of Hillel. The sayings, however, are quite independent of one another.

(2) *Said R. Ṣadoq, "..."*

M. Pes. 7:2

> Said R. Ṣadoq, "(M'ŚH B) Rabban Gamaliel once said to his slave Ṭabi, 'Go and roast for us the Passover-offering on the grill.'"

Ṣadoq's tradition immediately follows, and contradicts, an anonymous law stating that the Passover-offering may not be roasted on a grill. It is, however, independent of the anonymous law.

M. Ned. 9:1

> Said R. Ṣadoq, "Before they open [the way] for him [i.e., one] [to be released from a vow] in regard to the honor due to his father and mother, let them open [the way] for him in regard to the honor due to Heaven; if so, there are no [binding] vows."

Ṣadoq's remarks constitute a *reductio ad absurdum* of an opinion of Eliezer, and, hence, appears to refer to it. It is, however, not integral to what is otherwise a well-formulated dispute between Eliezer and the sages. With the exception of not providing an antecedent for "him", the remarks are as intelligible on their own as Eliezer's ruling. Nevertheless, there is some room for doubt whether Ṣadoq's lemma was formulated entirely *independent* of Eliezer's.

C. Narratives

As has already been mentioned, narratives in which Ṣadoq is involved constitute the greatest proportion of the sources (62.5% of the entire corpus, and 46.6% of the legal traditions). Seven are narratives of legal import; the remaining eight are non-legal, that is, they are historical, biographical or homiletical in character. The legal narratives may also be subdivided into two types on the basis of their function. Narratives may be used by a redactor as a "precedent" to support or contradict an opinion or legal statement, or they may be presented "unattached" to any legal view. In the latter case, the redactor has not made explicit the precise legal import of the narrative. Both Neusner and Porton in their studies of the traditions of Tannaim have remarked that narratives appear to have no definitive formal structure. The same holds true for the narratives involving Ṣadoq. (Hence, when referring to narratives, the word "form" will function merely as a term of convenience.)

(1) *Legal Narratives*

(a) *Narratives used as Precedents*

M. Suk. 2:4d, 5

> (M'Ś́H W...W) When they gave R. Ṣadoq less than an egg's bulk of food, he took it in a towel and ate it outside the *sukkah* and did not say the Benediction after it.

The pericope in which this incident appears begins with an anonymous law stating that snacks are not eaten in the *sukkah*. An incident involving Gamaliel and Yoḥanan b. Zakkai and which contradicts the law then follows. This incident involving Ṣadoq, which supports the anonymous law, is appended to the first narrative.

Tos. Sanh. 8:1

> Said R. Eleazar b. R. Ṣadoq, "When R. Gamaliel was sitting in Yavneh, my father and another [sat] at his right, and the elders at his left...."

This tradition follows a ruling concerning the proper seating arrangement to be adhered to in the Sanhedrin. Eleazar's narrative supposedly provides support for the ruling in question.

Tos. Kel. B.B. 2:1-3

And so R. Eleazar b. R. Ṣadoq used to say, "Two blocks were in the house of my father, one capable of becoming unclean, and the other incapable of becoming unclean. I said before my father. 'On what account is this capable of becoming unclean and the other incapable of becoming unclean?' He said to me, 'This one which is hollowed out is capable of becoming unclean, and the other which is not hollowed out is incapable of becoming unclean. And on it sat Haggai the prophet.'"

Eleazar's reminiscence is a precedent for his own ruling, which is given earlier in the pericope.

Sem. 12:9

[Eleazar b. R. Ṣadoq relates Ṣadoq's instructions for the latter's burial. Ṣadoq prescribes temporary burial, ossilegium and secondary burial He also informs his son that he himself must not perform the ossilegium. Eleazar relates how he carried out Ṣadoq's instructions, and that he spread dry herbs over the bones after they had been gathered. He concludes by stating that this procedure had been followed in his family for several generations.]

Eleazar's narrative follows a dispute about what may be spread on bones during ossilegium. The narrative supports the sages view that one does not use wine or oil, but does use dry herbs.

(b) *Unattached Narratives of Legal Import*

Tos. Suk. 2:3

[Eleazar b. R. Ṣadoq relates that when he studied with Yoḥanan b. Haḥoranit he once brought him olives on the instructions of Ṣadoq. Yoḥanan, seeing that they were moist (and, hence, susceptible to uncleanness according to the House of

Hillel), would not eat them. Eleazar, on informing Ṣadoq, is told by the latter that the jar in which the olives had been kept had indeed been broached but had become stopped by the lees. (Hence, the olives had not been rendered susceptible to uncleanness even according to the Hillelite opinion on the matter.)]

The narrative lends support to the Hillelite ruling of M. ʿEd. 4:6, and further serves to indicate that even Shammaites such as Yoḥanan (and Ṣadoq) agree that the Hillelite view is to be followed.

Tos. Nid. 4:3, 4

(MʿŚH B) A woman was discharging [what looked] like red scales, and they came and inquired of R. Ṣadoq, and R. Ṣadoq went and inquired of the sages, and the sages sent and called for the physicians, and [the physicians] said, "There is a wound within her; therefore she discharges [what looks] like red scales."

The narrative indicates that the discharging of red scales by a woman can be quite unrelated to either miscarriage or menstruation, and, therefore, need not necessarily render a woman unclean.

Tos. Nid. 4:3, 4

(ŠWB MʿŚH B) A woman was discharging [what looked] like red hairs, and they came and inquired of R. Ṣadoq, and R. Ṣadoq went and inquired of the sages, and the sages sent and called for the physicians, and [the physicians] said, "There is a mole in her belly; therefore she discharges red hairs."

What was said in regard to the immediately preceding narrative equally applies to this one. Only a difference in several details makes this narrative a different case from the preceding.

(2) *Non-legal Narratives*

Tos. Kip. 1:12

(M'ŚH B) [One priest murders another during the Temple service, and Ṣadoq delivers a short sermon based on Deut. 21:1, 2 serving to point out the depravity of the priesthood. The narrative then returns to the events of the incident. The priests are shown to be more concerned about the knife, which has been rendered unclean by the slaying, than about the slaying itself.]

Ṣadoq's sermon is used as a polemic against the priesthood. We indicated, however, that this narrative is not the original setting of the sermon. Its proper context could not be found.

b. Qid. 32b (Sifré Deut. 38; M. T. Deut. 11:10)

MYTYBY: (M'ŚH B) [Joshua allows himself to be served by Gamaliel the Patriarch at a feast. Eliezer objects to Joshua's behavior, and Joshua delivers a homily indicating that Gamaliel is doing what the *obligation* of hospitality (as exemplified by Abraham) demands of him. Ṣadoq delivers a similar homily likening Gamaliel's behavior to the grace of God.]

As was mentioned in our commentary, Ṣadoq is here represented by the redactor as being on the patriarchate's side of the conflict between the patriarchate and the circle of the sages.

b. Nid. 31a

TNW RBNN: At first they used to say, "[If] the woman reaches orgasm first, she gives birth to a male. [If] the man reaches orgasm first, she gives birth to a female." And they did not explain the matter [from Scripture] until R. Ṣadoq came and explained it.

These are the sons of Leah whom she bore to Jacob in Paddam Aram, with Dinah his daughter (Gen. 46:15). [Scripture] assigned the males to the females, and the females to the males.

b. Giṭ. 56a, b (Lam. R. 1:31)

[Some say that Martha the daughter of Boethius, a rich woman of Jerusalem, died during the siege after eating a dried fig left by Ṣadoq. Ṣadoq had fasted for forty years to prevent the destruction of Jerusalem. When he needed to refresh himself he sucked the juice from a dried fig and discarded the rest.

Yoḥanan b. Zakkai, having won Vespasian's favor, arranges for Ṣadoq's removal from the city before it is razed by the Romans. The emmaciated Ṣadoq is tended to by Roman physicians.]

Ṣadoq is represented as a "holy man." The narrative is of little historical value and is Amoraic.

b. Qid. 40a

[A Roman matron attempts to coerce Ṣadoq for immoral purposes; Ṣadoq resists.]

ARNa 16

[Ṣadoq was taken captive to Rome where he comes into the possession of a Roman matron. The matron attempts to mate Ṣadoq with one of her beautiful handmaids. Ṣadoq resists temptation by reciting words of Torah all night.]

This pericope with its Rabbinic overtones is similar to the Amoraic narrative listed immediately above (b. Qid. 40a). Priestly descent is claimed for Ṣadoq in this late source.

b. Bek. 36a

[Joshua and Gamaliel disagree over a case arising from the blemishing of a firstling belonging to Ṣadoq. Ṣadoq not only acts as an informant of the Patriarch but also allows himself to be the occasion by which Joshua is disciplined for his stance against Gamaliel.]

The narrative as we have it is a reconstruction by an Amoraic redactor using b. Ber. 27b as a model for the confrontation between Gamaliel and Joshua. Behind this historical narrative, however, stands some legal tradition concerning a case involving the firstling of Ṣadoq. This case seems to assume that Ṣadoq is of priestly descent.

Pesiqta Rabbati 29/30

(M'ŚH B) [Before the siege of Jerusalem, Ṣadoq had been the executor of the estate of the deceased husband of Miriam the daughter of Naqadimon. Weekly, Ṣadoq apportioned generous sums to the widow; nevertheless she cursed him for his stinginess. During the siege of Jerusalem, Ṣadoq saw this once wealthy woman wandering about the marketplace with her father. Her hair had fallen out due to the rigors of the famine. The narrative concludes with the direct discourse of Ṣadoq stating that he had seen her gathering bran-flour from amongst cattle-dung and that he applied Song of Songs 1:8 to her.]

This narrative is a late reformulation of an earlier source in which Ṣadoq plays no part whatsoever, and in which the concluding direct discourse is attributed to Eleazar b. R. Ṣadoq.

D. Testimonies

The remainder of the traditions of Ṣadoq (that is 16.5% of the entire corpus and 26.6% of the legal corpus) strictly adheres to the testimony-form, *testified authority x concerning* (ʿL)...*that* (Š).... None of the form's other variations appear in our sources.[17]

M. Ter. 10:9

> Testified R. Ṣadoq concerning (ʿL) brine [made] from unclean locusts that (Š) it is clean.

M. ʿEd. 7:1

> Testified R. Joshua and R. Ṣadoq concerning (ʿL) the redemption [lamb] for the firstling of an ass that died that (Š) there is nothing here for the priest.

M. ʿEd. 7:3

> Testified R. Ṣadoq concerning (ʿL) flowing [water] which exceeded [the amount of] dripping [water which had mingled with it] that (Š) it is fit [as flowing water].

M. ʿEd. 7:4

> Testified R. Ṣadoq concerning (ʿL) flowing [water] which one made gush forth through leaves of nuts that (Š) it is fit [as flowing water].

Relative to the formulation of the other traditions of Ṣadoq, the above have been most carefully and consistently formulated. Furthermore, as we mentioned at the outset of this chapter, only traditions of Joshua appear more often in this form than those of Ṣadoq. Of the six testimonies of Joshua, five are joint testimonies like M. ʿEd. 7:1 above. Five *different* authorities are involved with Joshua in these five traditions. These facts lead me to suspect that Joshua is not the integral authority in these five traditions, but that the appearance of his name is the work of the circle of his disciples. Perhaps this circle is responsible for the preservation of Ṣadoq's testimonies.

The Distribution of the Traditions Over the Forms

We may now return to an issue raised at the outset of our study of the forms assumed by the corpus of Ṣadoq's traditions, the distribution over the various forms. Our data may be summarized as follows:

FORMS		A	B	C	D
No. of	Legal	2	2	7	4
traditions	Non-legal		1	8	

The dispute, the most common form assumed by the traditions of the Houses, Eliezer and Ishmael, is the least common form in the Ṣadoq-corpus. Moreover, in one case the dispute-form has been "improperly" used. Not much more of the Sadoq-corpus is formulated as independent lemmas. The bulk of the traditions are, in fact, not preserved in direct discourse at all, but rather in the indirect discourse of testimonies and in narratives.

However, the lemma and its use in the dispute has been shown to be the "hallmark" of the redaction of the traditions of Yavneans and the Houses by the ʿAqivan circle of redactors.[18] The implication to be drawn in regard to the Ṣadoq-corpus, which does not exhibit these forms, is that it derives for the most part from some redactional circle other than that of the mainstream, ʿAqivan redactors.

This supposition is not inconsistent with a number of facts which we have accumulated in both Parts One and Two: (1) the corpus of Ṣadoq traditions, which has been preserved, is quite small; (2) whatever there is of it does not distribute well over the "ʿAqivan" formulary patterns; and (3) there has been a concerted effort on the part of redactors to demonstrate Ṣadoq's alignment with the mainstrem of tradition, the sages (cf. our discussion in Part One of M. ʿEd. 7:1-4).

A likely candidate for a circle in which Ṣadoq's traditions were formulated and preserved is that associated with the Patriarch, Gamaliel II. This too is consistent with a number of observations. In M. Pes. 7:2, a MʿŚ́H dealing with Gamaliel is attributed to Ṣadoq. In M. Suk. 2:4d, 5, Mʿ́ŚYWT of Gamaliel and Ṣadoq have been joined to form one single narrative. Ṣadoq is represented by b. Qid. 32b (= Sifré Deut. 38), y. Sanh. 1:4 and b. Bek. 36a as having close ties with the patriarchate of Gamaliel II. Finally, Gamaliel's corpus shows a similar trend to modes of expression which do not utilize direct discourse, in particular toward Mʿ́ŚYWT.[19]

In further support of our claim, we may point to a distinct correlation between traditions which relate Ṣadoq and Gamaliel and the narratives, the mode of expression seemingly associated with patriarchal redactors. All but one (4/5 = 80%) of the traditions which tie Ṣadoq to Gamaliel are in this "form." These stories comprise 27% of all of the Ṣadoq narratives, and 29% of the legal narratives. Moreover, that one tradition which we deemed an exception (M. Pes. 7:2) attributes a Gamaliel Mʿ́ŚH to Ṣadoq: "Said R. Ṣadoq, '(Mʿ́ŚH B) R. Gamaliel...'." The patriarchate, then, appears to have claimed Ṣadoq, a pre-70 master, as a supporter in its confrontation with the circle of the sages. We may safely assume, furthermore, that Ṣadoq was a far more important and influential figure in his day than one would surmise given the size of the extant corpus of his traditions in the Tannaitic (ʿAqivan) literature.

At this point, we shall allow ourselves a brief aside. Ṣadoq is not the only figure whose corpus of traditions exhibits a tendency to narratives. Neusner remarks that "while most laws assigned to the Houses are one-sentence lemmas, all laws attributed to named pre-70 masters (except the three sayings in standard [dispute] form of Shammai and Hillel, M. ʿEd. 1:3) are narratives of one kind or another."[20] Now here again there is a distinct correspondence between "form" and substance; with the exception of the Houses, in general the pre-70 masters are purported by the tradition to have held the position of either *nasi* (patriarch) or *'av bet din* (head of the court and subordinate to the *nasi*). The traditions of these pre-70, patriarchal figures assume the mode of expression we have associated with the post-70 patriarchal redactors. Perhaps the traditions of the pre-70 masters form the patriarchate's history of pre-70 Pharisaism, while those of the Houses represent the mainstrem Aqivan account of the same.[21]

If we were to hazard a guess concerning which traditions derive from a circle of Ṣadoq's disciples or from some circle of redactors to which Ṣadoq was a central rather than peripheral figure, the testimonies would, in my opinion, be the most likely candidates. They are the most carefully formulated of the corpus, and Ṣadoq is the figure most frequently associated with the testimony-form. (But, it must be stressed that we are still dealing with very few traditions, 4 of 33 testimonies.) I have suggested that (at least) in the case of the testimonies, Ṣadoq's traditions entered the redactional mainstream through a circle of redactors intimately related to Joshua.

VI. The Man Behind the Traditions

Thus far in our attempt to make the connection between the extant traditions concerning Ṣadoq and the man himself, we have utilized two approaches, each taking us further than the last. We discussed the distribution of the traditions of Ṣadoq over the various Rabbinic documents in which they appear. It was argued that the legal corpus is more likely to be representative of Ṣadoq than the non-legal traditions, which generally make their first appearance only in the latest strata of the rabbinic literature, and which are without demonstrable connection to Tannaitic sources. In our examination of the forms assumed by the corpus of Ṣadoq's traditions, implications were drawn regarding the circles responsible for the formulation and transmission of the traditions. We shall now take further steps in assessing the reliability of our sources for historical purposes.

A. Attestations

An attestation is a reference to a pericope, and provides a *terminus ante quem* for the tradition in question. For example, if an authority can be shown, in one way or another, to have known a particular tradition, he has, in "attesting" to that tradition, provided us with a rough date before which it must have existed.[22] A source can be attested to in three ways. First, tradition may be referred to directly by some figure outside the rabbinic tradition. There are no such attestations for the Jewish literature of late antiquity.[23] Second, by reason of its appearance in a (closed) collection, a tradition is provided a *terminus ante quem* by the date of the compilation of the text.[24] Thus a passage which first appears in Mishnah probably reached its present form by A.D. 200-220. Finally, a tradition may be referred to by an authority within the rabbinic circle; thus a source is provided with both a date and a "location" in which it was extant.[25]

In his study of the traditions of the Houses of Hillel and Shammai, Neusner established the existence of attestations of the third and final type for a great part of the Houses' legal traditions. A considerable proportion could be shown to be extant at Yavneh. Ushan attestations could be provided for still more.[26] Likewise, a great many of Eliezer b. Hyrcanus' traditions were attested to at a period soon after his death.[27] We have no attributions of this third type whatsoever for Ṣadoq's corpus of traditions. *None* of his traditions are attested to earlier than the final date which can be given for the compilation of the collections in which they appear. Thus, sources appearing in the Mishnah must have reached their present form no later than approximately A.D. 200-220. The

Tosefta may be dated ca. A.D. 250. The Tannaitic Midrashim may be given approximately the same date. Those sources appearing in the Palestinian Talmud date from the fifth century, those in the Babylonian Talmud a century or two later. Traditions which appear in the later midrashic collections are to be dated from the dates which can be given for the final compilation of the documents in question.[28] Our summary listing of all the traditions and the documents in which they appear (with which we began Chapter IV) provides, therefore, the *terminus ante quem* for each tradition. Hence, we are, as yet, unable to trace any traditions to a date earlier than some one and a quarter centuries after Ṣadoq's death.

B. Traditions Which May Be Better

Although by the method of attestations we cannot probatively date any of our sources earlier than 200-220, we are not precluded from estimating which traditions are likely to be earlier. For example, where it can be shown that a pericope in Mishnah containing a Ṣadoq tradition is a reformulation of another pericope in Mishnah in which the same tradition is found, we can surmise that the tradition in question can be dated earlier than A.D. 200-220. Just how much earlier admittedly cannot be ascertained with any degree of accuracy. Using this method, four traditions may be said to be "better" than the remainder of the traditions appearing in the Mishnah.

M. Ter. 10:9; M. ʿEd. 7:2

> Testified R. Sadoq concerning brine [made] from unclean locusts that it is clean.

M. ʿEd. 7:2 is dependent upon M. Ter. 10:9.

M. ʿEd. 3:8; M. Kel. 12:4, 5

> [Ṣadoq holds that the nail of a money-changer, the chest of a grist-dealer, and the nail of a sundial are unclean.]

The interdependency of the sources was discussed at length in Part One, pp. 70-74. All that need be said here is that the tradition has gone through considerable reformulation.

M. ʿEd. 7:1; M. Bek. 1:6

> Testified R. Joshua and R. Ṣadoq concerning the redemption [lamb] for the firstling of an ass that died that there is nothing here for the priest.

M. ʿEd. 7:1 and M. Bek. 1:6 are interdependent.

M. ʿEd. 7:3; M. Miq. 5:5

> Testified R. Sadoq concerning flowing [water] which exceeded [the amount of] dripping [water which had mingled with it] that it is fit [as flowing water].

If either of the sources is not dependent upon the other, then both at least are dependent upon an earlier common source.

It is interesting that in our list of the four traditions which may be deemed "better" using our "dependency method," we have accounted for three of the four traditions in testimony-form. We earlier provided reasons for suspecting that the testimonies entered the redactional mainstream through a circle of Joshua's disciples. This is not inconsistent with our finding here, namely that these traditions could well be quite early.

Still another tradition, M. Ned. 9:1, is likely to be early for a different reason. The pericope concerns itself with the ground whereby a sage may annul one's vow. Eliezer b. Hyrcanus gives a lenient ruling, and Ṣadoq provides a *reductio ad absurdum* of the view. We remarked that the importance of just this issue is attested to by the Gospels, documents which are contemporaneous with Yavneh. Moreover, the concern of Eliezer with many aspects of this issue further suggests the importance of the problem of the "release from a vow" to the Yavneans. For the above reasons, Ṣadoq's tradition on this subject *could* well be early.

We may now summarize our findings regarding the "reliability" of the corpus of Ṣadoq's traditions. Although we have provided evidence why five traditions may be suspected of being early, we have been unable probatively to establish that any of the corpus dates much earlier than A.D. 200-220, the accepted date for the final compilation of the Mishnah.

C. The Man Behind the Legal Agendum

As was mentioned in our Introduction, Ṣadoq may be deemed a minor figure for precisely the same reason the minor prophets were so designated. There are extremely few extant traditions of Ṣadoq in the rabbinic literature. Neusner lists two hundred and nineteen legal traditions for the Houses,[29] and two hundred and two hundred and twenty-eight for Eliezer b. Hyrcanus.[30] The legal corpus of Ṣadoq, on the other hand, totals only fourteen traditions. It is preposterous to imagine that the body of Ṣadoq's traditions preserved in the literature represents the total gamut of legal issues with which Ṣadoq concerned himself. We must have in our possession only a fraction of his legal rulings. Moreover, we can have no idea of what processes of selection (if any) were brought to bear in the preservation and transmission of those traditions of Ṣadoq which are extant. There is no reason to assume that the distribution of fourteen sources over various areas of concern in fact represents the relative concern of Ṣadoq about different issues. For example, that of the fourteen traditions none deal with tithes, heave-offering, *pe'ah* or the like, is hardly firm evidence that Ṣadoq was unconcerned with these issues or that he never expounded any legal opinions regarding them. In short, the connection between the extant legal agendum and the man is tenuous indeed.

Although the data will not permit the reconstruction of the personality of Ṣadoq, his policies regarding heated issues of his time or the trends of his thinking, rather general, even if qualified, statements concerning his alignment can be made. Hence, we shall now turn to the extant agendum.

1. Purity

M. Ter. 10:9: The brine made from unclean locusts is clean.

Tos. Suk. 2:3: A jar in which moist olives are kept must be broached in order that the olives not be rendered susceptible to uncleanness.

M. ʿEd. 3:8: A nail of a money-changer, a chest of a grist-dealer and a nailoof a sundial are all susceptible to uncleanness.

M. ʿEd. 7:3: If flowing water exceeds the amount of dripping water which had mingled with it, the whole is still considered flowing water for the purposes of immersion.

M. ʿEd. 7:4: Flowing water which is channeled through leaves of nuts is still considered flowing water for purposes of immersion.

Tos. Kel. B.B. 2:1-3: Hollowed out blocks are unclean.

Tos. Nid. 4:3, 4: Not all discharges of a woman can be attributed to miscarriage or menstruation.

2. Sabbath and Festivals

M. Shab. 20:2: The amount of drink which may be prepared on a Sabbath or Festival depends upon the number of guests to be served.

M. Pes. 7:2: The Passover-offering may be roasted on a grill.

M. Suk. 2:4d, 5: Less than an egg's bulk of food may be eaten outside the *sukkah*.

3. Agriculture

M. ʿEd. 7:1: If one has set aside a lamb to redeem the firstling of an ass, and the lamb dies, a substitute for the lamb need not be given to the priest.

4. Vows

M. Ned. 9:1: The honor due to one's parents is not valid grounds for one to be released from a vow.

5. Miscellaneous

Tos. Sanh. 8:1: "Elders" sit on the left of the patriarch, others on his right.

Sem. 12:9: During ossilegium, one does not gather the bones of one's parents oneself.

The analysis of the traditions of the pre-70 Pharisees and Eliezer b. Hyrcanus by Jacob Neusner and those of Ishmael by Gary Porton allows us to surmise what the legal agendum of a Pharisee at Yavneh would be. Of primary concern are laws pertaining to agriculture (such as proper tithing and donation of heave-offering) and purity. Second in importance would be festival law; other topics of concern would be vows, oaths and family law.

Admittedly, the distribution of the extant legal traditions does not exactly parallel this model agendum. Nevertheless, the agendum is that of a Pharisee. In Ṣadoq's legal traditions found in Mishnah-Tosefta, we do find a primary concern with purity; there is also one tradition dealing with agriculture. Festival law forms an important category, and, finally, we have one Mishnaic tradition dealing with vows. In short, there are no legal concerns which one would not expect of an Eliezer or Ishmael. However, although we can say with reasonable certainty that Ṣadoq was a Yavnean with Pharisaic leanings, I do not believe that the nature of the data allows us to proceed further in our attempt to describe the man beneath the traditions.

D. Conclusions

The study of Ṣadoq's traditions has revealed very little of the man himself. Most sources which purport to be of biographical significance appear to be quite late, and cannot be traced to earlier sources. Hence, they are virtually of no value in reconstructing the events of Ṣadoq's life, his attitudes and personality. The legal traditions, which, relatively speaking, are earlier, still cannot be shown with certainty to date much before the beginning of the third century. They are, nevertheless, the "best" data available to us. But even here the extreme paucity of the tradition makes it impossible to formulate any detailed picture of the man supposedly behind the tradition. Any statements concerning trends in policy and thought extrapolated from some dozen or so sources could have little claim to reliability. The claims which have been made are that Ṣadoq was a Pharisee at Yavneah, a contemporary of Joshua and Gamaliel II, and seemingly a figure of considerable worth to the patriarchate of the latter.

In our study we have pointed out where the often repeated notions[31] of Ṣadoq's priestly descent and Shammaite leanings find their basis. The first appears to underly an Amoriac pericope in b. Bek. 36a, and is explicitly mentioned in ARNa 16, a relatively late compilation. The second notion, that Ṣadoq was a Shammaite, solely relies upon possible implications of Tos. Suk. 2:3. No better evidence for these claims can be adduced; they deserve, therefore, to be forwarded only with severe qualifications.

Oddly enough, however, what is a hindrance in uncovering "the man" is of significance in other areas of concern, namely the formulation and transmission of Ṣadoq's traditions. Since, as has been proven by Porton, the tradition channels through the ʿAqivan redactional circle, the paucity of Ṣadoq's traditions indicates that, at least for the ʿAqivans, Ṣadoq was an unimportant and peripheral figure. Our study of the forms assumed by the traditions of Ṣadoq serves to support this claim. The sources show a general tendency to forms utilizing indirect discourse such as testimonies, and particularly to narratives. The lemma and its use in the dispute form, the "hallmark" of the ʿAqivan redactional circle, is much less common in the corpus of Ṣadoq's traditions. Hence, on formal grounds alone, we were able to claim that Ṣadoq's traditions are peripheral to the ʿAqivan tradents.

Since the traditions of Gamaliel II exhibit the same penchant for narratives as opposed to lemmas and disputes, and since several sources represent Ṣadoq as having strong ties with the patriarchate of Gamaliel II, we have *suggested* the circle of patriarchal redactors as an origin for the body of Ṣadoq's traditions. This was further confirmed by a correlation of the narrative mode of expression with pro-Gamaliel substance.

If any traditions may have originated from a circle with closer ties to Ṣadoq (such as a circle of his disciples), we have suggested the testimonies. We have also adduced some evidence for a claim that at least these traditions entered the redactional mainstream through the circle of Joshua's disciples. It is particularly with these traditions that we find the concerted effort to demonstrate Ṣadoq's alignment with the opinions of the sages. Such an effort is quite consistent with our notion that some strong relationship existed between Ṣadoq and Gamaliel II. Moreover, it would lead one to suspect that the relationship was historical as well as redactional.[32]

NOTES

ṢADOQ THE YAVNEAN

[1]J. Neusner, *Eliezer* II, pp. 1-17.

[2]A. Hyman, *Toledot Tannaim VeAmoraim* I (Jerusalem, 1964) pp. 201-5; "Zadok," *Enc. Jud.*, XVI, cols. 914, 915.

[3]A. Hyman, *Toledot*, pp. 201-5.

[4]"Zadok," *Enc. Jud.*, XVI, cols. 914, 915.

[5]We may cite the work of M. Margolioth ("R. Ṣadoq," *Encyclopedia of Talmudic and Geonic Literature* II, cols. 743-46) as an example of such attempts to harmonize sources. He holds that the "matron" stories of b. Qid. 40a and ARNa 16 and the dispute in M. Shab. 20:2 refer to a "R. Ṣadoq II," who is the grandson of the Ṣadoq with whom we are dealing. The matron stories (which appear in an Amoraic tradition and in a later Rabbinic compilation) represent Ṣadoq as having been taken captive by the Romans and sold to a Roman lady. Now this stands in contradiction to other late traditions (b. Giṭ. 56 and Lam. R. 1:31) which claim that Yoḥanan b. Zakkai had Ṣadoq removed from Jerusalem before its fall and that Vespasian provided physicians to heal Ṣadoq. If both sets of stories have a claim to veracity, then the Ṣadoq of the matron stories cannot be the Ṣadoq of the Jerusalem stories. In fact, the historical value of either set to a biography of Ṣadoq is negligible.

The problem presented by M. Shab. 20:2 is somewhat different. The tradition has Ṣadoq in dispute with Judah b. Ilai, an Ushan. Hence, according to Margolioth, this cannot be our Ṣadoq. But the relationship between authorities in a dispute is a redactional one. Indeed, redactors generally have contemporaries dispute with one another, but this is not always the case. Some disputes are more carefully formulated than others, and to have non-contemporaries in dispute with one another is not uncommon. In fact, we shall show that this particular dispute is not a "good" one for other reasons unrelated to the fact that Ṣadoq and Judah are not contemporaries.

[6]Neusner, *Pharisees* III, *Eliezer* II. Preliminary results for Ishmael can be found in Gary G. Porton, "The Legal Traditions of Rabbi Ishmael: A Form-Critical and Literary-Critical Approach," Doctoral Dissertation, Brown University, 1973, pp. 310ff.

[7]Neusner, *Pharisees* III, pp. 64ff.

[8]Neusner, *Eliezer* II, p. 60.

[9]Porton, "Legal Traditions," p. 310.

[10]Neusner, *Pharisees* III, pp. 14-16.

[11]Ibid., p. 5.

[12]Ibid., p. 6.

[13]Ibid., p. 7.

[14]Gary G. Porton, "The Artificial Dispute: Ishmael and ʿAqiva," in J. Neusner, ed., *Christianity, Judaism, and Other Greco-Roman Cults: Studies for Morton Smith at 60* (Leiden, 1975) Part IV, p. 18.

[15]Neusner, *Eliezer* II, pp. 18-62.

[16]Porton, "Legal Traditions," pp. 311ff.

[17]See Neusner, *Pharisees* III, pp. 14, 15.

[18]Neusner, *Eliezer* II, pp. 367-77.

[19]See Shamai Kanter, *Gamaliel of Yavneh* (Leiden, 1978).

[20]Neusner, *Pharisees* III, p. 23.

[21]This was suggested to me as a possibility by Professor Jacob Neusner.

[22]Neusner, *Pharisees* III, pp. 180ff.

[23]Ibid., p. 180.

[24]Ibid.

[25]Ibid., p. 181.

[26]Ibid., pp. 199-220.

[27]Neusner, *Eliezer* II, p. 87.

[28]The date of the final editing of the Mishnah is uncertain; the same may be said for the Tosefta. See J. Neusner, *The Modern Study of the Mishnah* (Leiden, 1973) and Y. N. Epstein, *Introduction to the Tannaitic Literature* (Hebrew) (Tel Aviv, 1957) pp. 241-62. The dates which we have provided are those commonly accepted. For discussion on the editing of the Babylonian Talmud, see J. Neusner, *The Formation of the Babylonian Talmud* (Leiden, 1970). In regard to the date of the final editing of the Palestinian Talmud, see Y. N. Epstein, *Introduction to the Amoraic Literature* (Hebrew) (Tel Aviv, 1962) pp. 271-334. Vis-a-vis the final compilation of the Tannaitic Midrashim, see Y. N. Epstein, *Introduction to the Tannaitic Literature*, pp. 545-746.

[29]Neusner, *Pharisees* II, pp. 344-53.

[30]Neusner, *Eliezer* II, p. 1.

[31]See "Zadok," *Enc. Jud.*, XVI, cols. 914, 915; Hyman, *Toledot*, pp. 201-5.

[32]Almost all of this work was read and discussed in Professor Jacob Neusner's graduate seminar at Brown University during 1972-1973. It is impossible to document page by page my reliance on his insights and constructive criticisms. The comments and remarks of Professors Baruch Bokser, William Scott Green, Gary G. Porton, Charles Primus, Dr. Shamai Kanter, Rabbi Tzvee Zahavy, and Mr. Joel Gereboff have been most helpful and appreciated. A debt of gratitude is also owed to Professors Horst Moehring, Wendell Dietrich, and Rabbi Joel Zaiman for their advice and guidance.

The generous support of the Canadian Foundation for Jewish Culture enabled me to bring this work to completion.

ELEAZAR ḤISMA

Diane Levine

PART ONE: THE TRADITION

Our analysis concerns the traditions of R. Eleazar Ḥisma, who is purported to be a Yavnean and disciple of R. Joshua. The number of extant traditions is very small, in all eighteen unparallel sources. We can hardly assume that this represents the whole of Eleazar Ḥisma's original materials. Rather, what we have before us is the result of a process of selection. What can we say about this redactional process? Why are these materials included, what could account for the suppression or elimination of other materials? What is characteristic of the manner in which the tradition has been preserved, and what, if anything, does it tell us about the man behind the tradition? These are the questions we shall attempt to answer.

This paper is divided into two parts. In Part One we shall analyze each individual unit of tradition and explain the principles of law involved, and the forms and literary traits out of which the tradition is constructed. Part Two is an examination of the tradition as a whole. I shall attempt to isolate the authentic sources and perceive any overall pattern among them according to analysis of both form and substance. From this analysis we hope to make some valid remarks about the authority behind the tradition.

(1)

A. 1. As to one who says, "[Let] the Heave-offering of this heap be within it

2. "and its tithes be within it

3. "and the Heave-offering of the tithe be within it"--

B. R. Simeon says, "He designated it [properly]."

C. But the Sages say, "Until he says 'to its north or south' [it is not properly designated]."

D. R. Eleazar Ḥisma says, "[As to] one who says [let] the Heave-offering of the pile [be given] from this [heap] for this [same heap], he has designated [properly]."

E. R. Eliezer b. Jacob says, "[As to] one who says [let] the tenth part of this tithe be Heave-offering of tithe for this [same tithe] he has designated it [properly]."

M. Ter. 3:5

Comment: A-C is a dispute between R. Simeon and the sages concerning the proper formula for designating tithes. Since tithes cannot be used as common produce once they are designated, it is important that they clearly be differentiated from common produce in order to avoid confusion of the two. Simeon claims that *within it* (BTWKW) is sufficient to designate tithes, but the sages are more stringent. If the designating formula does not clearly mark a place for the tithes separate from the common produce, it is as if the tithes were not designated at all (Maimonides, MT, Ter. 3:8).

Eleazar Ḥisma gives a different formula for the proper designation of tithes. He rules that the formula *MMNW ʿLYW* is sufficient for proper designations, for it guarantees the general law of M. Ter. 2:4 that tithes for given produce must be taken from that produce only.

Thus, Eleazar's opinion disagrees with that of the sages and Simeon, who hold a more stringent view. Simeon holds that *within it* is sufficient for proper designation for, although a generalized formula, it still is specific enough to distinguish one part of the produce from the rest. Eleazar, however, requires the person to state merely that the Heave-offering shall be given from that pile. Thus, he does not differentiate one part of the pile from the other. Compared to Simeon and the sages, Eleazar requires a minimal differentiation in order to properly designate Heave-offering.

As to Eliezer b. Jacob, TYY, Bertinoro, and Maimonides contend that he disagrees with Simeon in A. They explain that, according to Simeon, even if one has not separated tithes from the rest of the pile, if he says *Let the Heave-offering of this heap be within it*, he has designated it properly. Eliezer b. Jacob, however, requires one to first separate the tithe and then designate Heave-offering for a given pile. This explanation is based upon the language in Eliezer b. Jacob's statement "tenth part of this tithe" which indicates that the tithe has already been separated.

Mishnah Rishonah objects to this explanation and argues that also Simeon requires the prior separation of tithe before uttering the formula *Let the Heave-offering of this heap be within it*. The disagreement between Simeon and Eliezer b. Jacob is rather that since Eliezer b. Jacob follows the general principle of Eleazar Ḥisma's statement, he rules that the formula *for this same tithe* is sufficient.

Although the language and content in E is similar to Eleazar Ḥisma's saying in D, it is not dependent on it for its meaning. Thus, the pericope consists of the dispute A-C and two discrete sayings D and E. R. Simeon and R. Eliezer b. Jacob are Ushans.

(2)

A. A laborer may eat cucumbers even of a *denar*'s worth and dates of a *denar*'s worth.

B. R. Eleazar Ḥisma says, "A laborer should not eat more than [the value] of his hire."

C. But the Sages allow it.

D. Yet they teach a man that he should not be so gluttonous that the door is closed against him.

M.B.M. 7:5; b. B.M. 92a;
y. B.M. 7:4

A. [Concerning] a laborer who eats a bunch of grapes before he begins his work.

B. [If he eats] a bunch of grapes even of a *denar*'s worth, or cucumbers even of a *denar*'s worth.

C. Or dates even of three *ases*' worth (TRYSYT).

D. In behalf of R. Eleazar Ḥisma they said,

E. "A laborer should not eat more than [the value of] his hire."

F. But the Sages allow it.

Tos. B. M. 10:8, ed. Zuckermandel, p. 388, lines 9-11

Comment: In addition to his wage, a man is allowed to eat the fruit among which he works. In Mishnah, A limits this to a *denar*'s worth. B-C is a dispute independent of A. D appears to be a gloss connected to C by "yet" (Š).

Mishnah does not specify when the laborer is allowed to eat. If we accept Tos. as a single unit, however, it specifies that the issue concerns a laborer who eats before he begins his work. Thus, Tos. is an expansion and clarification of the case in Mishnah.

In contrast to Mishnah, Eleazar Ḥisma's statement is presented in the form of an indirect statement in his behalf.

A. *When you come into your neighbor's vineyard, then you may eat grapes until you have enough at your pleasure; but you shall not put them in your vessel* (Deut. 23:25).

B. The text says, *But you shall not put* [*produce*] *in your vessel.*

C. [This concerns] when you put [produce] into the owner's vessel.

D. *Your neighbor*

E. [This means produce] belonging to others.

F. *Your neighbor*

G. [This means produce] belonging to one of high [status] (employer).

H. *You may eat*

I. You may not press [them for making wine].

J. *Grapes*

K. And not figs.

L. From this you say, If he worked in dates, he shall not eat grapes. [If he worked] in grapes, he shall not eat figs; but he may restrain himself until he reaches the place of the nicest [fruits] and [then] eat.

M. R. Eleazar Ḥisma says, "From this [we learn] that a laborer shall not eat more than [the value of] his hire."

N. Scripture says, *As your soul* (KNPŠK).

O. But the Sages say, *Pleasure* (ŚBʿK).

P. This teaches that the laborer may eat more than [the value of] his hire.

Sifré Deut. #266, ed. Finkelstein, 286.

A. It is written, *When you come into your neighbor's vineyard...* (Deut. 23:25)

B. It is possible that this law concerns any man.

C. [But] the text says, *You shall not put them in your vessel.*

D. You shall not put [them in yours] but you do put them in the vessel of your comrade.

E. And if he [does] this, he is a worker.

F. *And you may eat grapes...*"

G. And is it not known that in a vineyard there is nothing to eat besides grapes?

H. What Scripture says, *And you may eat grapes.*

I. Rather from this [we learn] that if he works in grapes, he shall not eat figs.

J. *As your soul* (KNPŠK)

K. All which the passion desires.

L. *As your soul*

M. Any case in which (Š) he (the owner) is exempt from tithes, he is exempt from tithing what he eats; so also [if] the worker eats, he is exempt.

N. *Your soul.*

O. From this [we learn] that the laborer shall not eat more than [the value of] his hire.

P. From this R. Eleazar Ḥisma says, "A laborer shall not eat more than [the value of] his hire."

y. Ma. 2:4

Comment: Sifré is an exegesis of Deut. 23:25. Our concern is with M-P. In place of the simple dispute of Mishnah-Tosefta, the sayings of both the Sages and Eleazar Ḥisma have been transformed into a statement supplied with a prooftext. N should precede M so as to maintain the order of Scripture + opinion.

According to Eleazar Ḥisma, the meaning of *As your soul* is that one can consume an amount equal to the value of his labor.

In y. the order is correct--scripture + opinion, but this version lacks the opinion of the Sages. It is curious that Eleazar Ḥisma's saying appears anonymously in O and as an attributed statement in P.

(3)

A. R. Eleazar (Vilna MSS: Eliezer) (b.) Ḥisma says,

B. "[The laws of] bird-offerings and the onset of menstruation, these are the body of the laws.

C. "Astronomy and Gematria are the desserts of wisdom."

M. Avot 3:19, ARNa 27;
ed. Schechter, p. 24

Comment: Bird-offerings are obligatory offerings prescribed for the expiation of certain offenses and of certain conditions of uncleanness. Examples of such cases are one who comes into contact with corpse-matter, one sho suffers from an infectious skin disease, one who suffers as a Zab or a woman after childbirth. Similarly, menstruation requires bird offerings. Nearly 50% of the legal issues attributed to Eleazar Ḥisma in Mishnah-Tosefta are found in this category of cases. A detailed discussion of this will be found in Part Two.

Eleazar Ḥisma gives a curriculum for study. One should study the primary matters of *Halakah*, which are, according to Eleazar, matters of uncleanness. Once one has satiated his appetite, he is then allowed dessert--astronomy and gematria. TYY comments that in calling the sciences *desserts of wisdom*, Eleazar attacks those who consider these matters to be primary matters of study. Rather, one should delve into these issues after one has studied *Halakot*.

Thus, Eleazar Ḥisma's saying is not an outright condemnation of the study of scientific knowledge but a designation of their proper place in study.

(4)

A. [If] their appearance changed
B. Either to effect leniency or to effect stringency [in ruling]
C. How could it effect leniency?
D. [If] it was [white] as snow, and became [white] as the lime of the Sanctuary, as white wool or as the white of an egg.
E. [Or if] it became a scab of a fester or a scab of an intense white [spot].
F. How could it effect stringency?
G. [If] it was [white] as the white of an egg and became [white] as white wool, or as lime of the Sanctuary or as snow.

H. Rabbi Eleazar ben Azariah declares clean.

I. Rabbi Eleazar Ḥisma says, "[If the leprosy sign changed] to effect leniency, it is clean, but [if the sign changed] to effect stringency, it must be inspected anew."

J. Rabbi ʿAqiva says, "Whether [it changed] to effect leniency or stringency, it must be inspected anew."

M. Neg. 7:2

Comment: Leviticus 13 deals with various cases of malignant skin disorders that render a man unclean and result in his ostracism from the community. The suspect may be quarantined for up to two weeks. If after this time period the disease appears to be infected, the man is declared unclean. The signs of infection vary, depending on the nature of the disease. According to M. Neg. 3:3, in the case of a fester (Sʾ T), or a sore (MSPḤT), or a bright spot (BHRT), the infection is declared unclean due to one of three signs--at least two white hairs, raw flesh, or spreading.

The actual case involved in M. 7:2 is unclear. It appears to deal with the problem of M. 7:1 where the bright spot is assumed clean under certain instances and does not require inspection by the priest. In 7:2 the question is raised as to the validity of this ruling if the appearance of the bright spot should change. We can only assume that this is the intention of the superscription A-B, for it is not specifically stated.

C through G is a gloss describing the degrees of color that determine the severity of the infection. C-D and F-G are balanced opposites. The former describes the change in color from intense to dim white, and the latter from dim to intense white. These categories of color are found as a tradition of Rabbi Meir's in M. Neg. 1:1 and are therefore Ushan--

A. The two appearances of leprosy signs are four.

B. The intense bright white spot (BHRT) [which is] as snow; the second [shade] to it is as the lime of the Sanctuary.

C. The fester (S'T) [which is] as the white of an egg; the second [shade] to it is as white wool.

The categories of E are not found in M. 1:1, and in M. 7:2 only serve to destroy the balanced statements of C-D and F-G. It is probably a later gloss of C-G.

By ignoring the gloss we have simply a superscription and three rulings. Although B is a clarification of A, it still does not clarify the nature of the change in appearance. Mishnah 1:5 and 1:6 deal with changes that effect leniency or stringency and perhaps supply us with a definition of our superscription.

The case is concerned with a change in appearance occuring after the Sabbath. If the day for inspection after quarantine falls on the Sabbath, the priest must wait until the next day to examine the suspect. The criteria for judgment, either lenient or stringent, are not color, but are those found in M. 3:3 for a bright spot, sore or fester (i.e., white hairs, raw flesh, or spreading).

Because of the special nature of the case due to the fact that inspection could not occur at its appointed time, the question is whether the infection be examined by the priest at a later time.

In H, Eleazar ben Azariah declares that the infection is clean, that is, the suspect is not subjected to examination. ʿAqiva (J) is not at all concerned with the nature of change. Whether the infectious condition improved or worsened, it must be examined as if it were a newly discovered infection.

R. Eleazar Ḥisma's statement is a compromise between the two. The nature of change is important in the determination of his ruling. If the infection lessened in severity, it is clean and need not be examined. If it should grow worse, it must be examined and the suspect may be made to submit to the two weeks quarantine and possible isolation.

Thus, the original dispute form would be superscription A followed by the three opinions H-J. Such a variation on the dispute form, which normally consists of two opinions instead of three, can only be explained by the logic of the dispute. There are three possible solutions to A. The nature of the infection changes after the appointed time for inspection. One can ignore the change. This means that the infection is declared clean or it must be inspected anew without consideration of any previous inspection. The third possibility is to consider the nature of the change. If the infection improves, the law is according to H. If it worsens, it must be inspected anew.

Eleazar b. Azariah and R. ʿAqiva are pre-Ushan.

A. And God spoke to Moses and Aaron saying

B. *A man who has in the skin of his flesh...* (Lev. 13:2)

C. What does the text mean? As it is said

D. *And a man or a woman who has bright spots...*

E. The bright spots [in this case] are clean.

F. There is no need to speak of bright spots which do not have in them the appearance of leprosy signs and which are not subject to the law [of uncleanness] rather [we speak of] bright spots that do contain the appearance of leprosy signs that were [found in the case of] a non-Jew who converted.

G. Or of a child when it was born

H. Or in a fold [of the skin] and was discovered (later)

I. Or on the head or on a beard.

J. Or [in the case of] a boil, burn, or blister that healed (reads KRḤ; corrected to KDḤ as found in M. Neg. 7:1, 6:8, 8:5)

K. If their appearance changed either to effect leniency or to effect stringency
L. R. Eleazar ben Azariah declares clean.
M. R. Eleazar ben Ḥisma says, "[If the leprosy signs changed] to effect stringency, it must be inspected anew."
N. R. ʿAqiva says, "Whether [it changed] to effect leniency or stringency, it must be inspected anew."
O. For this reason it is said
P. *A man who will have...*

Sifra Taz. 1:1, ed. Weiss

Comment: Leviticus 13:2 describes the general law concerning one who suffers from a skin infection, that is, from a fester, sore, or bright spot. He is taken to the priest and examined. He is either declared unclean then or put into isolation for a week. If it remains the same, he is isolated another week and re-examined. The priest must then decide whether the disease has improved or worsened and declare him clean or unclean. Here, Lev. 13:2 is applied to Lev. 13:38 where the bright spots are found to be dull white (BHK) and the suspect is declared clean. But if the issue concerns bright spots that are clean, then the issue of K-N, which is identical to A-B and H-J in M. Neg. 7:2, is unclear. It cannot apply to A-E where the bright spot is declared clean by the priest, and is no longer subject to the law of uncleanness. F-J attempts to reconcile A-E to K-N by claiming that the case under debate is that found in M. Neg. 7:1 and not the case of dull white leprosy (BHK). The dispute is clearly made to apply to a case where one is accepted into the Israelite community, as in the case of the proselyte, and afterwards the malignant infection is discovered. This stands in contrast to M. Neg. 7:2 where no clear reference to M. 7:1 is made.

The three statements do not clearly apply to M. 7:1. The commentator Rabad recognizes that R. Eleazar ben

Azariah's statement is not concerned with the same issue as those of R. ʿAqiva and R. Eleazar Ḥisma. Since R. Eleazar ben Azariah simply declares clean, without concern for change of appearance, he is seen as referring to the case of dull white leprosy. Only M and N dispute M. 7:1. The problem we saw just previously however still remains. The bright spots are clean and the suspect need not be examined by the priest. M and N refer to a case where the subject is taken before the priest again or is exempt from examination. This implies the case of M. Neg. 1:5, 1:6 where the subject is to be examined after seven days of quarantine and the seventh day is the Sabbath.

(5)

A. [As to a house in which a leprosy sign appears] its stones and timber, and mortar render unclean [if they are] of an olive's bulk.

B. R. Eleazar Ḥisma says, "Whatever their bulk."

M. Negaim 13:3

Comment: Leviticus 14:33-45 states the law concerning a house infected by fungus or a similar type of growth. The house must be inspected by the priest and shut up for one week. The priest then returns, and if the infection remains, the infected stones are removed and replaced with clean ones. If the infection should return, the house is declared unclean and is destroyed.

The meaning of the reference *its* in A is supplied by the context of M. Neg. 13:3 in which A-B appears. The pericope deals with specific instances in which leprosy signs appear in a house with and without upper stories. Our pericope is otherwise unrelated to what precedes it. A-B considers the amount of infected material of a house sufficient to render unclean. A states that the stone, timber, and mortar render unclean if they are of an olive's bulk. Eleazar Ḥisma answers that they render unclean no matter what size they are. Maimonides explains that infected house materials render a man or vessel unclean by contact, carrying, or by entrance into the infected house. Thus, entering an unclean house is equivalent to entering an unclean tent.

Bertinoro points out that the measurement *of an olive's bulk* in A is the same prescribed for corpse matter, in order to render unclean. Thus, A equates unclean matter of a house to corpse matter.

To understand the measurement found in Eleazar Ḥisma's ruling, we turn to M. Oholoth 1:7.

A. The members [of a body] have no prescribed bulk (ʿŠYWR)
B. Even less than an olive's bulk of a corpse, and less than an olive's bulk of carrion, or less than a lentil's bulk of a creeping thing [suffice to] render unclean their uncleanness.

Mishnah Aharona and Sens compare the principle of law here to B of M. Neg. 13:3. The limb of a body has no measurement, and thus even the smallest amount renders unclean. The stones, timber, and mortar are not the complete house, but are only part, just as a limb is only part of the entire corpse. The ruling in each case is identical.

A-B is a carefully redacted dispute, with the superscription contained in the anonymous law A. If we reconstruct the dispute, we find that it is perfectly balanced, each statement of the apodosis containing four syllables.

A. Its stones and timber and mortar render unclean.
B. [If they are] of an olive's bulk (BKZYT)
C. R. Eleazar Ḥisma says, "Whatever their bulk (BMŠHN)."

A. [As to a house in which a leprosy sign appears] its stones, timber, and mortar render unclean like a creeping thing (KŠRṢ).

B. R. Eleazar Ḥisma says, "Whatever their bulk."

Tos. Neg. 7:2, ed. Zuckermandel, p. 626, lines 18-21

Comment: In the Tosefta, A-B is placed within a context different from the Mishnah. It deals with the house materials which may be saved from a house to be destroyed on account of a malignant infection.

Eleazar Ḥisma's statement remains the same. The apodosis in A, however, has been altered. *Of an olive's bulk* (BKZYT) has been changed to *like a creeping thing* (KŠRṢ). Since the amount necessary to render unclean like a creeping thing is of a lentil's bulk, the ruling in Tos. is less stringent than that found in Mishnah. Not only does a creeping thing require less of a quantity than an olive's bulk, in order to render unclean, but where an olive's bulk of house material renders unclean by contact and carrying, a lentil's bulk renders unclean only by carrying. Both, however, are Fathers of Uncleanness.

The alteration in Tos. is important in another respect. In Mishnah, we had a well-balanced dispute. In Tos., KŠRṢ contains only three syllables, and thus destroys the balance of 4-4 found in the Mishnah.

(6)

A. Concerning one who discharges thick drops from the member
B. He is unclean.
C. These are the words of R. Eleazar Ḥisma.
D. Concerning one who has impure thoughts [in a dream] at night and rose up and found his flesh heated
E. He is unclean.
F. Concerning [a woman] who discharges semen on the third day [after intercourse]
G. She is clean.
H. These are the words of R. Eleazar b. Azariah.

M. Miq. 8:3

Comment: A-H is a composite pericope containing three cases of law related to one another by thematic similarities only. All three are based on the principle of Leviticus 15:16. *And if the flow of seed go out from a man, then he shall bathe all his flesh in water, and be unclean until the evening.*

If potent semen is expelled outside of the act of intercourse, it renders the person unclean.

A-C, which is attributed to Eleazar Ḥisma, is preceded by M. Miq. 8:2 and stands in contrast to it. The previous Mishnah makes distinctions between urine and semen according to the criteria of appearance of the flow and at what point, during urination, it takes place. The ruling of Eleazar Ḥisma is much closer to the biblical law for he makes the simplest distinction between urine and semen. If a man discharges thick drops, at any time, he has expelled semen and is unclean.

The pericope has been placed into a neatly ordered form by the redactor. The pattern consists of a superscription A, the ruling B, and the attribution C. It is repeated in F-H. D-E, however, is missing the attribution and instead appears as an anonymous ruling.

(7)

A. Testified R. Yose b. Hameshullam in behalf of R. Nathan his brother who said in the name of R. Leazar Ḥisma

B. That (Š) they do not prepare [any] clean [foodstuffs] for an *am ha'areṣ*.

C. 1. One should not prepare for him the dough of Heave-offering in cleanness.

C. 2. But he does prepare for him the dough of common produce in cleanness.

D. He separates from it the Dough offering and places [it] in a basket (KPYSH) and the *am ha'areṣ* comes and takes both (Dough offering and vessel) [to the priest].

E. 1. One should not prepare for him olives of Heave-offering in cleanness.

E. 2. But he prepares for him the olives of common produce in cleanness.

F. He separates from it the Heave-offering and places [it] in the vessels of an associate (ḤBR) and the *am ha'areṣ* comes and takes both [to the priest].

Tos. Demai 3:1, Lieberman,
p. 73, lines 1-6

Comment: One suspected of neglecting tithes and of not keeping the laws of cleanness is known as an *am ha'areṣ*.

Preparation, here, means the proper preparation of produce such that it may be given as consecrated food or such that consecrated food may be given from it.

The pericope consists of two parts: A-B, which is Eleazar's statement, and C-F, which seems to be an anonymous law in dispute with A-B. This is clearly indicated by the change of verb form from third person plural perfect, to third person singular imperfect. We shall, therefore, discuss these two parts separately.

Since Eleazar does not specify in B any particular type of food which a person may not prepare, we assume that Eleazar prohibits the preparation of all food stuffs. We can explain his ruling as follows.

If a non-associate brought a lump of dough and said, "Prepare this such that I may give it as Dough offering for the remainder of my dough," he may not do this for two reasons. First, we assume that all dough has already become unclean in the hands of the non-associate. Second, even if we were to assume the lump of dough to be clean, we would prohibit its preparation as Dough offering, for by giving it for the rest of his dough, the non-associate gives clean for unclean. This is according to M. Ter. 2:1, 2:2.

Furthermore, if the non-associate brought a lump of dough to an associate and said, "Prepare it such that I may separate Dough offering from it and retain the remainder as common produce," Eleazar would prohibit this action. Once the non-associate touches the separated Dough offering, he renders it unclean.

The rulings of C2 and E2, however, seem to dispute B. According to these statements, one *may* prepare common dough in cleanness. The rulings of C1 and E1, on the other hand, agree with B. Thus, unless we assume that C2 and E2 are later additions to C-F, then C-F and B cannot both be Eleazar's original statement. Perhaps C-F is an anonymous law disputing Eleazar's ruling. As we shall see, the parallel to this pericope in b. has dropped B and thus has eliminated the difficulty of reconciling B to C-F.

C1 of Tos. states that one does not prepare the dough of Heave-offering. This term is meaningless. Lieberman (*Tosefta Kifshuṭa*, VI, p. 222) explains the use of this odd term *dough of Heave-offering* as an attempt by the redactor to maintain the parallel with *olives of Heave-offering* in E1. The meaning is that one does not prepare the Dough offering. As we shall see, the version of C1 of Tos. in b. reads *They do not prepare Dough offering....* Lieberman and GRA emend the text of Tos. according to the b. version.

Thus, according to C1, one may not prepare the Dough offering of a non-associate in cleanness. Lieberman explains that in this case a non-associate brought the dough, which he intended to give as Dough offering, to the associate and asked him to prepare it. The associate should not prepare it, since it has already been rendered unclean. Dough is flour mixed with water. Water renders flour susceptible to uncleanness, and since the non-associate has made the flour into dough, it is assumed unclean.

Similarly in E1, the associate should not prepare olives of Heave-offering in cleanness, for they have been rendered unclean during the process of pickling or pressing by the non-associate.

According to C2 and E2, one *may* prepare dough or olives of common produce in cleanness for a non-associate.

Lieberman explains that the non-associate brings unprocessed wheat or olives to the associate. These items have not yet been rendered susceptible to uncleanness and therefore may be prepared in cleanness. Once having completed preparations, he follows the procedure outlined in C-D and F-G. He places the offering in a vessel that does not receive uncleanness and gives it to the non-associate.

Thus, we see that Eleazar Ḥisma's ruling is a general prohibition against the preparation of foodstuffs in cleanness for a non-associate. C-F expands greatly on his statement and represents a more detailed consideration of the legal problem expressed in B. It guarantees the absolute purity of foods prepared for a non-associate by an associate while still allowing the associate to earn a livelihood from the non-associate.

A. Testified R. Yose b. Hameshullam in behalf of R. Yohanan his brother who said in behalf of R. Eleazar Ḥisma

B. 1. They do not prepare Dough offering for an *am ha'areṣ* in cleanness.

B. 2. But they do prepare for him the dough of common produce in cleanness.

C. And take from it [the given amount] as Dough offering and place [it] in a basket or on a board. And when the *am ha'areṣ* comes, he takes both.

D. And there is no fear [that it will be rendered unclean].

E. 1. And they do not prepare olives of Heave-offering in cleanness.

E. 2. But they do prepare olives of common produce in cleanness.

F. And take [the given amount] as Heave-offering and place [it] in the vessels of an associate. And when the *am ha'areṣ* comes to take [it], he takes both.

G. And there is no fear [that it will be rendered unclean].

b. Giṭṭin 62a

Comment: A of b. is almost identical to A of Tos. except that R. Nathan becomes R. Yohanan. The major difference between the two sources is that b. has dropped B of Tos. and thus C-F of Tos. is now the only saying of Eleazar. In doing so, b. has eliminated the difficulties pointed to above. Furthermore, b. has changed the verbs of C-F of Tos. All verbs are now in the third person plural perfect tense. In Tos., C1 and E1 are third person singular imperfect, which suggested that C-F was a spelling out of Eleazar's statement.

To get a clear idea of the development of Tos. in b., a synopsis is supplied below.

Tos.	*Bavli*
1. R. Yose b. Hameshullam testified in behalf of R. Nathan his brother who said in behalf of R. Eleazar Ḥisma	1. ...R. Yohanan...
2. That they do not prepare clean [food stuffs] for an *am ha'areṣ*.	2. - - - - -
3. One should not prepare for him the dough of Heave-offering in cleanness. But he does prepare for him the dough of common produce in cleanness.	They do not prepare Dough offering of an *am ha'areṣ* in cleanness. But they do prepare...
4. He separates from it the Dough offering and places [it] in a basket and when the *am ha'areṣ* comes, he takes both (ZW W ZW).	4. And takes from it [the given amount] as Dough offering and places [it] in a basket or on a board. And when the *am ha'areṣ* comes, he takes both (ŠTYHN).
5. - - - - -	5. And there is no fear.
6. One should not prepare for him olives of Heave-offering in cleanness.	6. And they do not prepare the Heave-offering of olives in cleanness.
7. But he prepares for him the olives of common produce in cleanness.	7. But they do prepare olives of common produce in cleanness.

8. He separates from it the Heave-offering and places [it] in the vessels of an associate and the *am ha'areṣ* comes and takes both.	8. And take [an amount] as Heave offering and place [it] in the vessels of an associate. And when the *am ha'areṣ* comes to take [it], he takes both (ŠTYHN).
9. - - - - -	9. And there is no fear.

(8)

A. Testified R. Yose b. Hameshulam in behalf of his brother Nathan who said in behalf of R. Eleazar Ḥisma

B. That (Š) one who leases (MQBL) from a gentile a field of his fathers to harvest olives gives to him [the prescribed amount of produce as rent] as they are [untithed].

Tos. Demai 6:7, ed. Lieberman, p. 95, lines 20-22

Comment: A man can work someone else's field either by hiring or by leasing it. If it is by hire, he must pay the owner a given amount of the produce regardless of the yield. By leasing a field, he agrees to pay a proportion of the entire yield.

Tos. states that a man who leases a field from a non-Jew must make payment for rent and then tithe his share of the produce. The importance of this ruling for both lessor and lessee can be seen in an example. Since the field is being leased, the Jew agrees to pay perhaps 50% of the entire yield as rent. The yield is 100 bushels. According to Tos., he gives 50 to the non-Jew and is left with 50, which he tithes, leaving approximately 45 bushels as his final yield. In the opposite case, he tithes 100 bushels first and is left with 90, out of which he pays the rent of 50% of 100, and is left with 40. Eleazar Ḥisma's ruling is thus to the benefit of the lessee.

There are two important details in Eleazar Ḥisma's statement. First, a field that is rented is a field of his fathers. We will explain this notion below. Second, a person intends to harvest olives. As we shall see, harvesting olives to produce olives is distinguished from harvesting olives to produce olive oil. Our initial explanation of the pericope will concentrate on the fact that the field rented is a field of his fathers.

Land once owned by a Jew is taken over by a non-Jew. If the Jew returns and leases the land, does the rightful ownership belong to the Jew or non-Jew? Eleazar claims that the fact that the field once belonged to the Jew's family does not make him legal owner and thus liable to tithe. He tithes only the portion left to him after he pays rent.

In M. Demai 6:2 we find the following:

> A. If he hired a field from a gentile, he must set aside Tithes and then make payment.
>
> B. R. Judah says, "Also if he leased from a gentile the field of his fathers he must set aside Tithes as well and then make payment."
>
> (Danby, p. 26)

Judah seems to oppose Eleazar's opinion, for he rules that the person must tithe the entire yield before giving the gentile his portion. Judah presupposes that the field is of Jewish ownership.

This interpretation of the sayings of Judah and Eleazar neglects the fact that Judah does not specify the purpose for leasing the field while Eleazar does specify a particular purpose. If we can discover why, in this case, Eleazar rules that one does not tithe all the produce and then pay rent, then Eleazar and Judah may not totally disagree. Rather, as we shall see, it is because of the special nature of the case that Eleazar rules as he does.

In Tos. Demai 6:6, which precedes Eleazar's statement, we find:

> A. [If] an Israelite leased a field from a ḤBR to reap [it] when it is [ripe] with ears of corn; a vineyard to cut grapes, olives to harvest olives [not to produce oil].

B. He gives [them] to him as they are [untithed] [for rent].

C. [If he leases] a field [from a ḤBR] to reap [it] [in order to thresh] wheat, a vineyard to cut [it] [in order to make] wine, olives to harvest [in order to make] oil

D. He tithes and then gives him [the prescribed amount of produce as rent].

Lieberman (*Tosefta Kifshuṭa*, p. 95) interprets MḤBRW not as *from an associate* but as *from a non-Jew*. He argues that we cannot understand why the Israelite must, in the case of C-D of Tos., tithe the produce before giving the portion to the ḤBR, for one assumes that a ḤBR tithes his produce. Thus, there would be no concern that the produce would go untithed. Lieberman therefore suggests that the field is leased from a non-Jew and the problem of untithed produce therefore exists.

From A and C of Tos., we see that the purpose for which the field was leased affects the Israelite's obligation to tithe the field. According to Lieberman, A concerns instances in which a Jew leased a field from a gentile without the intention of completely processing the produce (GMR ML'KH). Since, at the time the Jew gives the gentile his portion as rent, there is no GMR ML'KH, he does not have to tithe the gentile's portion. If, however, as in C, his intention is to completely process produce, he must first tithe all the produce and then give the gentile his portion as rent.

A-B of Tos. Demai 6:6 seems to agree with Eleazar Ḥisma. Thus it is perhaps because the Jew intends merely to harvest olives that Eleazar rules that he gives the gentile his portion prior to tithing. If this interpretation is correct, then the fact that the field is his fathers may be irrelevant. It seems that two separate issues have been combined in Eleazar Ḥisma's statement. As our exegesis has shown, an interpretation of the pericope on the basis of one issue renders the other irrelevant.

As in Tos. Demai 3:1, Eleazar Ḥisma's ruling appears in the form of a testimony (X testified that) and is attributed to him by R. Yose b. Hameshullam, an Ushan. The issue of one who leased a field of his fathers was peculiar to the post-Bar Kokhba war era in which many Jews who had lost their lands during the war returned. This supports our conclusion that this tradition is attested at Usha.

(9)

A. (M'ŚH B) R. Yoḥanan b. Beroka and R. Eleazar Ḥisma (who) came from Yavneh to Lod and greeted R. Joshua in PQY 'YN.

B. He said to them, "What was the new law in the House of Study today?"

C. They said to him, "We are your students and from your waters we drink up (receive) our knowledge."

D. He said to them, "It is not possible for the House of Study [to be]]without a new law."

E. "Whose turn to lecture was it?"

F. "It was the lecture of R. Eleazar b. Azariah."

G. He said to them, "And on what did he expound?"

H. *Assemble the people, the men, women, and children.*

I. "If men come to learn, and women come to listen, why do the children come?

J. "To receive a reward for their bringing."

Tos. Soṭah 7:9, Zuckermandel, p. 307, lines 7-12; b. Hagigah 3a

A. TNY'

B. R. Yoḥanan b. Beroka and R. Eleazar Ḥisma were going from Yavneh to Lod and received R. Joshua in BQY 'YN.

C. He said to them, "What legislation was there in the House of Study today?"

D. And they said to him, "Everyone is your student and drinks up your knowledge."

E. He said to them, "Even if this is so, it is not possible that there was nothing new in the House of Study all day.

F. "Who lectured there?"

G. They said to him, "R. Leazar b. Azariah."

H. "And what was his explanation?"

I. *Assemble the people, men, women and children.*

J. "And what did he say about it?"

K. "The men come to learn, the women to listen.

L. "Why does the child come?

M. "Rather to be given a reward for their coming."

N. He said to them, "The generation is not forsaken in which there is R. Eleazar b. Azariah."

y. Soṭah 3:4; y. Hagigah 1:1

Comment: R. Eleazar Ḥisma appears here as a disciple of R. Joshua and colleague of R. Yoḥanan b. Beroka. His role in the pericope is merely to report what happened at the House of Study. The concern of the pericope, which constitutes an integrated narrative, is in priase of R. Eleazar b. Azariah, as is made clear in y. Soṭah 3:4. The narrative reflects the developing interest in the lives of the rabbis and world of Torah study.

(10)

A. Concerning [beasts] forbidden [as offerings] on the altar, their young are permitted.

B. R. Eleazar forbids the young of a *terefah* [beast].

C. R. Eleazar says, "One does not sacrifice it upon the altar."

D. But the Sages say, "One does sacrifice it upon the altar."

E. And R. Eleazar agrees [that in the case] of a young bird that hatched from a *terefah egg*, it may be offered on the altar.

F. R. Ḥanina b. Antigonus says in behalf of R. Eleazar Ḥisma, "A fit [beast] which has sucked from a *terefah* [beast] is forbidden [as an offering] on the altar."

Tos. Tem. 4:10, ed. Zuckermandel, p. 556, lines 10-13

Comment: A-E, which supplies the context for Eleazar Ḥisma's statement in F, asks whether offspring of animals which have become unfit as offerings on the altar are themselves fit as offerings. Mishnah Tem. 6:1 lists the types of animals that may not be offered on the altar.

F is not directly concerned with the issue of offspring of non-fit animals. Rather, it deals with the broader case of any valid beast which has sucked from a non-fit beast. According to Maimonides and Bartinoro, the valid animal becomes unfit because it has received sustenance from an unfit animal. Thus, Eleazar Ḥisma holds a more stringent opinion, for *any* animal which has sucked from a non-fit beast can become non-fit.

In M. Tem. 6:5, F of Tos. is attributed to R. Ḥanina b. Antigonus alone.

(11)

A. R. Eleazar b. Yanni said in behalf of R. Eleazar Ḥisma before Rabbi

B. "The House of Shammai and the House of Hillel did not disagree concerning one who had an attack of one [issue] on the first [day], one on the second [day] and on the third [day] [the issue] ceased, and on the fourth [day] he suffered one [issue].

C. "Or instead [concerning] one who suffered one on the first [day] and on the second [day] [the issue] ceased, and on the fourth [day] suffered two [issues]. For this is not a complete *Zab*.

D. "Concerning what did they dispute?

E. "Concerning one who suffers two or one as profuse as two and on the second [day] ceased, and on the third and fourth [day] suffered one [issue]."

Tos. Zab 1:7, ed. Zuckermandel, p. 677, lines 1-5

Comment: This is the only existing tradition in the name of Eleazar Ḥisma that comments on a dispute between the Houses of Hillel and Shammai. The concern with Houses' traditions is almost entirely Ushan. See Neusner, *The Rabbinic Traditions About the Pharisees Before 70*, Volume II, p. 321.

(12)

A. Three things does R. Eleazar Ḥisma declare unclean in behalf of R. Joshua.

B. And the sages declare clean.

C. [If] a menstruant sat on a bed with one who was clean [wearing] a cap on her head

D. R. Eleazar Ḥisma declares [the cap] unclean in the behalf of R. Joshua.

E. And the Sages declare clean.

F. [If a menstruant] sat on board a freight ship, the rigging on top of the ship's mast (NW: Tos. Zuckermandel, p. 679; NS: Albeck, p. 770).

G. R. Eleazar Ḥisma declares [the rigging] unclean in the behalf of R. Joshua.

H. And the Sages declare clean.

I. [If she takes] a tub full of clothes when its weight is heavy

J. R. Eleazar Ḥisma declares [the clothes] unclean in the behalf of R. Joshua.

K. And the Sages declare clean.

Tos. Zabim 4:4, ed. Zuckermandel, p. 679, lines 1-5

Comment: In Tos. Zabim 4:4, Eleazar Ḥisma is presented as a tradent handing down Joshua material. M. Zabim 4:1 presents four cases of *midras* uncleanness in the name of Joshua. Three of them appear here and have been carefully redacted in the following manner: A defines the nature of the pericope. The list of *three things* is a cliché of tradition. C, F, and I are the protases and are followed, in each case, by the two disputing opinions. Thus, a perfectly balanced dispute is maintained throughout the pericope.

As we have seen in Tos. Soṭah 7:9, Eleazar Ḥisma appears as a disciple of R. Joshua.

(13)

A. Another [Baraita] taught (TNY')

B. [*And if a man eat of the holy things in error*] *he shall give the holy things to the priest* [*adding a fifth to its value*...] (Lev. 22:14)

C. 1. [This implies] something which is fit to be holy.

C. 2. Excluding (PRṬ) one who eats the Heave-offering of leaven on Passover.

D. For (Š) he is exempt from payment and from [liability for] the value of [fire] wood.

E. The words of R. Eliezer b. Jacob.

F. But R. Eleazar Ḥisma declares [him] liable.

G. R. Eliezer b. Jacob said to R. Eleazar Ḥisma, "Yet what benefit does he (priest) have in it?"

H. R. Eleazar Ḥisma said to R. Eliezer b. Jacob, "Yet what benefit does he have [in the case] of one who eats unclean Heave offering during the rest of the year for (Š) he pays?"

I. He said to him, "No, if you speak of unclean Heave-offering during the rest of the year where, although he (priest) does not have the right of eating, he does have the right [of its use for] heating, will you say [the same] in this [case] where he neither has the right of eating or [use for] heating?"

J. He said to him, "Also ('P) in this [case] he has the right of [use as] fuel for if he wishes, the priest can place it before his dog or burn it under his pot."

b. Pes. 32a

Comment: If a man eats clean Heave-offering by mistake, he must pay the proper restitution of its value (i.e., 1/5 value of object). If by mistake he eats unclean Heave-offering (which could not be consumed by the priest because of its uncleanness) he pays an amount equal to its value for fire wood, which the priest can then burn for fuel. This is because unclean Heave-offering could be burned as fuel. If, however, he eats Heave-offering deliberately, he pays nothing and is liable to extirpation.

B is the biblical law dealing with the first case. C clarifies B. C2-D deal with the specific case of one who eats by mistake Heave-offering of leaven on Passover. Since the Heave-offering is leaven and is, therefore, forbidden to the priest, the guilty party is exempt from both payment of restitution and payment for its value as firewood.

Eleazar Ḥisma disputes this, saying that one is liable, but he does not make clear in what manner the guilty party is liable. We can understand the meaning of F in terms of the debate G-J.

In G, Eliezer b. Jacob asks how one can be liable since the leaven is forbidden to the priest. Eleazar Ḥisma responds in H that the priest receives the value for fire wood in the case of one who eats unclean Heave-offering during the rest of the year although no benefit can be derived from it. This implies that the Heave-offering could be burned as fuel on Passover and thus the guilty party is liable. Eliezer b. Jacob then answers in I that during the rest of the year payment of the value of fire wood is made because the unclean Heave-offering could have been used for fuel, but on Passover the priest could not have used the Heave-offering of leaven as fuel. Eleazar Ḥisma responds in I and says that the priest may use it as fuel for his personal needs.

Thus, Eliezer b. Jacob and Eleazar Ḥisma disagree about what one does with leaven of Heave-offering on Passover. The problem is that although the substance is leaven, and therefore forbidden, it is still Heave-offering, which belongs to the priest. Normally, when one finds leaven after the time permitted to derive any benefit from it, one must burn or destroy the leaven (see M. Pes. 2:1). Does one neglect the fact that the leaven Heave-offering is leaven and destroy it himself, or does one, in consideration of the fact that it is Heave-offering, give it to the priest who then destroys it? Eliezer b. Jacob seems to agree with the first notion that the person himself destroys it--the priest receives no benefit from it; Eleazar Ḥisma, however, seems to require the person to give Heave-offering to the priest. Thus, for Eliezer b. Jacob, the fact that it is leaven is determinative while for Eleazar Ḥisma, the primary consideration is that it is Heave-offering.

If we drop the words PRṬ from C2 and Š from D, C2-F is a standard dispute.

C. 2. [Concerning] one who eats the Heave-offering of leaven on Passover

D. He is exempt from payment and from [liability for] the value of [fire] wood.

E. The words of R. Eliezer b. Jacob.

F. But R. Eleazar Ḥisma declares [him] liable.

This is similar to the tradition in Tos. Pes. 1:10:

A. [Concerning] one who eats Heave-offering of leaven on Passover

B. One does not pay the value of [fire] wood to the priest.

Here the case is clearly stated [Tos. Pes. 1:10]. The anonymous law of Tos. agrees with Eliezer b. Jacob.

C2 of b. does not specify whether the guilty party has eaten in error or deliberately. We can only assume on the basis of the biblical law in B of b. that he has done it in error. Moreover, C2 does not specify whether the Heave-offering was clean or unclean, but this fact seems inconsequential. The pericope assumes that Heave-offering of leaven on Passover is equivalent to unclean Heave-offering during the rest of the year since neither leaven nor unclean Heave-offering can be eaten by the priest.

Tos. Pes. 1:10 concludes with the following:

C. R. Yoḥanan b. Nuri said, "I said to R. ʿAqiva, 'Why does one who eats Heave-offering of leaven on Passover not pay the value of [fire] wood to a priest? What is the difference [between] Passover and the rest of the year, for during the rest of the year, one does pay the value of [fire] wood to the priest.'"

D. He said to me, "No, if you say during the rest of the year that he pays although he (priest) does not have the right of eating, he does have the right [to burn] [fire] wood, will you say [the same] in this [case] where he neither has the right of eating or use for [fire] wood?"

The tradition, redacted by ʿAqivan tradents, is not in the form of a dispute, but of a legal narrative in the first person. Yoḥanan b. Nuri's question is not rhetorical, but is asked as a disciple to a master. This tradition indicates that the question of what one must pay for eating leaven of Heave-offering on Passover is a concern of other Yavneans. Furthermore, ʿAqiva's alleged response in D to Yoḥanan seems to agree with Eliezer b. Jacob's opinion in I of b. Both agree that one does not pay the value of the fire wood.

Tos.	*Bavli*
D. He said to me, No, if you say during the rest of the year that he pays although he does not have the right of eating, he does have the right [to burn] [fire] wood, will you say [the same] in this case where he neither has the right of eating or use for [fire] wood?	I. He said to him, No, if you speak of unclean Heave-offering during the rest of the year where although he does not have the right of eating, he does have the right [of its use for] heating, will you say [the same] in this [case] where he neither has the right of eating or [use for] heating?

In b. Pes. 32a, we find the following tradition: KTN'Y

A. He who eats Heave-offering of leaven on Passover is free from payment and from [liability for] the value of the [fire] wood.

B. [These are] the words of R. ʿAqiva.

C. R. Yoḥanan b. Nuri declares him liable.

D. R. ʿAqiva said to R. Yoḥanan b. Nuri, "And what benefit does he [the priest] have in it?"

E. R. Yoḥanan b. Nuri said to R. ʿAqiva, "And what benefit does he [the priest] have that he who eats unclean Heave-offering during the rest of the year must pay?"

F. He said to him, "No, if you speak of unclean Heave-offering during the rest of the year, because although he [the priest] does not have the right of eating, he does have the right [to burn] [fire] wood, will you say [the same] in this [case] where he neither has the right of eating or use for [fire] wood?"

This tradition is identical to our reconstruction of the Eleazar Ḥisma-Eliezer b. Jacob tradition. The only difference is that the final retort (J) is missing, and the names of the authorities have been changed. Eliezer b. Jacob's sayings are in the name of ʿAqiva, and Eleazar b. Ḥisma's are in the name of Yoḥanan b. Nuri.

We could account for the duplication of the two *beraitot* in several ways. The Toseftan version could have generated the ʿAqivan version of b. and the Eleazar Ḥisma *beraita* was either a separate tradition or a mere substitute of the name of Eleazar Ḥisma and Eliezer b. Jacob in place of those found in the ʿAqivan tradition. Alternatively, Eleazar Ḥisma's tradition was separate from Tos. and later someone formulated a new tradition in b. on the basis of both traditions.

(14)

A. Has not R. Isaac b. Samuel b. Marta said
B. "[Concerning] one who reads the *shema*ʿ
C. He shall not blink his eyes, move his lips, or point with his finger."
D. WTNYʾ
E. R. Eleazar Ḥisma says
F. "[Concerning] one who reads the *shema*ʿ and blinks his eye or moves his lips and points with his finger,
G. Concerning him Scripture says
H. *and you did not call upon me, Jacob* (Is. 43:22)."

b. Yoma 19b

Comment: The material preceding A-H refers to the repeating (MTNY) of M. Yoma 1:6 before Rav. The story of the mispronunciation of Kebutal's name is made to apply to the issue of the proper recitation of the *shema*ʿ in E-G.

Our pericope contains two similar traditions concerning the recitation of the *shema*ʿ. In A-C, the legal saying is presented in the form of a superscription B followed by a declarative statement C. It is not in the standard form *x says* but in the past tense (ʾMR).

Eleazar Ḥisma's statement E-H is attributed in a simple declarative sentence. We expect a ruling, such as "He has not fulfilled his obligation," yet what is presented is a scriptural reference to Isaiah 43:22. It is one of the few instances where Eleazar Ḥisma is presented as an exegete.

(15)

A. Why does Scripture say, *Today you will not find it in the field*? (Ex. 16:25)

B. They (Sages) said, "The heart of our forefathers was broken at that moment for they said, 'Since we could not find it today, perhaps we shall not find it tomorrow.'"

C. He said to them, "This day you do not find it, but tomorrow you will find it" (D. Hoffman MSS inserts, "These are the words of R. Joshua").

D. E. Eleazar Ḥisma says, "You will not find it in this world, but you will find it in the world to come."

Mekh. De R. Ishmael, Vayassa, 5, ed. and trans. Lauterbach, v. II, p. 119. Mekh. de R. Simeon b. Yochai, ed. Epstein-Melamed, p. 113, lines 18-21

Comment: Exodus 16:25 refers to the story of the gathering of *mana* by the Israelites during their wanderings in the desert. Each day they would go out into the field and find enough food to support them that day. On the sixth day, however, they collected twice as much so they should have food on the Sabbath.

B-D are three exegeses of the verse in A. According to Lauterbach's translation, B-C both are the statement of the Sages, for C represents Moses' comforting answer to the Israelites who fear that God will no longer provide for them. In Hoffman's edition, C appears without *He said to them* and is represented not as the words of Moses, but as an exegesis of R. Joshua's.

Eleazar Ḥisma offers a third exegesis. Just as Israel was reassured that they would receive *mana* in the future, although they lack it presently, so the Jewish people must be assured that they will gain salvation in the world to come.

(16)

A. *Then came Amaleq* (Ex. 17:8)

B. R. Joshua and R. Eleazar Ḥisma say

C. "This verse is drawn [as an allegory] and explained in connection with Job where it is said,

D. *Can the rush shoot up without mire? Can the reed grass grow without water?* (Job 8:11)

E. "For is it possible for the rush to grow without mire and water, or is it possible for the reed grass to exist without water? So also is it impossible for Israel to exist unless they make themselves busy in the words of the Torah.

F. "And because they separated themselves from the Torah, so the enemy came upon them.

G. "For the enemy comes only because of (ʿL) sin and transgression."

H. As it is said

I. *Then came Amaleq.*

Mekh. de R. Ishmael, Amaleq 1, ed. and trans. Lauterbach, v. II, p. 135

Comment: A-I represents the standard homiletic exegesis and is a complete unit with a well-written literary style.

First, the biblical verse is related to a verse in the book of Job and explained allegorically in relation to it. This interpretation concentrates on the end of the verse in Exodus, *and fought Israel in Rephidim*. Lauterbach explains that *Rephidim* is interpreted as feebleness of hands in upholding the Torah (RPYWN YDYM).

The message of the exegesis is twofold. First, Israel must busy itself in Torah. Second, when it fails to do so, disaster comes. Thus, the events of Israel's history are interpreted in terms of adherence to Torah.

In the entire tradition of Eleazar Ḥisma, this is the only statement given a joint attribution. The appearance of Eleazar Ḥisma with R. Joshua again suggests the conception of Eleazar Ḥisma as his disciple.

(17)

(*And I charged your judges at that time saying, Hear* [the cases] *between your brothers and judge righteously*) (Deut. 1:16)

A. *At that time saying*

B. You used to have your own authority. Behold, now you are slaves made to serve the public.

C. (M'ŚH B) R. Yohanan b. Nuri and R. Eleazar Ḥisma whom Rabban Gamaliel appointed to the academy (HWŠYBM BYŠYBH), but the disciples paid no attention to them.

D. That evening they went and sat among the disciples.

E. And such was the character of Rabban Gamaliel:

F. When he would enter and speak, they would question [him] knowing that this was not disrespect.

G. When he would enter and not speak, they would question [him] knowing this was disrespect.

H. He entered and found R. Yohanan b. Nuri and R. Eleazar Ḥisma sitting among the disciples.

I. He said to them, "Yohanan b. Nuri and Eleazar Ḥisma, you have harmed yourself for the public, for you do not seek to impose authority on the public.

J. "You used to have your own authority. Behold, now you are slaves made to serve the public."

Sifré Deut. 1:16, Finkelstein, ed., pp. 25-26.
Midrash Tannaim, ed., Hoffman, p. 9

Comment: B is an anonymous exegesis of Deut. 1:16. Its attribution to Rabban Gamaliel in H is solely for the purpose of presenting the narrative as an illustration of the exegesis.

The narrative relates the appointment of Eleazar Ḥisma to the academy (*Yeshivah*) of Rabban Gamaliel. Eleazar is ignored by the students (C). In I-J, it is the Patriarch himself who says that those in power are mere servants of the people. Thus, the narrative is an attack on the Patriarchate. The role of Eleazar Ḥisma is negligible.

A. Since it is stated *In the house of freedom* (II Kings, 15:5) it must be inferred that until then he was a servant.

B. As this [is shown in the case] of Rabban Gamaliel and R. Joshua.

C. They were travelling on a ship.

D. R. Gamaliel had some bread. R. Joshua had bread and flour.

E. When R. Gamaliel's bread was consumed, he depended on R. Joshua's flour.

F. He (R. Gamaliel) said to him, "Did you know that we would be so delayed that you brought flour with you?"

G. He said to him, "A certain star rises once in seventy years and leads the sailors astray and I suspected it might rise and lead us astray."

H. He said to him, "(Joshua), You possess so much [knowledge] yet you travel on a ship."

I. He said to him, "Rather than wonder at me, I wonder at two of your disciples on dry [land], R. Eleazar Ḥisma and R. Yohanan b. Gudgada who are able to calculate how many drops there are in the sea, yet they do not have bread to eat or clothes to put on."

J. He decided to appoint them supervisors.

K. When he landed, he sent for them but they did not come.

L. He sent for them again and they came.

M. He said to them, "Do you imagine that I offer you rulership? I offer you servitude."

N. As it is said *And they spoke to him saying, 'If you will be a servant to the people this day'* (I Kings 12:7).

b. Hor. 10a-10b

Comment: Previous to this portion of the *gemara* is a reference to II Kings 15:5. A is an exegesis of the part of the biblical verse, and states that the role of a king is one of servitude to the people. B is the work of the redactor, who supplies the narrative because of its similarity to the theme of the exegesis in A. In N, the narrative is associated with I Kings 12:7. The narrative is independent of any exegesis. It contains two independent traditions, each dependent on an apophthegm placed in a narrative setting. The two narratives have been blended into one story by the use of a continual dialogue and similar setting.

The first narrative, C-G, centers around the saying in G. The metaphor of the star refers to R. Gamaliel as Patriarch, and the fact that Joshua claims it leads men astray suggests a conflict between the masters.

H-M is identical in character. I may once have circulated independently as a short biographical saying about the irony of Eleazar Ḥisma's life. He was very wise but very poor. K-L adds to this motive. Gamaliel had to call for him twice because he was too modest to accept the position of supervisor. As it appears before us, the narrative has been formed by the unification of these elements in the words of Joshua tradents.

The point of the story is contained in M. The Patriarch himself confesses that to hold a position of authority is to be a servant of the people. In N, Gamaliel is compared to King Rehobam, against whom the people rebelled, for he rejected the advice of the elders and placed a heavy yoke of authority on the people.

This narrative is an example of many story elements joined together to form one story line. The final redaction was done by Joshua tradents.

(18)

A. R. Eleazar Ḥisma came to a certain place.
B. They said to him, "Do you know how to recite [the blessings accompnaying] the *shema*ʿ?"
C. He said to them, "No."
D. "Do you know how to pass before the Ark? [read the prayers preceding the *shema*ʿ]"
E. He said to them, "No."
F. They said, "It is for nothing that he is called Rabbi."
G. His face turned pale and he went before R. ʿAqiva, his master.
H. He asked him, "Why is your face so pale?"
I. He told him what happened, and said to him, "Are you willing to teach me, Master?"
J. He said to him, "Yes."
K. After he learned, he returned to that place.
L. They said to him, "Do you know how to recite [the blessings accompanying] the *shema*ʿ?"
M. He said to them, "Yes."
N. "Do you know how to pass before the Ark?"
O. He said to them, "Yes."
P. They said, "Eleazar has received a steel edge (NTḤSM--recovered the power of speech; Jastrow, p. 488). And they called him R. Eleazar Ḥisma.

Lev. Rabbah 23:4

Comment: This narrative is the only tradition in later compilations which refers to Eleazar Ḥisma. Composed entirely in Aramaic, it is a simple story constructed mostly from dialogue. It depicts Eleazar as a student of R. ʿAqiva and explains the meaning of his name. It is the only biographical narrative in which Eleazar plays a central role.

PART TWO: ANALYSIS OF THE TRADITION

I. The Tradition as a Whole

We have thus far analyzed each of Eleazar Ḥisma's traditions individually. Our purpose now is to examine the tradition as a whole, to analyze the manner in which it has been preserved and to discover who is responsible for its preservation.

We shall begin with a summary of the entire tradition presented according to the order in which each item ap peared in Part One, and categorized according to the strata in which they appear. There are eighteen items in all.

Item	I Mishnah- Tosefta	II Tannaitic Midrashim	III *Beraitot*	IV Amoraic Material	V Later Complications
1. Proper designation of Heave offering from a pile.	M. Ter. 3:5				
2. A laborer should not eat more than the value of his hire.	M.B.M. 7:5	Sifré Deut. 23:25		y.Ma. 2:4	
3. The laws of bird offerings and the onset of menstruation are the body of the law.	M.Avot. 3:19				
4. If a leprosy sign changed to effect leniency.	M.Neg. 7:2	Sifra Taz. 1:1			
5. As to a house in which a leprosy sign appears.	M.Neg. 13:3 Tos.Neg. 7:2				
6. One who discharges thick drops from the member is unclean.	M.Miq. 8:3				
7. They do not prepare any clean foodstuffs for an *Am ha'areṣ*.	Tos.Dem. 3:1		b. Giṭṭin		
8. One who leases from a gentile a field of his father's to harvest olives.	Tos.Dem. 6:7				

Item	I	II	III	IV	V
9. R. Eleazar Ḥisma and R. Yohanan b. Nuri greeted R. Joshua.	Tos.Sotah 7:9		b.Hag. 3a y.Sotah 3:4 y.Hag. 1:1		
10. A fit beast which has sucked from a *terefah* beast is forbidden on the altar.	Tos.Tem. 4:10				
11. The House of Shammai and the House of Hillel did not disagree...	Tos.Zab. 1:7				
12. Three things did Eleazar Ḥisma declare unclean in behalf of R. Joshua.	Tos.Zab. 4:4				
13. Concerning one eats unclean leaven on Passover.			b. Pes. 32a		
14. *And you did not call upon me, Jacob*.			b. Yoma 19b		
15. You will not find it in this world, but you will find it in the world to come.		Mekh.deR. Ishmael, vayassa 5.			
16. *Then came Amaleq*.		Mekh.deR. Ishmael, Amaleq 1.			

Item	I	II	III	IV	V
17. R. Eleazar Ḥisma and R. Yohanan ḅ. Gudgada restored to *Yeshiva*.		Sifré Deut. 1:16	b.Hor. 10a-10b		
18. R. Eleazar Ḥisma learns to recite the blessings of the *shema*'.					Lev. Rabbah 23:4

Having assigned the traditions according to the strata in which they appear, we can now begin our analysis by dividing the traditions into legal and non-legal categories. Ten of the eighteen traditions are legal sources and first make their appearance in Mishnah-Tosefta. Thus, the bulk (91%) of the legal material occurs in the earliest stratum. The remaining 9% is accounted for by the appearance of one legal tradition in Amoraic materials. Of the eight non-legal sources, we find two (29%) in Mishnah-Tosefta, three (43%) in the second strata, and one (14%) in both the Amoraic material and later compilations.

II. Forms

Our traditions are set into five kinds of pericopae, each exhibiting unique formal characteristics: (A) Independent Sayings, (B) Disputes, (C) Debates, (D) Testimonies and (E) Narratives.

As we examine each form, we shall also take into consideration any recurring formulary patterns, phrases, or clichés out of which the large elements of the pericope may be built.

A. Independent Sayings

An independent saying is any statement which appears autonomously in a pericope. It may also appear with statements of other authorities, but it is not dependent on those statements for its context or meaning. These sayings are normally presented in the form *authority x says + direct discourse*. We shall examine this form and then its variations.

(1) *Authority x says...*

M. Ter. 3:5

> Eleazar Ḥisma says, As to one who says [let] the Heave-offering of the pile...

This saying appears in a pericope containing a dispute and another discrete saying. The sole issue of the pericope is the proper designation of Heave-offering. Eleazar Ḥisma's saying contains a statement of the legal issue and his opinion.

M. Avot 3:19

R. Eleazar (b.) Ḥisma says, [The laws of] bird offerings and the onset of menstruation...

b. Yoma 19b

R. Eleazar Ḥisma says, [Concerning] one who reads the *shema*'...

This saying is preceded by a ruling in the form of a declarative sentence. Eleazar, however, states the protasis and gives a prooftext instead of the expected ruling.

Mekh. de R. Ishmael, Vayassa, 5

and Moses said... (Ex. 16:25)

Eleazar Ḥisma says, You will not find it in this world, but you will find it in the world to come.

This saying is juxtaposed with an exegesis in the name of the Sages.

Mekh. de R. Ishmael, Amalek, 1

R. Joshua and R. Eleazar Ḥisma say, [What follows is an exegesis of Ex. 17:8]

This saying comprises the entire pericope.

(2) *Words of authority x*

M. Miq. 8:3

[Concerning] one who discharges thick drops....These are the words of R. Eleazar Ḥisma.

Eleazar's statement occurs in a collection of three independent rulings which are thematically related. This phrase *words of*... is a redactional formula which functions in the same manner as *x says*.

(3) *Authority x says/ said in behalf of authority y*

Tos. Tem. 4:10

R. Ḥanina b. Antigonus says in behalf of R. Eleazar Ḥisma...

This statement follows a dispute but is not at all concerned with the issue of that dispute, and is, therefore, an independent saying. The reliability of the attribution is doubtful for this saying appears in M. Ter. 6:5 as a saying of R. Ḥanina b. Antigonus.

Tos. Zab. 1:7

R. Eleazar b. Yanni said in behalf of R. Eleazar Ḥisma before Rabbi...

The entire pericope is a comment on a Houses' dispute, which by the time of the establishment at Usha, was no longer an important element.[1] The use of the past tense *said* is unusual in this form. Here, it reflects a one-time historical occurrence. The use of the form *x said* is used consistently in this chapter of Tos. when relating the formation of a Houses' tradition.

From this survey we see that five of the eight independent sayings are in the standard form *x says*. The form is not restricted to any one type of material but functions as both a legal and non-legal saying.

B. Disputes

The standard version of this form is as follows:

Superscription
Authority x says + ruling, in direct discourse
Authority y says + ruling, in direct discourse

The superscription states the legal issue or problem about which the authorities dispute. The first variation of this form occurs when the superscription is removed and the statement of law is assigned to authority x. We also find the case in which an authority disputes an anonymous statement of law and is not followed by a contrasting statement of a second authority. Third, the direct discourse in the standard legal form is replaced by an intensive transitive verb in the present tense, such as *declare liable*. Let us now examine the use of this form in Eleazar Ḥisma's tradition.

(1) *Standard Dispute Form*

M. Neg. 7:2

[If] their appearance changed

R. Eleazar ben Azariah declares clean.

R. Eleazar Ḥisma says...

R. ʿAqiva says...

As we noted in Part One, the appearance of three disputing opinions is unusual but is called for here by the logic of the dispute.

Tos. Zab. 4:4

[If] a menstruant sat on a bed...

R. Eleazar Ḥisma declares unclean in behalf of R. Joshua.

And the Sages declare clean.

As we have seen in Part One, this dispute concerns Joshua material and occurs in a list of three disputes with the Sages concerning *midras* uncleanness. The use of *declare clean* vs. *declare unclean* is a standard formulary pattern out of which a balanced dispute is constructed. The Sages' opinion, lacking in Joshua's pericope (M. Zab. 4:1) has been tacked on to Joshua's legal opinions by the redactor.

b. Pes. 32a

For he is exempt from payment and from [liability] for the value of [fire] wood.

The words of R. Eliezer b. Jacob.

In our discussion of this pericope in Part One, we postulated what the original dispute could have been. As it appears here it has been redacted into a fully developed pericope generating a debate. A similar tradition is attributed to R. ʿAqiva and Yoḥanan b. Nuri.

(2) *Authority x + legal opinion*
Authority y + intensive transitive verb

M.B.M. 7:5

R. Eleazar Ḥisma says, A laborer should not eat more than the value of his hire.

But the Sages allow it.

This tradition occurs in many formulary patterns. In Tos. B.M. 10:8, Eleazar's statement appears in the attributive formula *In behalf of x, y said.* The statement of Eleazar Ḥisma could stand independent of the Sages' ruling. In y. Ma. 2:4, this is the case. In Sifré Deut., each disputant is supplied with a prooftext to support their statement. The Sages' statement appears in the form of a complete opinion in direct discourse.

(3) *Anonymous Law*
Authority x says...

M. Neg. 13:3

[As to a house in which a leprosy sign appears]

R. Eleazar Ḥisma says, Whatever their bulk.

This tradition is an excellent example of the process of redaction involved in its formulation and demonstrates an important point in our survey, namely, that the traditions before us do not represent a verbatim account of Eleazar Ḥisma's opinions. His statement in M. Neg. 13:3 is dependent for its meaning and content on the anonymous law preceding it and never circulated as an independent saying. The use of balanced opinions (BKZYT/BMSHN) is the work of the redactor. The case in Tos. Zab. 4:4 is another example of this. The dispute is formed by supplying *And the Sages declare clean* after each of Joshua's opinions. Joshua's opinions stand alone in M. Zab. 4:1. This suggests that M.B.M. 7:5 may originally have circulated independently.

Eliminating Joshua's tradition, we are left with four traditions (40%) which assume the dispute form.

C. Debate

The debate is generated from the contents of the preceding dispute. It substitutes the present tense *says* for the past tense *said*. The form is *x said to y...y said to him*.

b. Pes. 32a

R. Eliezer b. Jacob said to R. Eleazar Ḥisma
Yet what benefit...
R. Eleazar Ḥisma said to R. Eliezer b. Jacob,
Yet what benefit...
He said to him, No, if you speak...
He said to him, Also in this...

This is the only debate found in our traditions.

D. Testimony Form

Testimony form functions in the same manner as the *x says* form by substituting HʿYD for ʾWMR and the past tense for the present. Being in the past tense, it represents a one-time historical occurrence. The form present in Eleazar Ḥisma's traditions is a variation of the standard form.

Tos. Demai 3:1

Testified R. Yose b. Hameshullam in behalf of R. Nathan his brother who said in the name of R. Eleazar Ḥisma...for an *am haʾareṣ*.

Tos. Demai 6:7

Testified R. Yose b. Hameshullam in behalf of his brother Nathan who said in behalf of R. Eleazar Ḥisma...

The paucity of material in this form limits its importance in this study. It is peculiar to Tos. Demai and is attested to by the same authority.

E. Narrative

The narrative lacks any strict formal structure. In Tos. Sot. 7:9 and Sifré Deut. 1:16, the redactional formula *ma'aseh b* introduces a narrative which illustrates a scriptural verse.

Tos. Sot. 7:9

> [Eleazar Ḥisma and Yoḥanan b. Beroka return from Yavneh to their master Joshua's residence and relate the lecture of Eleazar b. Azariah]

Eleazar Ḥisma is depicted as a Yavnean and disciple of Joshua.

Sifré Deut. 1:16

> [Eleazar Ḥisma and Yoḥanan b. Nuri are restored to the *Yeshiva* by R. Gamaliel but are ignored by the students].

Eleazar appears with another Yavnean in a tradition that depicts the poor lot of one who works for R. Gamaliel.

b. Hor. 10a-10b

> [Eleazar Ḥisma and Yoḥanan b. Gudgada are appointed supervisors by the Patriarch].

It is unlikely that Eleazar could have appeared with Yoḥanan b. Gudgada, a late Ushan.

Lev. Rabbah 23:4

> [Eleazar learns the blessings which accompany the *shema'* from R. 'Aqiva and gains the name Ḥisma].

Except for the narrative found in Lev. Rabbah, the use of Eleazar Ḥisma's name, associated with some Yavnean named Yoḥanan, is used merely as a name. He plays no substantial role in the narratives.

We can summarize the forms as follows:

FORMS		A	B	C	D	E
No. of traditions	Legal	3	4	1	2	
	Non-legal	4				4

The most common form is the independent saying, constituting 50% of all non-legal forms and 30% of all legal forms. 40% of the legal traditions assume the dispute form. One of these traditions is a discrete saying to which the Sages' contrary opinion is merely tacked on. Only two disputes are with named authorities.

Examining the tradition as a whole, we see that approximately 39% (7) constitutes independent sayings (A) and 23% (4) are disputes (B). 23% (4) are non-legal narratives (E), 11% (2) are testimonies (D) and 6% (1) are debates (C).

The importance of these results, if any, can only be seen in relation to other Tannaitic traditions. Neusner has shown that the dispute form is the trademark of the ʿAqivan redactors in the Eliezer tradition.[2] This is not characteristic of Eleazar Ḥisma's traditions. Rather, Neusner's data imply that our materials probably derive from a redactional circle apart from that of the mainstream, i.e., ʿAqivan redactors. What that circle was is difficult to say, for we discern no predominant form which could suggest anything characteristic of the manner in which Eleazar Ḥisma's tradition was preserved.

III. The Man Behind the Tradition

A. Attestations

An attestation is a reference to a pericope and supplies an approximate date at which a tradition attributed to a given authority may have been known. There are three ways in which a tradition may be attested.[3] A tradition may be cited by an authority external to rabbinic tradition; second, an authority within rabbinic literature may comment on a pericope and yet stand outside the framework of the pericope; third, we may fix the final date for the present forms of our sources according to the final date of compilation of the collection in which the materials are found. Thus a pericope which first appears in Mishnah-Tosefta appeared in its present form by 200-250 C.E. We have no such attestations, as found in the first case, for our materials. The third type of attestation can readily be seen by examining the chart supplied in the beginning of Part Two.

As for the second case, no attestation to non-legal traditions exist. We do, however, have instances of attestation of Eleazar Ḥisma's legal sayings, but these do not occur in the form described above. Rather, we find the pattern, *Authority x says/said that Authority y says that R. Eleazar Ḥisma says.* This is known as a chain of tradition. It differs from an attestation in that it gives more precise information about the authorities responsible for the preservation and transmission of Eleazar Ḥisma's traditions.[4] We have three chains of tradition.

Tos. Zab. 1:7

> R. Eleazar b. Yanni said in behalf of R. Eleazar Ḥisma before Rabbi...

What follows is a comment on a Houses' dispute. As we saw in Part One, the formation of the Houses' traditions was a Yavnean concern. Yet, the earliest *terminus ante quem* that can be supplied is the time of Judah at *Bet Shearim*.

Tos. Demai 3:1

> Testified R. Yose b. Hameshullam in behalf of R. Nathan his brother who said in the name of R. Eleazar Ḥisma...

We find the identical chain in Tos. Demai 6:7. These two chains are a variation of the standard formulary pattern *x said*. It appears that R. Yose was concerned with transmitting those traditions which involve the issue of Heave-offering. We have seen that the problem of leasing land once owned by the father could be an Ushan issue. The reliability of the tradition is supported by the fact that R. Yose is an Ushan and would have been familiar with Eleazar's traditions not long after their formulation. The fact that these two traditions involve Heave-offering may suggest a special Ushan interest which determined the legal agendum preserved from the larger corpus of Eleazar's traditions. If we examine the four pericopae in which he appears with another authority, we find that he appears with Ushans twice; in both cases the issue involves Heave-offering. In b. Pes. 32a he appears in dispute with Eliezer b. Jacob and in M. Ter. 3:5 he appears with R. Simeon and again with Eliezer b. Jacob. It thus appears that Heave-offering was a live issue at Usha. This may account for the preservation of these traditions.

We cannot postulate from such a small amount of material whether any other traditions date earlier than 200-250 C.E., the date fixed for the final compilation of the Mishnah-Tosefta. We have very little understanding of the process by which our other traditions were incorporated into the body of extant traditions. Yet, if we examine the legal agendum of Eleazar's traditions, we may discern a specific pattern of legal interests.

B. Legal Agendum

1. Agricultural tithes and offerings

M. Ter. 3:5: Proper designation of Heave-offering.

Tos. Demai 3:1: One does not prepare foodstuffs (Dough offering or Heave offering of olives) for an *am ha'areṣ*.

Tos. Demai 6:7: One who leases from a gentile a field of his father's to harvest olives.

2. Purity

M. Neg. 7:2: If a leprosy sign changed

M. Neg 13:3: As to a house in which a leprosy sign appears

M. Miq. 8:3: One who discharges thick drops is unclean.

3. Sabbath and Festivals

b. Pes. 32a: Concerning one who eats unclean leaven of Heave offering on Passover.

4. Miscellaneous

M.B.M. 7:5: A laborer should not eat more than [the value] of his hire.

Tos. Zab. 1:7: The House of Shammai and the House of Hillel.

From this list, we see that the primary concerns of Eleazar's tradition are agricultural tithes and ritual purity. The other two areas of concern can be subsumed under these two categories. b. Pes. 32a concerns agricultural tithes and Tos. Zab. 1:7 concerns a Houses' dispute of what constitutes a true *Zab*. This is exactly the type of legal agendum which could be attributed to a Pharisee.[5]

We have dealt thus far with the legal sources attributed to Eleazar Ḥisma. Do we find similar Pharisaic tendencies in the non-legal traditions as well?

C. Non-legal Agendum

We noted in Part One that M. Avot. 3:18 depicts Eleazar's major legal concerns to be with purity laws, and this view was supported in our analysis of his legal agendum. It is the concern with the importance of study reflected in this same saying that represents a new element in these traditions. Mekh. de R. Ishmael portrays Eleazar as an exegete concerned with the study of Torah as the means of salvation for Israel (#15, 16). These rabbinic sayings are representative of the developing interest at Usha in rabbinic history and Torah study. In contrast to these non-legal traditions, we saw that the legal traditions can be associated with the legal agendum of a Pharisee.

D. Conclusion

Our purpose in this study has been to analyze the traditions attributed to Eleazar Ḥisma and examine how they developed. We have seen that the attribution of a given body of materials to a named authority is not arbitrary. Indeed, we were able to perceive certain overall patterns among the traditions. The corpus of legal materials is set in a small number of forms and exhibits an interest in a limited number of legal issues. The majority of legal opinions were simply juxtaposed with rulings of other authorities on thematically similar issues. Thus, those opinions were preserved by some circle which did not play a major role in the ultimate redaction of the larger body of materials. The only attested sayings are found at Usha, and they did not supply us with sufficient data to assume what circle is responsible for the formulation and transmission of Eleazar Ḥisma's traditions.

Of the tradition as a whole, we noticed that the legal traditions tend to associate Eleazar Ḥisma's opinions with Pharisaic concerns of ritual purity and agricultural tithes. The non-legal traditions suggest rabbinic concerns. Of the man behind these traditions, we can say nothing.

NOTES

ELEAZAR ḤISMA

[1]Neusner, *Eliezer* II, p. 351.

[2]Neusner, *Pharisees* III, pp. 5-14; *Eliezer* II, pp. 1-62.

[3]Neusner, *Pharisees* III, p. 180.

[4]Neusner, *Eliezer* II, p. 73.

[5]Ibid.; Porton, *Ishmael*.

THE BERURIAH TRADITIONS

David Goodblatt
Haifa University

Learned women do not abound on the pages of talmudic literature. Among the very few is Beruriah.[1] This in itself is sufficient justification for a study of the Beruriah traditions, especially in an age of women's liberation.[2] Furthermore, these materials offer valuable evidence for the status of women in what Salo Baron has dubbed "the world of the Talmud."[3] Despite their intrinsic interest and importance, the sources relating to Beruriah have yet to be systematically and critically evaluated.[4] The latter task is the object of this paper.

I. The Family Connections of Beruriah

The first step in any study of biographical materials must be discarding sources which do not refer to the subject of the study. In the present case, this means we must begin with the issue of the family connections of Beruriah. It is believed that the latter was the daughter of Rabbi Ḥananyah ben Teradyon[5] and the wife of Rabbi Meir.[6] Hence passages which mention "the daughter of Rabbi Ḥananyah ben Teradyon" or "the wife of Rabbi Meir" without specifying her name are assumed to refer to Beruriah. However, as I shall show, this assumption is far from assured.

There are two pericopae which explicitly identify Beruriah as both daughter of Ḥananyah and wife of Meir, while a third describes her simply as the wife of Meir. All three are anecdotes in Babylonian Aramaic occurring in the Babylonian Talmud (hereafter: BT). I shall cite the three passages, beginning with the one making a single identification.

I.1 b. Berakhot 10a

> Certain brigands who were in the neighbourhood of Rabbi Meir used to trouble him greatly. He prayed [lit.: sought mercy] that they die. Beruriah his wife (*devethu*) said to him, "What is your opinion [i.e., on what do you base your prayer?] Because it is written [Psalms 104:35], 'let sins cease...?' Is 'sinners' written? [Rather] 'sins' is written. Furthermore, cast your eyes to the end of the verse, 'and they are wicked no more.' Since sins will cease, they will be wicked no more. So pray that they repent and be wicked no more. He prayed for them, and they repented.

Another Beruriah anecdote, cited below as IV.2, follows. It also contains an exegesis of a verse and the formula "cast your eyes etc." However, it does not mention any family connection. Both of the anecdotes are anonymously cited, and no named master comments upon or alludes to them.

I.2 b. Pesahim 62b

> Rabbi Simlai came before Rabbi Yoḥanan and said to him, "Let the master teach me the Book of Genealogies (*sefer yuḥasin*)." He said to him, "Where are you from?" He answered, "From Lod." "And where is your residence?" "In Nehardea." He said to him, "One engages in discussion neither with Lodites nor with Nehardeans. How much more so with you who are from Lod and whose residence is in Nehardea." He pressed him, and he consented. He [Simlai] said to him, "Let the master teach me [the material] in three months." He [Yoḥanan] picked up a clod, threw it at him, and said to him, "If Beruriah, the wife (*devethu*) of Rabbi Meir,

> the daughter of Rabbi Ḥananyah ben Teradyon, learned 300 traditions in a day from 300 masters, and even so did not fulfill her obligations in three years--how can you say in three months?" As he [Simlai] was getting up to go he said to him, "Master, what is [the difference] between 'for its own sake' and 'not for its own sake,' [between] 'for those who eat it' and 'not for those who eat it' [referring to Mishnah Pesaḥim 5:2-3]?" He said to him, Since you are a disciple of the masters (*ṣurba merabbanan*), come and I will tell you..."

The section quoted above is neither commented upon nor cited by any named master. Still, *prima facie*, it records a reference to the learning and family connections of Beruriah by a late third century Palestinian master. However, the version of this anecdote appearing in the Palestinian Talmud (hereafter: PT) does not mention Beruriah. The passage, from y. Pesaḥim 5:3, 32a-b, is as follows:

> Rabbi Simlai came to Rabbi Yonatan [*sic*] and said to him, "Teach us *aggadah*." He said to him, "I have in hand a tradition from my ancestors that one teaches *aggadah* neither to a Babylonian nor to a Southerner, for they are coarse in spirit and lacking in Torah. And you are a Nehardean and dwell in the South!" He said to him, "Tell me one thing. What is [the difference] between 'for its own sake' and 'not for its own sake?' What [is the difference] between 'for those who eat it' and 'not for those who eat it?'" He said to him...

It is difficult to decide whether the Palestinian version is more accurate than the Babylonian one by placing Simlai's origins in Babylonia and his residence in Lod (the South). But the PT reading Yonatan is probably preferable to BT's Yoḥanan.[7] Another difference between the two versions is the subject Simlai wants to learn. PT refers to *aggadah* in general, while BT specifies the Book of Genealogies. Concerning the latter work, we read the following in another passage from b. Pesaḥim 62b:

> Rami ben Rav Yud[8] quoted Rav who said, "From the day when the Book of Genealogies was hidden away (*nignaz*), the strength of the sages has been weakened and the light of their eyes has dimmed." Mar Zuṭra said, "We loaded 400 camels with exegeses [on the text] from 'Aṣel' [I Chronicles 8:38a] to 'Aṣel' [I Chronicles 8:38b]."[9]

The Book of Genealogies is mentioned nowhere else in talmudic sources. Commentators have generally seen in the comment of Mar Zuṭra a reference to the contents of this work, viz., exegetical traditions relevant to the genealogical sections of Chronicles.[10] For my purposes the most important difference is that the PT version does not allude to Beruriah, as noted. Thus I doubt whether BT Pesaḥim constitutes an attestation of a Beruriah tradition by a Palestinian master. The allusion to her, like the specification of the subject Simlai wanted to learn, is probably part of the Babylonian reworking of a Palestinian source.

I.3 b. ʿAvodah Zarah 18a-b

Beginning on folio 17b, b. ʿAvodah Zarah cites two versions of the martyrdom of Ḥananyah ben Teradyon.[11] The first is mainly in Hebrew, and the second entirely so. Both versions mention an unnamed daughter of Ḥananyah (see below). The first account relates that the wife of the latter was also sentenced to death, while his daughter was condemned to prostitution. After the second account comes the following story which is entirely in Babylonian Aramaic,

> Beruriah the wife (*devethu*) of Rabbi Meir was the daughter of Rabbi Ḥananyah ben Teradyon. She said to him [Meir], "It is a disgrace for me that

my sister sits in a house of prostitution." He took three qabs of denarii and went [to Rome]. He said, "If no forbidden thing has been done to her, a miracle will occur. If she has done what is forbidden, no miracle will occur for her." He went and presented himself as cavalryman [or: member of the equestrian class]. He said to her, "Submit to me." She said, "I am menstruating." He said to her, "I am very aroused [and do not care]." She said to him, "There are many more beautiful than I." He said, "One may infer that she has not done what is forbidden. She says this to whoever comes." He went to her keeper and said, "Give her over." He said, "I fear the government." He said to him, "Take the three qabs of denarii. Use half for bribes and keep half." He said, "When the half [for bribing] is gone, what shall I do?" He said to him, "Say 'God of Meir, answer me,' and you will be saved." He said to him, "Who says that it is so?" Some man-eating dogs were there. He picked up a clod and threw it at them. They came to eat him, and he said, "God of Meir, answer me,"--and they left him alone. So he gave her to him. Eventually the matter became known to the palace. They brought him [the keeper] and crucified him. He said, "God of Meir, answer me," and he brought him down. They said to him, "What is this?" He told them what happened. They carved the likeness of Rabbi Meir on the gates of Rome and said that whoever sees this face should bring him [to the authorities]. One day they saw him and ran after him. He ran away from them and entered a house of prostitution. Some say he saw gentile food, dipped one finger in it, and licked another [giving the impression that he ate food unfit for Jews]. Others say that Elijah appeared in the

> form of a prostitute and embraced him. They said, "If that were Rabbi Meir, he would never have done that." He arose and fled to Babylonia. Some say because of this matter, while others say because of the Beruriah incident.

For "the Beruriah incident," see IV.5 below. The flight of Meir to Babylonia is unknown to Palestinian sources. The latter do refer to a flight, but without specifying the destination and under varying circumstances. The closest parallel to our study is an account in Galilean Aramaic preserved in Midrash Kohelet Rabbah 7:11,

> Rabbi Meir was sought by the government and fled. He was passing a tavern of Arameans, and he found them sitting and eating from "that species" [viz., pork]. They saw him. [Some] said, "That is he." [Others said], "That is not he." They said, "In case it is he, let us call him and [see] whether he eats with us." He would dip one of his fingers in the blood of the pig and put another finger in his mouth. He dipped this one and licked the other. They said to each other, "If this were Rabbi Meir, he would not do this." They let him go, and he fled. And he recited this verse concerning himself (Ecclesiastes 7:12), "and the advantage of knowledge is that wisdom preserves the life of him who has it."

This source agrees with the BT passage that Meir fled from the Roman government. On the other hand, y. Beṣah 5:3, 63a reports that Meir fled after a dispute with the patriarch. A third Palestinian source, y. Mo'ed Qaṭan 3:1, 82a, alludes passing to the flight of Meir. None of these pericopae hints at the location to which he fled. Since "Arameans" can mean "pagans," the reference to "a tavern of Arameans" is too vague to help. According to y. Kilayim 9:9, 32c and parallels, Meir died in the vicinity of Eilat in Provincia Arabia.[12] In sum, the theme of Meir's flight is well attested in Palestinian sources. However, the details of the BT story, including the connection with Beruriah, are unique to the Babylonian document.

The above three Babylonian sources are the only ones which specify the family connections of Beruriah. Only in I.3 are these connections necessary to the plot. They explain why Meir in particular tried to rescue the (other) daughter of Ḥananyah ben Teradyon. In I.2 the family tie is completely irrelevant. As for I.1, the wife probably is part of the original story. One wonders whether Beruriah was. That is, if we find grounds to doubt her relationship to Meir, we could explain the appearance of her name in this passage as a gloss on the basis of later tradition. And grounds for doubt do exist. As noted already, all these stories are part of the Babylonian Amoraic stratum of talmudic literature. The Palestinian sources, both early (Tannaitic) and late (Amoraic, midrashic), make no mention whatsoever of the family ties of Beruriah. They do mention the latter, as well as an unnamed daughter of Ḥananyah ben Teradyon and an unnamed wife of Meir. But they nowhere hint, let alone state, that these three are one and the same person. In the following sections I shall cite those pericopae which refer to the daughter of Ḥananyah and wife of Meir.

II. The Daughter of Ḥananyah ben Teradyon

Four passages refer to an unnamed daughter of Ḥananyah ben Teradyon. All are in Hebrew. Certainly two of them, probably three, and possibly all belong to the Tannaitic (i.e., early Palestinian) stratum.

II.1 Tosefta Kelim Bava Qamma 4:17

> An oven...which he plastered in cleanness and [which] became unclean--from when is its purification? Rabbi Ḥalafta of Kefar Ḥananyah said, "I asked Shimʿon ben Ḥananyah who asked

the son of Rabbi Ḥananyah ben Teradyon, and he [the latter] said when they move it from its place. But his daughter said when they disassemble its parts."

When these things were said before Rabbi Yehudah ben Bava, he said, "His daughter said better than his son."

Compare IV.1 below.

II.2 Sifré Deuteronomy, §307, ed. Finkelstein, p. 346

Another matter: "The Rock, his work is perfect" (Deut. 32:4a),--when they arrested Rabbi Ḥananyah ben Teradyon, he was sentenced to be burned together with his book. They said to him, "You have been sentenced to be burned with your book." He recited this verse, "The Rock, his work is perfect [for all his ways are justice]." They said to his wife, "Your husband has been sentenced to be burned, and you [have been sentenced] to be killed." She recited this verse, "A God of faithfulness and without iniquity, [just and right is he] (Deut. 32:4b)." They said to his daughter, "Your father has been sentenced to be burned, your mother to be killed, and you [have been sentenced] to 'do work.'"[13] She recited this verse (Jer. 32:19), "Great in counsel and mighty in deed; whose eyes are open to all the ways of men, rewarding every man according to his ways and according to the fruit of his doings."

Rabbi [Yehudah the Patriarch] said, "How great are these three righteous people! In the hour of their distress they summoned three verses vindicating [God's] judgment--which is unprecedented in all of Scripture. The three of them directed their hearts and vindicated the judgment for themselves."

This story is cited with minor variations in b. ʿAvodah Zarah 17b. The BT version adds an explanation why Ḥananyah and his daughter deserved their fate. It also (correctly) glosses "to do work" with "to sit in a house of prostitution." This latter point provides the background for I.3 above.

II.3 Massekhet Semaḥot, Chapter 12, end[14]

> It happened that the son of Rabbi Ḥanina ben Tardion [*sic*] fell into evil ways. Brigands seized him and slew him. His mutilated body was found after three days. They wrapped it in a net and placed it on a bier. They then brought him into the city and acclaimed him by praising his father.
>
> His father cited this verse for him: And thou moan, when thine end cometh, when thy flesh and thy body are consumed, and say: 'How have I hated instruction, and my heart despised reproof, neither have I hearkened to the voice of my teacher, nor inclined my ear to them that instructed me! I was nigh in all evil' (Prov. 5:11-14). Having finished, he went back to the beginning of the verse.
>
> His mother cited this verse for him: A foolish son is a vexation to his father, and bitterness to her that bore him (ibid., 17:28).
>
> His sister cited this verse for him: Bread of falsehood is sweet to a man; but afterwards his mouth shall be filled with gravel (ibid., 20:17).

A parallel at Ekhah Rabbah 3:6 explains that the son actually joined a band of robbers. They killed him when he betrayed them. Masseket Semaḥot may be as old as the late third century.[15] The parallel structure in II.2 and II.3, in which father, wife, and daughter all cite verses appropriate for the occasion, should be noted.

II.4 b. ʿAvodah Zarah 18a

> Our masters taught (*teno rabbanan*): When Rabbi Yosi ben Qisma took sick, Rabbi Ḥananyah ben Teradyon came to visit him....They [the Roman authorities] found Rabbi Ḥananyah ben Teradyon sitting and engaging in Torah, convening public assemblies, and a Torah scroll was in his breast pocket. They brought him, wound the Torah scroll around him, surrounded him with bundles of twigs, and set them on fire. They brought wool sponges, soaked them in water, and laid them on his breast so that he would not die quickly. His daughter said to him, "Father, how can I see you thus!" He said to her, "If I were being burned alone, the matter would be hard for me. But now that I am burned together with the Torah scroll--he who seeks [to avenge] the humiliation of the Torah scroll will seek [to avenge] my humiliation."...

The daughter mentioned in II.2 is obviously not Beruriah, at least according to I.3 above. On the basis of the similarity between II.2 and II.3, W. Bacher decided that the same daughter appears in both anecdotes. Hence II.3 also does not refer to Beruriah.[16] In any event, neither of these sources hints that there were other daughters. Nor do II.1 and II.4.

II.1 and II.2 certainly belong to the Tannaitic stratum of talmudic literature. The *baraita* superscription introducing II.4 claims Tannaitic provenance for the latter source also. If we accept the view that Massekhet Semaḥot is early, then II.3 also is Tannaitic. At the very least this last pericope is Palestinian, as the parallel in Ekhah Rabbah indicates. The Tannaitic and/or Palestinian provenance of all these passages makes their failure to mention Beruriah all the more significant.

III. The Wife of Rabbi Meir

Only one passage known to me refers to an unnamed wife of Meir. Two other parallel pericopae allude to one. I begin with the former.

III.1 Midrash Mishle *ad* 31:10

> Another matter; "A good wife who can find (Prov. 31:10)?" It once happened that Rabbi Meir was sitting and lecturing in the house of study on Sabbath afternoon, and his two sons died. What did their mother[17] do? She laid the two of them on the bed and spread a sheet over them. After the departure of the Sabbath, Rabbi Meir came home from the house of study. He said to her, "Where are my two sons?" She said, "They went to the house of study." He said, "I was watching the house of study, and I did not see them." She gave him a cup for *havdalah*, and he recited the *havdalah* prayer. He again said, "Where are my two sons?" She said to him, "They went to another place and will soon come." She set food before him, and he ate and blessed. After he blessed, she said, "Master, I have a question to ask you." He said to her, "Ask your question." She said to him, "Master, some time ago a man came and gave me something to keep for him. Now he comes and seeks to take it. Shall we return it to him or not?" He said to her, "Daughter, whoever has an object in trust must return it to its owner." She said to him, "Master, I would not have given it to him without your knowledge." What did she do? She took him by the hand and led him up to the room. She led him to the bed and removed the sheet that was on them. When he saw the two of them lying dead on the bed, he began to cry and say, "My sons, my sons..." At that time she said to Rabbi Meir,

"Master, did you not say to me that I must return the trust to its master?" He said, "The Lord gave and the Lord has taken away; blessed be the name of the Lord (Job 1:21)."

R. Ḥanina[18] said, "In this way she comforted him, and his mind was set at ease. Regarding such an instance does it say, "A good wife who can find?"

The provenance of Midrash Mishle is a matter of dispute, though all agree that in its present form it is medieval.[19] It may preserve older material. In any case, I find it striking that even so late a work lacks any reference, even a gloss, to Beruriah in a text mentioning the wife of Meir.[20] If, as I shall argue below, the identification of Beruriah as the wife of Meir is a Babylonian invention, then our source's failure to allude to that connection could indicate that it is of Palestinian provenance.

III.2a y. Demai 2:1, 22c

Rabbi Ze'ira [cited] Rabbi Ḥiyya [who said] in the name of Rabbi Yoḥanan. "Rabbi [Yehudah the Patriarch] permitted Bet She'an [i.e., declared it exempt from certain agricultural dues and restrictions incumbent on the land of Israel] on the basis of Rabbi Yehoshu'a ben Zeroz, son of the father-in-law of Rabbi Meir, who said, 'I saw Rabbi Meir take a vegetable from a garden in the seventh year.' And he permitted it all."

III.2b b. Ḥullin 6b

Rabbi Yehoshu'a ben Zeroz, son of the father-in-law of Rabbi Meir, testified before Rabbi [Yehudah the Patriarch] about Rabbi Meir that he ate the leaf of a vegetable [from which tithes had not been separated]. And Rabbi permitted all of Bet She'an because of him.

According to these sources, the father-in-law of Meir was not Ḥananyah ben Teradyon, but Zeroz. Of course, it is possible that Meir was married more than once.[21]

IV. The Remaining Beruriah Sources

Besides the three pericopae cited in Section I above, four more talmudic passages refer to Beruriah. An eighth tradition is attested only in post-talmudic sources.

IV.1 Tosefta Kelim Bava Meṣi'a' 1:6

> A *claustra*--Rabbi Tarfon declares unclean, but the sages declare clean. And Beruriah says, "One removes it from this door and hangs it on another."
>
> On the Sabbath these things were said to Rabbi Yehoshu'a.[22] He said, "Beruriah said well."

The similarity between this pericope and II.1 above is obvious. However none of the named individuals occur in both passages. Thus I do not see why we must assume that Beruriah and the daughter of Ḥananyah are identical--unless we assume *a priori* that they are one and the same.

IV.2 b. Berakhot 10a

> A certain Sadducee said to Beruriah, "It is written [Is. 54:1], 'Sing, O barren one, who did not bear.' Because she did not bear [should she] sing?" She said to him, "Fool! Cast your eyes to the end of the verse where is written, 'For the children of the desolate one will be more than the children of her that married, says the Lord.' What then does 'barren one who did not bear' mean? [It means,] rejoice, sons of the assembly of Israel, who resemble a barren woman who did not bear sons of gehenna like you."

This anecdote follows II.1 above. Both are in Babylonian Aramaic, and both contain the formula "cast your eyes etc."

IV.3 b. ʿEruvin 53b

> Rabbi Yosi the Galilean was going along the road. He met Beruriah. He said to her, "By which road shall we go to Lod?" She said to him, "Galilean fool! Did not the sages say, 'Do not talk too much with a woman' [M. Avot 1:5, b. Nedarim 20a]? You should have said, 'By which to Lod?'"

IV.4 b. ʿEruvin 53b-54a

> Beruriah found a certain disciple who was reciting his lesson in a whisper. She kicked him and said to him, "Is it not written [2 Samuel 23:5], 'Ordered in all and secure?' [That is,] if it is ordered by means of [all] your 248 limbs, it will be preserved. But if not, it will not be preserved."

IV.4 follows immediately on IV.3. Both anecdotes are in Babylonian Aramaic. Neither is cited or commented upon by a named master. A *baraita* is cited to illustrate the second story, but this cannot fix the provenance of the latter.

IV.5 Rashi ad loc. b. ʿAvodah Zarah 18b, s.v. "And some say because of the Beruriah incident."

> One time she [Beruriah] mocked what the sages said [cf. b. Qiddushin 80b], "Women are flighty." He [Meir] said to her, "By your life! You will eventually concede [the correctness of] their words." He instructed one of his disciples to tempt her to infidelity. He [the disciple] urged her for many days, until she consented. When the matter became known to her, she strangled herself, while Rabbi Meir fled because of the disgrace.

This story is not attested prior to the citation by Rashi (eleventh century).

Now that all the pericopae mentioning Beruriah have been examined, we can proceed to evaluate the material and draw conclusions.

V. The Traditions in Chronological Sequence

In the foregoing sections, thematic considerations determined the order in which I discussed the Beruriah traditions. At this point, I wish to arrange the passages in chronological sequence, i.e., according to the relative antiquity of the sources. This will enable the reader to follow the development of the talmudic tradition on Beruriah. Jacob Neusner has pioneered--and brought to a high level of sophistication--the study in chronological sequence of rabbinic traditions relating to a specific figure. In the course of his work, he devotes considerable attention to the relative dating of talmudic materials by means of attribution and attestation.[23] The methods developed by Neusner will be followed here.

The task of dating the sources mentioning Beruriah is relatively simple. None of these traditions is attributed to a named tradent or attested by a named master. Consequently the only available attestations are those afforded by the documents in which the traditions appear. The dates of the documents provide *termini ante quem* for the passages appearing in them. For the purposes of this article, I shall accept the usual dates assigned to the various documents. This approach avoids the question whether later documents preserve early sources. For example, it is agreed that both BT and PT contain, in addition to sources from the Amoraic period, material of Tannaitic provenance. The indicators of Tannaitic origin include special superscriptions (usually involving forms of the root *tny*) and Hebrew language. However neither of the latter elements, nor both together, can prove that a source appearing in BT, say, is of early Palestinian origin.[24] In any case, I shall indicate the language of the sources and presence of Tannaitic superscriptions.

Traditions Mentioning Beruriah

Subject	Document	Language	Number Above
A. First attested ca. 250			
1. Beruriah tells how to deal with *claustra*	Tosefta Kelim B.M. 1:6	Hebrew	IV.1
B. First attested ca. 500			
2. B. cites exegesis of Psalms 104:35 to her husband Meir	b. Berakhot 10a	Babylonian Aramaic	I.1
3. B. cites exegesis of Is. 54:1 to a Sadducee	b. Berakhot 10a	Babylonian Aramaic	IV.2
4. B. cites rabbinic saying on women to Yosi the Galilean	b. ʿEruvin 53b	Babylonian Aramaic	IV.3
5. B. cites exegesis of 2 Sam. 23:5 to a disciple	b. ʿEruvin 53b-54a	Babylonian Aramaic	IV.4
6. B. wife of Meir and daughter of Ḥananyah ben Teradyon learned 300 traditions a day from 300 masters	b. Pesaḥim 62b	Babylonian Aramaic	I.2
7. B. wife of Meir and daughter of Ḥananyah ben Teradyon asks husband to rescue her sister from house of prostitution in Rome	b. ʿAvodah Zarah 18a-b	Babylonian Aramaic	I.3
C. First attested eleventh century			
8. B. mocks rabbinic saying on women and is tempted to infidelity by disciple of her husband Meir	Commentary of Rashi *ad* b. ʿAvodah Zarah 18b	Hebrew	IV.5

Traditions Mentioning an Unnamed Daughter of Ḥananyah ben Teradyon

A. First attested ca. 250			
1. Dtr. of Ḥ.b.T. on purification of unclean oven	Tosefta Kelim B.Q. 4:17	Hebrew	II.1
2. Dtr. of Ḥ.b.T. like her father and mother cites a verse *re* theodicy after sentencing in Roman persecution	Sifré Deut. 307	Hebrew	II.2

Subject	Document	Language	Number Above
B. First attested ca. 500, though perhaps by 250-300.[25]			
3. Dtr. of Ḥ.b.T. like her father and mother cites a verse *re* death of brother	Semaḥot 12, end = Ekhah Rabbah 3:6	Hebrew	II.3
4. Dtr. of Ḥ.b.T. witnesses father's execution	b. ʿAvodah Zarah 18a superscription: *teno rabbanan*	Hebrew	II.3

VI. Conclusions

A. The Family Connections of Beruriah

On this issue the traditions reviewed above fall into two categories: those which refer separately to Beruriah, the daughter of Ḥananyah ben Teradyon, and the wife of Meir, and those which identify the latter three (or two of them) as one person. Those which asserted the identification are all part of the Babylonian Amoraic stratum of talmudic literature. Those which in no way hint at this identification come from all strata, including several Tannaitic pericopae. In other words, it is precisely the latest and geographically farthest removed sources which assert the family connections of Beruriah. The earliest sources (as well as some later ones) do not mention them. There are two possible interpretations of these facts. First, we can assume that Beruriah in fact was the daughter of Ḥananyah ben Teradyon and wife of Meir, as the three BT passages claim. The other passages, including the Tannaitic ones, suppressed the filial and conjugal status of Beruriah. However, this status was not forgotten. It "resurfaced" later on in Babylonia. Alternatively, we can argue that the ascription of these family ties to Beruriah is a later elaboration of the tradition, or the conflation of several separate traditions. On the first alternative we must explain why talmudic sources censored references to Beruriah's family ties. If we adopt the second explanation, we must explain why Beruriah in particular was identified with the daughter of Ḥananyah and wife of Meir.

I prefer the second alternative, the "elaboration" theory. The assimilation of an unnamed character with a named one is not unprecedented in folklore. Such a process is especially understandable in the present case, for women in general and learned women in particular do not appear frequently in talmudic sources. Thus, references to a knowledgeable daughter of Ḥananyah ben Teradyon and to a contemporary learned woman named Beruriah could easily be assumed to refer to the same person. Admittedly I am less clear on how Meir comes into the picture. However, even with this loose end dangling, the second explanation is preferable to the "suppression" theory. This is because I find the assumption that the tradition censored out the family status of Beruriah intrinsically difficult to accept. True, the "Beruriah incident" reported by Rashi could constitute grounds for censorship--on the unlikely assumption that Rashi preserves a source which dates back to second century Palestine. But even granting this point, the censorship which resulted borders on the capricious. First of all, stories about Beruriah, the daughter of Ḥananyah, and the wife of Meir continued to circulate. Only the identification of the three was suppressed. This is the opposite of what we find in the case of Elishah ben Abuya. In traditions referring to the latter, it was precisely his name which was suppressed, while his relationship with his disciple Meir, for example, was freely mentioned. Furthermore, if the censorship was to be selective, then why suppress the filial relation? The embarrassing connection was the one to her husband. Thus the inner logic of the censorship is difficult to understand. Still more difficult is the assumption that biographical data suppressed in second century Palestine resurfaced in fifth (?) century Babylonia, to say nothing of eleventh century France (Rashi). It is much more reasonable to assume that what appears in an early source is early and what appears only in a late source is late. In view of the work of Jacob Neusner, this latter assumption is practically a proven fact.[26] In sum, the "suppression" theory seems to me untenable.

One final point should be noted. The one source in which the family ties of Beruriah were essential to the plot, I.3, is so blatantly folkloristic as to lack all credibility as an historical source. On the basis of the facts noted above, I conclude that the identification of Beruriah with the daughter of Ḥananyah ben Teradyon and the wife of Meir is a late Babylonian elaboration of the Beruriah tradition. As such, it is of no value with respect to research on the historical Beruriah who lived in second century Palestine.

B. The Education of Beruriah

The reader may object, with justice, that the above discussion revolves around a rather minor point. While it may be of interest to trace the development of a biographical tradition, the historian is more interested in what we can learn from these sources. Even if they are not reliable biographical data about an historical person, they still contain valuable evidence about the possible educational achievements of women in rabbinic society. That evidence will relate to the time(s) and place(s) in which the sources originated. Thus I must determine the provenance of the relevant passages. First, however, I will attempt to ascertain precisely what level of education is (implicitly) attributed to Beruriah by our sources. The types of learning she displays will indicate the level of her education. A survey of her learning, then, is my point of departure.

Only one of the eight Beruriah pericopae, I.3, does not in any way allude to her learning. A second passage is problematic. The story preserved by Rashi, IV.5, has Beruriah mock the rabbinic assertion that women are flighty.

This could mean that she knew a specific dictum, such as the (apparently later) one preserved at b. Qiddushin 80b. On the other hand, it could mean no more than that Beruriah was aware of the misogynistic attitude of her husband's colleagues. And this would not require a formal education. In IV.3, Beruriah explicitly cites a rabbinic dictum, apparently the same one preserved at Mishnah Avot 1:5 and b. Nedarim 20a. The latter saying also expresses rabbinic misogyny. In light of this last pericopa, it is not impossible that in IV.5 Beruriah also quotes a specific maxim. In IV.1, Beruriah exhibits knowledge of a fine point of the rabbinic purity laws. In the remaining pericopae, she displays knowledge of rabbinic scriptural exegesis, *midrash*. In I.1, IV.2, and IV.4, she quotes exegeses of specific verses: Ps. 104:33, Is. 54:1, and 2 Sam. 23:5 respectively. I.2 alludes to how Beruriah learned the Book of Genealogies, a *midrash* relating to Biblical genealogies. I stress these passages describe not knowlege of the verses *per se*, but knowledge of the rabbinic exegesis thereon.

What degree of formal education is reflected in the contents of Beruriah's learning just surveyed? At first glance, IV.1 suggests considerable rabbinic training. Actually it need not indicate any formal education at all. Details of rabbinic law relating to the kitchen and house would be known by a woman who grew up in a rabbinic household. Girls would learn these rules from their mother when they helped out with the housework. As we would expect on the basis of this hypothesis, talmudic literature refers to several women who possess knowledge of this type.[27] So rather than portraying a woman with extensive knowledge of rabbinic law and thus considerable formal training, IV.1 may simply suggest that the practical, informally acquired knowledge of a housewife is preferable to the academic knowledge of a master. The case of IV.3 and IV.5 is more complex. The former definitely and the latter possibly attribute to Beruriah knowledge of specific rabbinic maxims. Normally the acquisition of such knowledge would require a formal rabbinic training. What makes the issue unclear is the subject matter of the maxims. Both concern the place of women in rabbinic society. Thus one could argue that acquaintance with them was not restricted to academic circles. These sayings could easily penetrate into the kitchens and women's quarters of rabbinic homes. One could imagine girls being told to beware of men who engage them in conversation since men should not talk too much with women. One could imagine girls being told that certain rights and duties were denied them because they were flighty. Thus in the absence of other evidence, I would hesitate to take the sources examined in this paragraph as proof that Beruriah was unusually learned or possessed of a formal education.

Other, better, evidence is forthcoming in the remaining pericopae. I.2 is most explicit. It describes how Beruriah learned a specific corpus of rabbinic tradition from many masters over a definite period of time. Here this is no doubt that what I call formal education is meant. The other three passages are less explicit, but equally clear. Exegesis of specific verses, especially from the Prophets and Writings, was not something that a girl would learn from her mother in the kitchen, nor was it part of an indoctrination for modesty. It had to be formally learned, like the Book of Genealogies. Furthermore, *midrash* was an advanced subject. It was not part of the curriculum of elementary education. The latter consisted of learning how to read Scripture, i.e., how to read out loud with correct vocalization, punctuation, and cantillation from the consonantal text of Scripture. Only at more advanced levels of education did the student learn interpretation and exegesis.[28] Several talmudic passages indicate that elementary education was open to women, but not advanced training.[29] The uniqueness and importance of the Beruriah tradition is that it portrays a woman whose learning would require just such an advanced education.

The sources surveyed thus offer evidence of the possibility of a woman attaining a rabbinic education.

The question now is, to what point in history can we date this possibility? The answer depends on the provenance of the pericopae portraying Beruriah as learned in rabbinic tradition. If we limit ourselves to the passages which unequivocally ascribe formal learning to her, then we may consider only those which allude to her knowledge of *midrash*. These are I.1, I.2, IV.2, and IV.4. The first two are from the Babylonian Amoraic stratum of talmudic literature, as noted above. So too are the latter two passages. Both are in Babylonian Aramaic and are unparalleled in rabbinic literature. Thus all the anecdotes which portray Beruriah as possessing an advanced education are of Babylonian Amoraic origin.[30] From this I conclude that the historical situation they reflect is not second century Palestine, i.e., the time and place of the historical Beruriah, but Sassanian Babylonia. I cannot determine exactly when in the Sassanian period, though I doubt it was early. My guess, based on the absence of comments by named masters, is that these sources are relatively late, say late fourth or fifth century. Admittedly, this is only a guess. In any event, it was in Sassanian Babylonia that the existence of a woman learned in rabbinic tradition was a possibility, however uncommon. The remaining Beruriah pericopae, which come from various times and places including second century Palestine, do not require us to ascribe to her an advanced rabbinic education.

If my argument in the preceeding section is correct, then the Babylonian tradents elaborated the biographical tradition on Beruriah received by them by raising her educational level, as it were. This conclusion lends further plausibility to my argument in the previous section that the ascription of family ties to Beruriah was also a Babylonian elaboration. Regarding the substantive issue, I do not dissent from the universally held view that Beruriah was an exception to the rule regarding the degree of education of women in rabbinic society. I only argue that the background of this exception is Sassanian Babylonia, not Roman Palestine.

NOTES

THE BERURIAH TRADITIONS

[1]The name Beruriah, BRWRYH/', is usually taken as a Latin name. Most scholars derive it from Valeria, among them Wilhelm Bacher, *Die Agada der Tannaiten* I[2] (Strassbourg, 1903) p. 353; Louis Ginzberg, *The Legends of the Jews* VI (Philadelphia, 1946) p. 412; Heinrich Graetz, *Geschichte der Juden* IV[4] (Leipzig, 1908) p. 172; Marcus Jastrow, *Dictionary of the Targumim, The Talmud Babli and Yerushalmi and the Midrashic Literature* (New York, 1886-93) p. 171, s.v. BLWRY'; and Henrietta Szold, "Beruriah," *Jewish Encyclopaedia*, III (New York, 1902) p. 109. Ginzberg and Jastrow call attention to the similar name Beluriah, BLWRYH/', which appears as the name of a convert to Judaism at Massekhet Gerim 2:4, Mekhilta de Rabbi Yishma''el, Bo 15, edited Horovitz and Rabin, p. 57, and b. Yevamot 46a. I could not determine who was the first to suggest the derivation from Valeria. A minority view is expressed by S. Krauss, *Griechische und lateinische Lehnwörter im Talmud, Midrasch und Targum*, Teil I (Berlin, 1898) §105, p. 76, who derives the name from Veluria.

On the other hand, Professor Geza Vermes asks whether a Semitic etymology should be ruled out. A root BRR exists in Hebrew and other Semitic languages. The final element, YH, could be theophoric. Names apparently based on BRR do appear, though not frequently, in the Semitic onomasticon. See, for example, F. Gröndah, *Die Personnennamen der Texte aus Ugarit* (Rome, 1967) pp. 30, 121 for the name BRRN and G. Lankester Harding, *An Index and Concordance of Pre-Islamic Names and Inscriptions* (Toronto and Buffalo, 1971) p. 99 for BRR, BRRM, and BRRN. Note also H. Ranke, *Early Babylonian Personal Names* (Philadelphia, 1905) p. 75, for the name Bi-ru-ru-tum. In Hebrew the only comparable form I can find is the place name BRWR ḤYL, which appears at Tosefta Ma'asrot 2:1 and elsewhere. Finally, in view of the frequent exchange of B and P [in connection with rabbinic sources, see the examples collected by Y. N. Epstein, *Mavo' Lenusaḥ Hammishnah* II[2] (Jerusalem and Tel Aviv, 1964) pp. 1220-23], mention may be made of Semitic names apparently connected with a root PRR. Best known is the (Edomite?) name of the brother of King Herod, Φερώρας, see W. Pape and G. Benseler, *Wörterbuch der Griechischen Eigennamen*[2] (Reprint, Graz, 1959) p. 162. Compare the names Φρηρ, Φρηριος = *farir, fariri* in Heinz Wuthnow, *Die semitischen Menschennamen in griechischen Inschriften und Papyri des Vorderen Orients* (Leipzig, 1930) pp. 118, 162 and Harding, *Index*, op. cit., p. 46.

[2]For references to Beruriah in discussions of the place of women in Judaism and Christianity of late antiquity, see Judith Hauptman, "Women in the Talmud," *Response* 18 (Summer, 1973) p. 162; and Wayne A. Meeks, "The Image of the Androgyne: Some Uses of a Symbol in Earliest Christianity," *History of Religions* 13 (1974) p. 175. Already at the turn of the century, Wilhelm Bacher made of Beruriah a martyr for the feminist cause; see his *Agada der Tannaiten* I^2, op. cit., p. 353, n. 1.

[3]See Salo W. Baron, *A Social and Religious History of the Jews* II (Philadelphia, 1952) pp. 215-92.

[4]No such critical evaluation is attempted in encyclopaedia articles by Szold, cited above n. 1, by Zvi Kaplan, "Beruryah," *Encyclopaedia Judaica* IV (Jerusalem, 1971) col. 701, or by Aaron Hyman, *Toldoth Tannaim Ve'amoraim* I (Reprint, Jerusalem, 1964) pp. 294-95. Other scholars, e.g., Graetz, *Geschichte*, op. cit., pp. 172-73; Bacher, *Agada* I, op. cit., pp. 353, 396-97, and II (Strassbourg, 1890) p. 5; George Foot Moore, *Judaism in the First Centuries of the Christian Era* II (Cambridge, Mass., 1962) p. 128; and Salo W. Baron, *Social and Religious History* II, op. cit., pp. 239, 275 in effect merely mention Beruriah in passing. I was not able to obtain three works cited by Szold in her *Jewish Encyclopaedia* article: Adolf Blumenthal, *Rabbi Meir*; M. Kayserling, *Die jüdischen Frauen in der Geschichte, Literatur und Kunst*; and H. Zindorf, *Some Jewish Women*. However, to judge by the article written on the basis of these works, I doubt that the latter engaged in a critical analysis either.

[5]The first element frequently appears as Ḥanina instead of Ḥananyah, i.e., ḤNYN' instead of ḤNNYH. The name of the father, TRDYWN is variously vocalized. I have followed the form and vocalization adopted by H. Yalon in the edition of the Mishnah edited by H. Albeck, 6 vols. (Jerusalem and Tel Aviv, 1958-59). See M. Ta'anit 2:4 and Avot 3:6.

[6]That Beruriah was the daughter of Ḥananyah ben Teradyon and wife of Meir is asserted by all the scholars cited in n. 4 above.

[7]Regarding the origin of Simlai, cf. A. Hyman, *Toldoth*, op. cit., III, pp. 1150-51, who prefers the BT version; M. Margalioth, *Encyclopaedia of Talmudic and Geonic Literature* II (Tel Aviv, 1960) col. 837, who prefers the PT version; and Ch. Albeck, *Introduction to the Talmud, Babli and Yerushalmi* (Tel Aviv, 1969) p. 190, who leaves the question undecided. That b. Pesaḥim 62b should read Yonatan instead of Yoḥanan is argued among others by W. Bacher, *Die Agada der palästinenschen Amoräer* I (Strassburg, 1892) p. 60, no. 4; A. Hyman, *Toldoth* III, p. 1151; and Saul Lieberman, *Hayyerushalmi Kifshuto* (Jerusalem, 1935) pp. 457-58, ad loc. the PT passage.

[8]See R. Rabbinovicz, *Diqduqe Soferim. Variae Lectiones in Mishnam et in Talmud Babylonicum* III (Reprint, New York, 1960) ad loc.

[9]I follow the interpretation of Natan ben Yeḥi'el in his *'Arukh*, s.v. Rashi, ad loc., interprets that the reference is to the section from I Chron. 8:37 to 9:43.

[10]For a full discussion of the nature of this work, including a review of the suggestions of medieval commentators, see S. Klein, "Leshe'elat 'Sefer Yuḥasin,'" *Sefer Hayyovel...le B.M. Lewin* (Jerusalem, 1939) pp. 86-92. Klein concludes the *sefer yuḥasin* was a collection of midrashic material relating to Biblical genealogy, not just to Chronicles.

[11]For this material, see Saul Lieberman, "The Martyrs of Caeserea," *Annuaire de l'Institut de philologie et d'histoire orientales et slaves* VII (1939-44) pp. 418, 420, 429, and "On Persecution of the Jewish Religion," *S. W. Baron Jubilee Volume* III (Jerusalem, 1974) pp. 218-22.

[12]See G. Alon, "*Ṣava'ato Shel R. Me'ir*," *Meḥqarim Betoldot Yiśra'el* I (Ṭel Aviv, 1957) pp. 320-28.

[13]See Lieberman, "The Martyrs of Caeserea," op. cit., p. 418, n. 10, and "On Persecution of the Jewish Religion," op. cit., p. 218, n. 32 and 219, n. 37.

[14]I have used the translation appearing in *The Tractate "Mourning,"* edited and translated by Dov Zlotnick (New Haven and London, 1966) p. 83. See Zlotnick's notes on pp. 162-63. The Hebrew text appears on pp. 198-99. For a critical edition of the Hebrew text, see *Treatise Semaḥot*, edited Michael Higger (Reprint, Jerusalem, 1970) pp. 199-200.

[15]See the discussion in Zlotnick, op. cit., pp. 1-9.

[16]*Agada der Tannaiten* I, pp. 396-97.

[17]The text published by S. Buber, *Midrasch Mischle* (Wilna, 1893) pp. 108-9, reads 'MW, "his mother," which would mean Meir's mother (and not his wife). Buber makes no comment, and I suspect that this is simply a misprint for *'MN*, "their mother," i.e., the boys' mother (and Meir's wife). The letters W and N are very similar. The reading 'MN appears in the parallel at *Yalqut Shim'oni*, Vol. II, §964. Moreover, the quotation from Proverbs--"a good wife"--requires that the heroine be the wife of Meir.

[18]Buber, *Midrasch Mischle*, op. cit., p. 109, n. 17.

[19]See ibid., p. 9, and cf. Y. L. Zunz, *Hadderashot Beyiśra'el*, edited and translated Ch. Albeck (Jerusalem, 1954) pp. 133, 413.

[20]A. Hyman's assertion, *Toldoth* III, p. 876, that the wife mentioned in this story is "without doubt" Beruriah has no other basis than the sources surveyed in Section I above.

[21]Cf. Hyman, loc. cit.

[22]See Saul Lieberman, *Tosefet Rishonim* III (Jerusalem, 1939) p. 355.

[23]See Jacob Neusner, *Development of a Legend. Studies on the Traditions Concerning Yohanan Ben Zakkai* (Leiden, 1970); *The Rabbinic Traditions about the Pharisees Before 70* I-III (Leiden, 1971); *Eliezer Ben Hyrcanus. The Tradition and the Man* I-II (Leiden, 1973). On attributions and attestations, see *Rabbinic Traditions about the Pharisees* III, pp. 180-85 and *Eliezer Ben Hyrcanus* II, pp. 92-94.

[24]Compare E. Margaliyot, "*'Ivrit Ve'aramit Batalmud Uvamidrash*," *Leshonenu* 27-28 (1963-64) pp. 20, 33 and H. Albeck, *Mavo' Latalmudim* (Tel Aviv, 1969) pp. 28, 34-36.

[25]For the BT source, note the superscription. For the Semaḥot source, see n. 15 above. Attestation by 500 for the latter passage is provided by the parallel in Ekhah Rabbah which is dated to the end of the fifth century by M. D. Herr, "Lamentations Rabbah," *Encyclopedia Judaica* 10 (Jerusalem, 1971) col. 1378.

[26]See Neusner, *Development of a Legend*, op. cit., pp. 297-98, and compare the remarks of Morton Smith, quoted in Neusner, *Eliezer Ben Hyrcanus* II, p. 444.

[27]See II.1 above: the daughter of Ḥananyah ben Teradyon knew a rule concerning the purification of ovens; y. Shabbat 4, 6d end: the sister of Shim'on ben Rabbi knew a law concerning an egg laid on an holiday; and y. Beṣah 4:4, 62c end: the daughter of Ḥiyya the Great knew a law concerning cleaning an oven on the Sabbath.

[28]See the remarks of Birger Gerhardsson, *Memory and Manuscript. Oral Tradition and Written Transmission in Rabbinic Judaism and Early Christianity* (Copenhagen, 1964) pp. 60-62 and the literature cited there.

[29]See, e.g., Mishnah Nedarim 4:2-3, Qiddushin 4:13, and Tosefta Megillah 3:11 and parallel in b. Megillah 23a. Cf. Nathan Morris, *A History of Jewish Education* I (Tel Aviv, 1960) pp. 103-13.

[30]The doubtful cases IV.3 and IV.5 in which Beruriah apparently quotes rabbinic *dicta* are also late. The former seems to be of Babylonian Amoraic origin, while the latter is attested for the first time by Rashi.

THE MEN OF THE GREAT ASSEMBLY

Ira Jeffrey Schiffer

Page

PART ONE: THE TRADITION

PART TWO: ANALYSIS OF THE TRADITION

PART ONE: THE TRADITION

The collection of traditions in rabbinic literature about the Men of the Great Assembly is small. There are three items in Mishnah Avot 1:1-2, ten spread through the Palestinian and Babylonian Talmuds, and nine in the later midrashic collections. Our inquiry attempts to uncover and evaluate the history of this tradition.

I. Mishnah Avot 1:1-2

A. 1. Moses received the Torah from Sinai
   2. and handed it on to Joshua,
   3. and Joshua to the Elders,
   4. and the Elders to the Prophets,
   5. and the Prophets handed it on to the Men of the Great Assembly

B. They said three things, "Be careful in judgment, raise up many disciples, and make a fence around the Torah."

C. Simeon the Just was of the remnants of the Great Assembly. He used to say, "On three things the world stands: on the Torah, on the [Temple-] cult, and on deeds of loving kindness."

M. Avot 1:1-2

Comment: A5 establishes the Men of the Great Assembly as the link of Pharisaic tradition with the end of Scriptural tradition, the Prophets.

A-C begins the chain of Pharisaic tradition presented in M. Avot 1:1-18. The list continues:

D. Antigonus of Sokho received from Simeon the Just. He used to say...

E. Yose b. Yoʿezer of Ṣeredah and Yose b. Yoḥanan of Jerusalem received from them. Yose b. Yoʿezer says...
Yose b. Yoḥanan of Jerusalem says...

F. [M. Avot 1:6-17 cites nine more authorities: Joshua b. Peraḥiah and Nittai the Arbelite, Judah b. Ṭabbai and Simeon b. Sheṭaḥ, Shemaʿiah and Abṭalion, Hillel and Shammai, Rabban Gamaliel.]

G. Rabban Simeon b. Gamaliel says, "On three things the world stands: on truth, on judgment, and on peace, as it is written (Zech. 9:16), *Execute the judgment of truth and peace*."

M. Avot 1:3-18

B is independent of A. Its placement attributes rabbinic concerns to the Men of the Great Assembly with a three-part moral apothegm. The form of the chain from Simeon on is a list of names with three-part sayings.

The four pairs of authorities in M. Avot 1:6-17 are presented in the form of E: Authority x + Authority y received from them.

x says + three-part apothegm

y says + three-part apothegm.

(For a complete discussion of the chain, see *Phar*. I, pp. 15-23.)

Neusner argues in *Phar*. I, p. 19, that of A-C only A is original to the list, followed by E. The "them" of E would then refer to the Men of the Great Assembly, "a single mythologumenon which bridged the gap from the prophets to the Pharisees."

A. (W) But why have the sages said, Until midnight?

B. To distance [oneself] from a transgression [of the law], and to make a fence around the Torah.

C. And to confirm the words of the Men of the Great Assembly who used to say three things, Be careful in judgment, raise up many disciples, and make a fence around the Torah.

Mekh. de R. Ishmael, Pisha 6, Lautherbach, p. 46, lines 36-40

Comment: The phrase in B, "make a fence around the Torah," invites the gloss C, which cites M. Avot 1:1.

A. (Deut. 1:16) *And I charged your judges at that time saying, Hear* [*the claims*] *between your brothers and judge righteously.*

B. I said to them, "Be careful in judgment so that if the claim came before you a second and third time, do not say, 'This claim already came before me, and it is its second and third [time before me].' Rather, be careful in judgment."

C. Thus the Men of the Great Assembly say, "Be careful in judgment, raise up many disciples, and make a fence around the Torah."

Sifré Deut. 1:16, Finkelstein, p. 25, lines 9-12

Comment: C, M. Avot 1:1, serves as a proof-text for B, though it could stand as its own comment on A.

A. There we learned (TMN TNYNN):

B. Simeon the Just was of the remnants of the Great Assembly. He used to say, "On three things the world stands: on the Torah, on the [Temple-] cult, and on deeds of loving kindness."

y. Ta. 4:2 = y. Meg. 3:6

Comment: "The context is a discussion of the saying of R. Jacob b. Aha in the name of R. Yasa, 'The world stands only on account of the sacrifices,'" (*Phar*. I, p. 29). Simeon the Just's saying is introduced by the TMN TNYNN formulary and is quoted as contrary evidence. B cites M. Avot 1:2.

A. (Qoh. 12:11) *The words of the sages are like goads* (KDRBWNWT).

B. Said R. Huna, "Like a jewel of girls' [read KDRWR BNWT, so Jastrow, p. 322]."

C. There they call a pearl a *derah*.

D. Another interpretation: KDRBWNWT: like this ball (KKDWR) among the girls (HBNWT).

E. As this ball is thrown from hand to hand and finally comes to rest in the hand of another, so

F. Moses received the Torah from Sinai and handed it to Joshua, and Joshua to the Elders, and the Elders to the Prophets, and the Prophets handed it on to the Men of the Great Assembly.

y. Sanh. 10:1

Comment: Our pericope is a word play on *kadarbonoth*, which are goads used in prodding cattle. B reads it *kadror banoth* (so Jastrow), a "jewel of girls." D is a separate pun introduced by DBR 'ḤR, another interpretation, which reads *kaddur banoth*, a girls' toy ball.

C glosses B. F cites M. Avot 1:1. E-F makes the word play of D into an analogy between a game of catch and the passing of the tradition. As the ball is passed from person to person, so too the tradition is passed from generation to generation.

A. (Qoh. 12:11) *The words of the sages are like goads* (KDRBNWT).

B. [That is,] like a girls' ball (KDWR BNWT).

C. As this ball is received from one hand to the other and does not fall to the ground, so too (Joshua 21:45) *Not one thing fell*, etc. ['ḤD not in the Bible text].

D. As this ball is thrown by hand (BYDYM) and does not fall, so Moses received the Torah from Sinai and handed it on to Joshua, and Joshua to the Elders, and the Elders to the Prophets, and the Prophets handed it on to the Great Assembly, etc.

Qoh. R. 12:11

Comment: *Kaddur banoth* is the only word play on *kadarbonoth* in this exegesis of Qoh. 12:11. C and D provide separate analogies based on the pun.

C misquotes Joshua 21:45, adding an 'ḤD. The use of M. Avot 1:1 by D is similar to y. Sanh. 10:1.

A. [Extended discussion on a chain of tradition following the order: Moses; Joshua; Elders; Judges; Prophets; Haggai, Zechariah, and Malachi.]

B. The Men of the Great Assembly (QBLW) received [the tradition] from Haggai, Zechariah, and Malachi.

C. And they [i.e., the Men of the Great Assembly] said three things, Be careful in judgment, raise up many disciples, and make a fence around the Torah.

ARNa 1

Comment: ARN's discussion follows an expanded version of the earliest links of Pharisaic tradition from that in M. Avot 1:1. ARN adds the Judges and introduces the post-exilic prophets, making them the link with the Men of the Great Assembly. C is as we find it in M. Avot 1:1.

A. Moses received the Torah from Sinai and handed it on to Joshua, and Joshua to the Elders, and the Elders to the Judges, and the Judges to the Prophets, and the Prophets to Haggai, Zechariah, and Malachi. Haggai, Zechariah and Malachi handed it on to the Men of the Great Assembly.

B. And the Men of the Great Assembly (HYW) used to say three things, Be careful in judgment, raise up many disciples, and make a fence around the Torah.

C. [discussion on the links of the chain, concluding with:]

D. And Haggai, Zechariah, and Malachi (MSRW) handed it on to the Men of the Great Assembly.

E. And they used to say three things, Be careful in judgment, etc.

ARNb 1

Comment: In A, ARNb preserves the longer chain. B attributes the three-part saying to the Men of the Great Assembly. The verb tense of the saying varies with that of M. Avot.

Simeon the Just was of the remnants of the Great Assembly [ARNa 4 adds "Men of"]. He used to say, On three things the world stands, on the Torah, on the [Temple-] cult, and on deeds of loving kindness.

ARNa 4 = ARNb 5

Comment: The respective chapters of ARNa and b begin with the direct quote of M. Avot 1:2.

II. Traditions in the *Gemarot*

(1)

A. Bar Kappara said, "To call Abraham, Abram is to violate a positive law [i.e., one requiring an action]."

B. R. Levi said, "[It is to violate both] a positive law and a prohibitory law."

C. (Gen. 17:5a) *And you will not be called anymore by your name Abram*--behold, [this is a] prohibitory law.

D. (Gen. 17:5b) *But your name will be Abraham*--behold, [this is a] positive law.

E. They raised the following objection, "Behold, the Men of the Great Assembly called him Abram."

F. (Neh. 9:7) *You are the Lord God who chose Abram.*

G. [There] it is a different case, [it means] that while he was still Abram, [God] chose him.

y. Ber. 1:6

Comment: E-F claims that the men listed in Neh. 9:4-5 to whom are attributed the extended confession and prayer of Neh. 9:5-38 are to be labeled the Men of the Great Assembly.

The pericope is concerned with violations involved in calling Abraham, Abram. We find a similar tradition in b. Ber. 13a:

y.	b.
1. Bar Kappara said, "To call Abraham, Abram is to violate a positive law."	1. Taught Bar Kappara, "All who call Abraham, Abram violate a positive law."
2. ----	2. As it is written, Gen. 17:5b.
3. R. Levi said, "A positive law and a prohibitory law."	3. R. Eliezar says, "Violates a prohibitory law."
4. ----	4. As it is written, Gen. 17:5a
5. Gen. 17:5a--behold, a prohibitory law.	5. ----
6. Gen. 17:5b--behold, a positive law.	6. ----
7. ----	7. [Discussion on the names Sarah and Jacob.]
8. They raised the following objection, "Behold, the Men of the Great Assembly called him Abram."	8. The following objection was raised by R. Yosi b. Abin, and some say R. Yose b. Zebida, Zebida,
9. Neh. 9:7	9. " " "
10. It is a different case, while he was still Abram, [God] chose him.	10. It was said to him, There the prophet praises the Lord by referring to the past, which was originally.

By the third century, y. has identified the Men of the Great Assembly in Neh. b. does not know that tradition here though it cites late fourth century Palestinian Amoraim using the Neh. proof-text. If y. is primary, I do not know why b. would omit mention of the Men of the Great Assembly.

A. (Gen. 17:5) *And you will not be called anymore by your name Abram, but your name will be Abraham.*

B. Bar Kappara said, "All who call Abraham, Abram violate a positive law."

C. Said R. Levi, "[It is to violate both] a positive law and a prohibitory law."

D. *And you will not be called anymore by your name Abram* is a prohibitory law.

E. *But your name will be Abraham* is a positive law.

F. (W) But behold, the Men of the Great Assembly called him Abram.

G. (Neh. 9:7) [*God*] *who chose Abram.*

H. [There] it is a different case, [it means] that while he was still Abram, [God] chose him.

Gen. R. 46:8

Comment: Our pericope is essentially that of y. Ber. 1:6 used for Gen. R.'s discussion of Gen. 17:5. B-H is also found in Gen. R. 78:3. There it lacks the attribution to the Men of the Great Assembly in F and reads, "But behold it is written" + proof-text.

(2)

A. R. Simeon in the name [of] R. Joshua b. Levi:

B. Why are they called Men of the Great Assembly? Because they restored the greatness to its original state.

C. Said R. Pinḥas, Moses established the formula of *Tefillah*: (Deut. 10:17) *God, the great, the mighty, and the awe-inspiring.*

D. Jeremiah said (Jer. 32:18), *God, the great* [*and*] *the mighty, and did not say the awe-inspiring.*

E. Why did he say *the mighty*? It is fitting to call him mighty when he sees the destruction of his House and is silent.

F. And why didn't he say *awe-inspiring*? Only the Temple can be awe-inspiring.

G. As it is said (Ps. 68:36), *God, awe-inspiring in your Sanctuary.*

H. Daniel said (Dan. 9:4), *God, the great and the awe-inspiring*, and did not say *the mighty.*

I. His sons are bound in chains. Where is his might?

J. And why did he say awe-inspiring? It is fitting to call him awe-inspiring because of the awe-inspiring acts which he did for us in the heated furnace [i.e., Dan. 3:19-27].

K. And when they arose, the Men of the Great Assembly restored the greatness to its original state (Neh. 9:32), *God, the great, the mighty, and the awe-inspiring.*

y. Ber. 7:3

Comment: A-B gives an etymology of the name Men of the Great Assembly. It is based on a word play between greatness (HGDWLH) and the HGDWLH in the Men of the Great (HGDWLH) Assembly. It is attributed to a first generation Palestinian Amora. C-K is attributed to a fifth generation Palestinian Amora and is a development of A-B. It clearly sees the Men of the Great Assembly in Neh. as it provides an exegetical *aggadic* tradition on the development and redaction of the use of attributes in praise of God. The greatness in B is thus understood as the accepted attributes in the first benediction of *Tefillah*.

The tradition assumes that the Men of the Great Assembly were involved in liturgical affairs. This possibly arose after the identification of the Men of the Great Assembly in Neh. when it was noted that the language attributed to them in Neh. 9:32 was identical to the formula attributed to Moses in Deut. 10:17.

A. R. Simeon in the name [of] R. Joshua b. Levi:

B. Why are they called Men of the Great Assembly? Because they restored the greatness to its original state.

C. Said R. Pinḥas, Moses established the formula of *Tefillah*: (Deut. 10:17) *God, the great, the mighty, and the awe-inspiring.*

D. Jeremiah said (Jer. 32:18), *God, the great* [*and*] *the mighty*, and did not say *the awe-inspiring*.

E. And why is he *mighty*? It is fitting to call him mighty when he sees the destruction of his House and is silent.

F. And why didn't he say awe-inspiring? Only the Temple can be awe-inspiring.

G. As it is written (Ps. 68:36), *God, awe-inspiring in your Sanctuary.*

H. Daniel Said (Dan. 9:4), *God, the Great and the awe-inspiring.*

I. And why didn't he say *mighty*? His sons are bound in chains. Where is his might?

J. And why did he say awe-inspiring? It is fitting to call him awe-inspiring because of the awe-inspiring acts which he did for his people in the heated furnace [i.e., Dan. 3:19-27].

K. And when they assembled, the Men of the Great Assembly restored the greatness to its original state (Neh. 9:32), *And now God, God the great, the mighty, and the awe-inspiring, guardian of the covenant and mercy,* [*may our troubles*] *not be diminished before you, etc.*

y. Meg. 3:7

Comment: This is a better developed version of y. Ber. 7:3. H-J more carefully balances D-F. G is improved from "said" in Ber. to "written."

A. Said R. Joshua b. Levi,

B. Why are they called by the name of the Great Assembly? Because they restored the crown to its original state.

C. Moses came [and] said (Deut. 10:17), *God, the great, the mighty, and the awe-inspiring.*

D. Jeremiah came and said, "Strangers are destroying his Temple. Where are his awe-inspiring acts?" [So he did] not say awe-inspiring [as an attribute].

E. Daniel Came [and] said, "Strangers are enslaving his sons. Where are his mighty acts?" [So he did] not say mighty [as an attribute].

F. They [the Men of the Great Assembly] came and said, "On the contrary, here is the might of his mighty acts. He observes self-restraint (ŠKWBŠ 'T YṢRW) that (Š) he shows long-suffering to the wicked."

G. And these are his awe-inspiring acts. Were it not for the awe of the Blessed be He, how is the one nation [Israel] able to endure among the nations."

b. Yoma 69b = Yalqut Shimoni 856

Comment: b. does not use the word play in B. C-G proceeds with a similar though different development of the *aggadic* tradition found in y.

y. (Meg. 3:7)	b.
1. R. Simeon in the name of R. Joshua b. Levi:	1. Said R. Joshua b. Levi,
2. "Why are they called Men of the Great Assembly? Because they restored the greatness to its original state."	2. "Why are they called by the name Men of the Great Assembly? Because they restored the crown to its state."
3. Said R. Pinḥas, Moses established the formula of *Tefillah*: Deut. 10:17.	3. Moses came and said, Deut. 10:17
4. Jeremiah said, Jer. 32:18, and did not say the awe-inspiring.	4. Jeremiah came and said, "Strangers are destroying his Temple, where are his awe-inspiring acts?" So he did not say awe-inspiring.
5. And why is he mighty? It is fitting to call him mighty when he sees the destruction of his House and is silent.	5. ----
6. And why didn't he say awe-inspiring? Only the Temple can be awe-inspiring. As it is written, Ps. 68:36.	6. ----
7. Daniel said, Dan. 9:4. And why didn't he say mighty? His sons are bound in chains. Where is his might?	7. Daniel came and said, "Strangers are enslaving his sons. Where are his mighty acts?" So he did not say mighty.
8. And why did he say awe-inspiring? It is fitting to call him awe-inspiring because of the awe-inspiring acts which he did for his people in the heated furnace.	8. ----

y. (Meg. 3:7)

9. And when they assembled, the Men of the Great Assembly restored the greatness to its original state, Neh. 9: 32.

b.

9. They came and said, "On the contrary, here is the might of his mighty acts. He observes self-restraint that he shows long-suffering to the wicked. And these are his awe-inspiring acts. Were it not for the awe of the Blessed be He, how is the one nation able to endure among the nations."

The explicit identification of the Men of the Great Assembly in Neh. by y. is only implicit in b. Pseudepigraphic quotes are given to Jeremiah, Daniel, and the Men of the Great Assembly instead of their respective proof-texts.

C-F are in the form, Came x and said. D-E are balanced and F-G provides counter-examples. While there is little to suggest dependence of one version on the other, both may be drawing from a common tradition.

A. R. Phinehas the Priest bar Ḥama taught: "Moses instituted the order of prayer for Israel when he said: *The Lord your God, He is God of gods, and Lord of lords, the great God, the mighty, the awesome* (Deut. 10:17). *Great*: God did great things in Egypt; *mighty*: God brought mighty things to pass on the sea; *awesome*: in the days of Moses the Tabernacle was set up, of which it is said *Awesome is God out of thy holy place* (Ps. 68:36).

B. Jeremiah, in his order of prayer, said, *The great, the mighty God* (Jer. 32:18), but not *the awesome God*. Why did Jeremiah say *God the mighty*? Because, he explained, 'This One, though He saw His children put in chains and His Temple destroyed, remained silent; hence it is proper to call Him *mighty*.' But he did not say *God the awesome* because the Temple--of which it is said *Awesome is God out of thy holy place*

(Ps. 68:36)--was destroyed. Where, then, is the awe, if enemies came into His house and were not awed?

C. Daniel, [in his order of prayer], said, *O Lord, the great and awesome God* (Dan. 9:4), but not *God the mighty*. Why not? Because, as Daniel asked: When His children were put in chains, where was God's might? And why did Daniel say *God the awesome*? Because, as he explained, 'This One did awesome things for us in the lions' den and in the fiery furnace; hence it is proper to call Him *awesome*.'

D. However, when the Men of the Great Assembly arose, they restored the manner of praising God's greatness to its ancient form, saying: *Now, therefore, our God, the great, the mighty, and the awesome God* (Neh. 9:32). Why? Because, as they explained, 'God remains above every praise by which men would exalt Him.'

Midrash Ps. 19, trans.
Braude, pp. 273-74.

Comment: Midrash Ps. gives us an expanded account of the *aggadic* history first presented in y. Ber. 7:3. Moses' use of great, mighty, and awe-inspiring is explicated. The analysis of Jer. and Dan. remains the same. The explanation offered in D makes no sense in the limited context of A-D. That God remains above every praise of man cannot serve as a justification for the Men of the Great Assembly establishing three attributes in prayer.

(3)

A. Said R. Yona, "It is written (Is. 53:12), *It is for this purpose I will divide for him* [*a portion*] *with the many and with the mighty he will divide his gain.*

B. "This [applies to] R. ʿAqiva who instituted legal interpretation (MDRŠ HHLKWT) and *aggadic* interpretation (WHGDWT)."

C. There are those who say, These the Men of the Great Assembly instituted.

y. Sheq. 5:1

Comment: In this fourth century or later Palestinian tradition, we see the link between the Prophets and the Men of the Great Assembly (see M. Avot 1:1) used to couple the inception of rabbinic methods with the conclusion of the Scriptural tradition.

(4)

A. R. Shaman b. Abba said to R. Yohanan,

B. "Now the Men of the Great Assembly instituted for Israel blessings, *tefillot*, sanctifications, and *havdalot*."

C. "Let us see where [the Men of the Great Assembly] instituted [the *havdalah*]."

D. He said to him, [ms M omits C-D]

E. "In the beginning they established the [*havdalah*] prayer in the *Tefillah*. When they became rich, they established the prayer over a cup [of wine]. When they became poor again they re-established [the *havdalah*] in the *Tefillah*.

F. "And they said, '[He] who makes *havdalah* in the *Tefillah* must also make *havdalah* over a cup [of wine].'"

G. ('YTMR NMY) Likewise it is said:

H. ('MR) R. Hiyya b. Abba said [in the name of] R. Yohanan,

I. "The Men of the Great Assembly instituted for Israel blessings, *tefillot*, sanctifications, and *havdalah*,

J. "In the beginning they established the [*havdalah*] prayer in the *Tefillah*. When they became rich they established the prayer over a cup [of wine]. When they became poor again they re-established [the *havdalah*] in the *Tefillah*.

K. "And they said, '[He] who makes *havdalah* in the *Tefillah* must also make *havdalah* over a cup [of wine].'"

L. ('YTMR NMY) Likewise it is said:

M. Rabba and R. Joseph both said, "[He] who makes *havdalah* in the *Tefillah* must also make *havdalah* over a cup [of wine]."

b. Ber. 33a

Comment: A-B and H-I are third century Palestinian attributions crediting the Men of the Great Assembly with four liturgical activities. E-F and J-K give the same account of their role concerning *havdalah*. F is an independent ruling that *havdalah* must be made in two places. Its location in the pericope suggests that the "they" refers to the Men of the Great Assembly. E offers an explanation for the double *havdalah*, though it contradicts F. In E the *havdalah* is restored to the *Tefillah* because they could not afford wine. F requires *havdalah* both in the *Tefillah* and over the wine. The redactor provides a correction with L-M where he cites F attributed to Rabba and R. Joseph. The lemma is attributed to Samuel in b. Shab. 15b.

Our pericope is part of the *gemara* concerned with M. Ber. 5:2. The end of that *mishnah* is a dispute between 'Aqiva and Eliezer on the location of the *havdalah* in the *Tefillah*. Neusner comments on this in his study of Eliezer ben Hyrcanus, "Eliezer and 'Aqiva had no firm tradition on where to insert *havdalah*" (*Eliezer* II, p. 352). He further demonstrates that the formulation of the liturgy was a live issue during the Yavnean period (ibid., p. 201). On the basis of the M. Avot chain, the Men of the Great Assembly would allegedly be eight generations prior to Yavneh.

(5)

A. A man went down to lead the service in the presence of R. Ḥanina, and he said, "God, the great, the mighty, and the awe-inspiring, the glorious and the majestic, the feared, the strong, and the powerful, the prideful, and the honored."

B. He waited for him until he had finished. When he had finished, he said to him, "Have you finished all your praise of your Master?

C. "Why do I want all of that? [Even] these three [attributes] that we do say [i.e., great, mighty, and awe-inspiring]--if Moses our teacher had not said them in the Torah, and the Men of the Great Assembly [had not] come and instituted them in the *Tefillah*, we should not have been able to say even these. And you say all these and continue."

D. (MŠL) This is analogous to a human king (lit. king of flesh and blood) who had a million gold *denarii* and someone praised him [for having a million] of silver. Would not this be an insult to him?

b. Ber. 33b

Comment: The Men of the Great Assembly are again seen as the legitimizing authority of the formula of attributes in the *Tefillah* (see discussion of y. Ber. 7:3, y. Meg. 3:7, b. Yoma 69b). It is attributed to a third century Palestinian Amora.

The pericope is located in a discussion of pharses not permitted in public prayer. The rabbis are concerned that the phrases suggest either two powers, a good and evil power, or a limit to the power of God. R. Ḥanina may be objecting to the use of any attributes in prayer because they suggest limits concerning God. The point of the MŠL, D, is that praise of God is always inadequate.

A. A man went down to lead the service in the presence of R. Ḥanina, and he said, "God, the great, the mighty, and the awe-inspiring, the glorious, the strong, and the powerful."

B. He said to him, "Have you finished the praises of your Master?

C. "Now [as regards] these three that we say, if Moses had not written them in the Torah, and the Men of the Great Assembly come and instituted them, we could not say [even] these, and you said all those."

D. (MŠL) This is analogous to a man who had a million gold "denarii" and someone praised him [for having] a thousand silver *denarii*. Would not this be an insult to him?

b. Meg. 25a = Yalqut Shimoni 856

Comment: Stylistic differences make this a shorter version of the b. Ber. 33b pericope. Yalqut uses R. ʿAqiva instead of R. Ḥanina.[1]

(6)

Said R. Joshua b. Levi, Twenty-four fasts were observed by the Men of the Great Assembly concerning copyists of Biblical scrolls, *tefillin*, and *mezuzot*, so they should not become rich. Because if they would become rich, they would not write.

b. Pes. 50b

Comment: Our pericope makes the Men of the Great Assembly concerned with the unbroken continuation of the tradition.

(7)

A. The *Megillah* is [sometimes] read on the eleventh [of Adar].

B. From whence do we know this?

C. From whence do we know this!? It ought to be said [that we know it from] what is stated below.

D. The Sages dealt leniently with the villages allowing [the *Megillah* to be read] earlier [than the fourteenth, such that it coincided with] the day of assembly [i.e., Monday or Thursday] so that they could supply water and food to their kinsmen in the fortified cities.

E. We say here that all [the days permitted for the reading of the *Megillah*] the Men of the Great Assembly enacted.

F. For if you should think that the Men of the Great Assembly established [only] the fourteenth and the fifteenth [how is it possible that the later] Rabbis could abolish an enactment which the Men of the Great Assembly established?

G. For we have learned: One *Bet Din* cannot abolish the decision of a *Bet Din* of their colleagues unless [they are] greater than it in wisdom and in number.

H. Rather, it is clear that all [the days permitted for the reading of the *Megillah*] the Men of the Great Assembly enacted.

b. Meg. 2a

Comment: Our pericope uses the Men of the Great Assembly to sanction all the days permitted for the reading of the *Megillah*. F takes for granted the tradition that the Men of the Great Assembly wrote the Book of Esther (see b. B.B. 15a). This credits them with the Scriptural dates for reading derived from Esth. 9:17-19. A quotes M. Meg. 1:1 which extends the days permitted to the 11th, 12th, 13th, 14th, or 15th.[2] While D credits the Sages with the enactment of the additional days, G, M.ʿEd. 1:5, raises the problem of conflicting rulings. E, F, and H legitimize M. Meg. 1:1 with the authority of the Men of the Great Assembly. D is also found in b. Meg. 4a attributed to R. Ḥanina. There it is a commentary on a quote from M. Meg. 1:2, "villages read it earlier on the day of the assembly" (Danby, p. 201).

(8)

A. (Esth. 1:1) (WYHY) *And it came to pass in the days of Aḥasuerus.*

B. Said R. Levi, and some say R. Jonathan,

C. "This matter is a tradition in our hands from the Men of the Great Assembly:

D. All the places where it says WYHY, [and it came to pass,] it means nothing but the language of trouble [i.e., it indicates trouble]."

b. Meg. 10b

Comment: This is the only Talmudic reference that the Men of the Great Assembly are responsible for an exegetical interpretation (see y. Sheq. 5:1). They are credited with an old common exegesis. Neusner suggests in *Hist*. V (p. 205) that this interpretation of WYHY is an old native-Babylonian tradition. R. Ashi comments on it in b. Meg. 10b, and Rab gives an interpretation of WYHY in b. Meg. 11b.

(9)

The Men of the Great Assembly wrote Ezekiel, the Twelve [Minor Prophets], Daniel, and the Scroll of Esther.

b. B.B. 15a

Comment: I do not know any basis for this tradition.

(10)

Three kings and four commoners have no share in the world to come.

M. Sanh. 10:2, trans.
Danby, p. 397

A. Who enumerated them?

B. Said R. Ashi, "The Men of the Great Assembly enumerated them."

C. Said R. Judah said Rav, "They desired to include another..."

b. Sanh. 104b

A. Who enumerated them?

B. Said Rav, "The Men of the Great Assembly enumerated them."

C. Said R. Judah said Samuel, "They desired to join Solomon with these..."

Num. R. 14:1

Comment: b. A-B is another example of the Men of the Great Assembly being used to establish an older authority for a tradition. I have no idea why they are supposedly the authors of this decision. A-B was probably added to specify the anonymous "they" in C. Num. R. corrects the anachronism of having R. Ashi, an early fifth century Babylonian Amora, serve as the basis for a saying attributed to R. Judah, a late third century Amora.[3]

III. Traditions in Later Compilations

(1)

A. Where are the spheres of the sun and moon set?

B. In the second firmament.

C. As it is written (Gen. 1:17), *And God put them* ('WTM) *in the firmament of the heavens.*

D. R. Pinḥas [said] in the name of R. Abbahu, "The reading from Scriptures is in plene spelling (MQR' ML').

E. "And the Men of the Great Assembly explained (Neh. 9:6), *Thou art the Lord, even Thou alone. You made the heaven* [*and the*] *heaven of heavens and all their hosts, etc.*

Gen. R. 6:6

Comment: E identifies the Men of the Great Assembly in Neh. It further claims that they are involved in agadic exegesis. Following Albeck's definition of MQR' ML',

D notes that ʾWTM in C is spelled with a W.[4] Since it has an extra letter, the verse is an applicable proof-text for A-B.

(2)

A. (Gen. 9:12) *And said God, This is the sign of the covenant*, etc. [*for generations* (LDWRWT) *forever* forever.]

B. Said R. Yudan, "[Generations] is written LDRT. This excludes two generations, the generation of Hezekiah and the generation of the Men of the Great Assembly." [Yalkut Shimoni adds: They existed on their own merit.]

C. R. Hezekiah deletes the generation of the Men of the Great Assembly and substitutes the generation of R. Simeon b. Yoḥai.

Gen. R. 35:2 = Yalqut Shimoni 61

Comment: B sees the Men of the Great Assembly as being so worthy that they did not need a sign to sustain them. It is attributed to a fourth generation Palestinian Amora. Hezekiah and the Men of the Great Assembly represent two generations credited with reform activity.

(3)

A. What is [the meaning of] (Ex. 32:18), *The sound* [*of them*] *that sing do I hear*?

B. The sound of blasphemy and reviling I hear.

C. The Men of the Great Assembly arose and explained it (Neh. 9:18) *Even when they made the molten calf and said This is your god who brought you up from Egypt*.

D. [Is this] lacking anything?

Ex. R. 41:1

Comment: The Men of the Great Assembly are again identified in Neh. and credited with *aggadic* exegesis.

(4)

A. Why is tabernacle [mentioned] two times [in Ex. 38:21]?

B. Said R. Samuel b. Martah, Because the tabernacle [was taken as a pledge] two times on their [the Israelites'] account.

C. This is what the Men of the Great Assembly say (Neh. 1:7), *We have wronged against you, and we have not kept the commandments, nor the statutes, nor the laws.*

Ex. R. 51:3

Comment: C assumes the traditions that the Men of the Great Assembly wrote Neh. and are involved in *aggadic* exegesis.

(5)

And Shemaiah and Abṭalyon, who were among the descendants of Sisera, taught Torah to multitudes just as the Men of the Great Assembly did.

Midrash Ps. 1:1

Comment: On the basis of the traditions which locate the Men of the Great Assembly in Neh., our pericope identifies them with the group in Neh. 8:8 who teach the people Torah.

(6)

Said R. Abba bar Kahana, "Two generations pronounced the Ineffable Name (BŠM HMPWRŠ), the Men of the Great Assembly and the generation of persecution."

Midrash Ps. 36:8

Comment: The Men of the Great Assembly are named because Neh. 8:8 says, "they read the scroll of the law of God (MPRŠ)." The pericope comments on Ps. 36:10, *Continue your loving kindness to them that know you.* The independent saying is attributed to a third generation Palestinian Amora.

(7)

(Song 7:14) *And at our entrances are all [kinds of] precious fruits.*

A. And the Rabbis said, "[Compare this] to the king who had an orchard and gave it to a tenant. What did the tenant do? He filled baskets of figs from the fruit of the orchard and placed them at the entrance of the orchard. When the king passed and saw all this profit he said, All this profit in the entrance of the garden, how much more so must be in the orchard itself.

B. "So in the first generations, the Men of the Great Assembly, Hillel, Shammai, and Rabban Gamaliel the Elder. In the later generations, R. Yohanan b. Zakkai, R. Eliezer, R. Joshua, R. Meir, and R. ʿAqiva, and their disciples how much more so."

Song R. 7:14

Comment: The list in B seems to be taken from the chain of tradition in M. Avot 1:1-18.

(8)

How did the Men of the Great Assembly act? They wrote a document and spread it out in the Temple court and in the morning they rose and found it sealed.

Ruth R. 4:5

Comment: The context of this saying is a discussion of three things which the earthly court decreed and the heavenly court approved. The Men of the Great Assembly are cited as an authoritative council in reference to tithing while in exile.

[Discussion of the merits of the Months.]

A. The merit of the Men of the Great Assembly brought *Shebat*.

B. On the twenty-third all of Israel gathered concerning the concubine of Gibeah and concerning the idol of Micah.

Esth. R. 7:11 = Abba Gorion 3:85, A only

Comment: I do not know why *Shebat* should bring the merit of the Men of the Great Assembly.

B is taken from *Megillath Ta'anith* and refers to Judges chapters 20 and 17.[5] If A-B is a unit, then the Men of the Great Assembly are being identified in the gathering in Judges 20.

PART TWO: ANALYSIS OF THE TRADITION

IV. The Distribution of the Tradition as a Whole

In Part One we analyzed each of the items in the tradition of the Men of the Great Assembly. We shall now examine the tradition as a whole. Below is a summary listing of the traditions and their distribution. The order of the items follows their presentation in the first chapter.

Item	Mishnah	Tannaitic Midrashim	y.	b.	Later Compilations
1. Chain of tradition.	M. Avot 1:1a		y. Sanh. 10:1		Qohelet R. 12:11, ARNa 1
2. They said three things.	M. Avot 1:1b	Mekh. deR. Ishmael, Pisḥa 6, Sifré Deut. 1:16			ARNa & b 1
3. Simeon the Just was of the remnants of the Great Assembly.	M. Avot 1:2		y. Ta. 4:2 = y. Meg. 3:6		ARNa 4 = ARNb 5
4. Called him Abram + Neh. 9:7.			y. Ber. 1:6		Gen. R. 46:8
5. Restored the greatness (crown) + Neh. 9:32.			y. Ber. 7:3 y. Meg. 3:7	b. Yoma 69b	Yalqut Shim. 856 (without proof-text) Midrash Ps. 19
6. Instituted legal & *aggadic* interpretation.			y. Sheq. 5:1		
7. Instituted blessings, *tefillot*, sanctifications & *havdalot*.				b. Ber. 33a	
8. Instituted the three attributes in the *Tefillah*.				b. Ber. 33b b. Meg. 25a	Yalqut Shim. 856

Item	Mishnah	Tannaitic Midrashim	y.	b.	Later Compilations
9. Observed fasts concerning copyists.				b. Pes. 50b	
10. Enacted the days for reading the *Megillah*.				b. Meg. 2a	
11. Are responsible for the exegesis of WYHY (based on Esth. 1:1).				b. Meg. 10b	
12. Wrote Ezekiel, the 12, Daniel, and Esth.				b. B.B. 15a	
13. Enumerated the 3 kings and 4 commoners.				b. Sanh. 104b	Num. R. 14:1
14. Explained the spheres in the second firmament + Neh. 9:6.					Gen. R. 6:6
15. Did not need the sign of the covenant.					Gen. R. 35:a = Yalqut Shim. 61
16. Explained Ex. 32:18 + Neh. 9:18.					Ex. R. 41:1
17. Concerning the tabernacle they say + Neh. 1:7.					Ex. R. 51:3
18. Taught Torah to the multitudes.					Midrash Ps. 1:1
19. Used HŠM HMPWRŠ.					Midrash Ps. 36:8

Item	Mishnah	Tannaitic Midrashim	y.	b.	Later Compilations
20. First generations.					Song R. 7:14
21. They wrote a document and spread it in the Temple court.					Ruth R. 4:5
22. Their merit is in the month of *Shebat*.					Esth. R. 7:11 = Abba Gorion 3:85

This small collection of traditions breaks down into five legal items (y. Ber. 1:6, y. Ber. 7:3, b. Ber. 33a, b. Ber. 33b, and b. Meg. 2a) which constitute 23% of the collection. The remaining 77% are *aggadic* materials offering biographical-historical information. No legal activity is ascribed to the Men of the Great Assembly in Mishnah Avot. This picture contrasts sharply to the traditions of individual authorities.[6] More than 70 percent of those traditions are legal, and roughly 90 percent of the legal traditions occur in the Tannaitic stratum. The biographical-historical materials largely appear later and are less likely to be representative of the authority. Our tradition occurs uniformly in the later documents and is much less *halakhic* than the traditions of the named authorities.

V. The History of the Tradition

Although no forms are peculiar to the tradition of the Men of the Great Assembly, perhaps the discrete items of which it is composed exhibit an internal logic or consistency. We begin our analysis with M. Avot 1:1a. In this chain of tradition the Men of the Great Assembly serve merely as a name which bridges the large gap between the Prophets and Simeon the Just, a period of roughly two hundred years.[7] The Simeon tradition, M. Avot 1:2, is thus essentially part of 1:1a as it moves the chain forward from the Men of the Great Assembly. This is the only appearance in Mishnah of the Men of the Great Assembly. Since the tradition lacks any attestations, the only date we can assign it is the redaction of Mishnah, ca. 200-250.[8] It can be noted, though, that the interest in a history of the Oral Torah from Moses to the Rabbis is a dominant theme of Ushan historians.[9] Our M. Avot tradition is probably from this later stratum of Mishnah. While the need for a name to bridge the generations is understandable, the reason for the specific choice of this name remains unknown. M. Avot 1:1b then ascribes rabbinic concerns to the Men of the Great Assembly.

We can group the non-mishnaic items around a number of themes. These are (1) the Men of the Great Assembly identified in Neh., (2) their role in liturgical affairs, (3) the Men of the Great Assembly as exegetes, and (4) their responsibility for the writing of Esther. y. Ber. 7:3 and b. Yoma 69b, "the restoration of the greatness (crown)," will be counted as two items since the y. pericope includes a proof-text.

Nehemiah	*Liturgy*	*Exegetes*	*Esther*
y. Ber. 1:6		y. Ber. 1:6	
y. Ber. 7:3	y. Ber. 7:3	y. Ber. 7:3	
b. Yoma 69b	b. Yoma 69b		
		y. Sheq. 5:1	
b. Ber. 33a	b. Ber. 33a		
b. Ber. 33b	b. Ber. 33b		
	b. Meg. 2a		b. Meg. 2a
		b. Meg. 10b	b. Meg. 10b
			b. B.B. 15a
Gen. R. 6:6		Gen. R. 6:6	
Ex. R. 41:1		Ex. R. 41:1	
Ex. R. 51:3		Ex. R. 51:3	
Midrash Ps. 1:1			
Midrash Ps. 36:8			

Other

b. Pes. 50b
b. Sanh. 104b
Gen. R. 35:2
Song R. 7:14
Ruth R. 4:5
Esth. R. 7:11

We see from the chart that four of the five items concerned with liturgy, and five of the seven under the theme of exegetes are based on the identification of the Men of the Great Assembly with those mentioned in Neh. 9 (except Ex. R. 51:3 which quotes Neh. 1:7). The items under Neh. make up 50% of the non-mishnaic traditions. y. Sheq. 5:1 does not bear a direct relationship with Neh. but assumes an exegetical activity based on Neh. 8-9. b. Meg. 2a and 10b reflect the liturgical and exegetical concerns established in Neh. and the tradition about the writing of Esther. The tradition that the Men of the Great Assembly wrote Esther, Ezekiel, Daniel and the twelve minor Prophets (b. B.B. 15a) also grows out of the identity of the Men of the Great Assembly in Neh. The books of Esther, Ezekiel, and Daniel claim to be from this period, and the minor Prophets range from the eighth to the fifth centuries B.C.E. It was an easy step to assign the authorship of these books to the assembly of that period, the Men of the Great Assembly. The Midrash on Psalms also suggests the identification of the Men of the Great Assembly in Neh. 8.

Thus we can explain the history of 70% of the non-mishnaic traditions. First comes the name in M. Avot 1:1. The period bridged by the Men of the Great Assembly is between the end of the Prophets and the time of Simeon the Just, that is, the period of Ezra-Nehemiah. The tradition then identifies the Men of the Great Assembly with the assembly in Neh. 8-9. It ascribes to them primarily matters of exegesis and liturgy and so reflects the description of the assembly's activity in Neh. 8-9. Neh. 8:8 describes the group as giving the clear sense of the Torah to the people. Having located an authoritative assembly in this period, the tradition understands the Men of the Great Assembly to be the author of the books it believes were written in that period.

There are six items still unaccounted for. While they do not relate to the traditions which grow out of the identification in Neh., they all presuppose the name in M. Avot 1:1. Four are in late midrashim. Three of these are general honorific traditions, while only one, Ruth R. 4:5, gives them a legal concern. This leaves two items in the Talmud. b. Pes. 50b, "They observed fasts concerning copyists," perhaps presupposes the fast in Neh. 9:1, or their role in the continuation of the tradition. I cannot account for the enumeration of kings and commoners in b. Sanh. 104b.

Two basic elements are thus seen in the tradition. The first are those items which presuppose the identification of the Men of the Great Assembly in Neh., and all that follows from that. The second are the pericopae in which they are only a name. Can we suggest anything about the dating of these two elements? y. Ber. 7:3 and b. Yoma 69b which identify the Men of the Great Assembly with those in Neh. 9 are attributed to Joshua b. Levi, a first generation Palestinian Amora. b. Meg. 10b which derives from the Neh. theme is attributed to R. Levi, and some say R. Jonathan. This is possibly R. Levi the fifth generation Tanna and the first generation Palestinian Amora, R. Jonathan. It can be attributed no later than R. Levi the third generation Amora. b. Ber. 33a is an expansion of the liturgical activities ascribed to the Men of the Great Assembly in y. Ber. 7:3 and b. Yoma 69b. It is attributed to second or third generation Palestinian Amora, R. Shaman b. Abba (third generation) said to R. Yohanan (second generation), or R. Hiyya (third generation) reported in the name of R. Yohanan. Midrash Ps. 36:8 is attributed to R. Abba b. Kahana, another third generation Palestinian Amora. If we assume the reliability of the attributions, we see the identification of the Men of the Great Assembly in Neh. established by the earliest generations of Palestinian Amoraim. Further, if the lateness of the M. Avot list is correct, then we show that the bulk of the tradition, the naming, identification, and concern with liturgy and exegesis, derives from this late Tannaitic, early Amoraic period. On the other hand, of the six other items, four are in late *midrashim* and probably not part of the early active period of the tradition's formulation. Gen. R. 35:2 is attributed to the fourth or fifth generation Amora, R. Yudan, and supports this contention. b. Sanh. 104b is attributed to the sixth generation Babylonian Amora, R. Ashi, and bears no relationship to anything. This leaves us with b. Pes. 50b which is attributed to Joshua b. Levi. As we suggested before, this fast concerning copyists may be tied to the identification in Neh.

VI. Conclusions

This analysis of the traditions concerning the Men of the Great Assembly suggests that the name was created by Mishnaic masters interested in establishing a continuous chain of authority from Moses to the Pharisees. The early Amoraic masters then identified this name with the assembly described in Neh. 8-9. They ascribed to it liturgical and exegetical concerns based on the activity of the group in Neh. Once this had become established, related activities not specified Neh. could be credited to them. This included the writing of books which the rabbis believed were from the period of the Men of the Great Assembly. We thus have an active and formative period of development probably at the end of mishnaic times and during the early Amoraic generations. The items in which the Men of the Great Assembly are merely a name and not part of the viable tradition are mostly found in the later compilations or have late attributions.[10]

VII. Bibliographical Study

In this preliminary examination of previous studies of the Men of the Great Assembly I shall examine the major articles in English which have dealt with the subject. Most of the articles are characterized by the quest for the historical Men of the Great Assembly. The notable exception is G. F. Moore's "The Rise of Normative Judaism," *Harvard Theological Review* 17 (1924) pp. 307-73. There he states,

> The idea of this 'Great Synagogue,' to which various institutions and regulations of fundamental importance in Judaism are attributed, in all probability originated in the assembly described in Neh. 9-10..." (p. 310)

S. Krauss in "The Great Synod," *Jewish Quarterly Review* 10 (1897/98) pp. 347-77, holds that the Talmudic traditions are historical records of the Men of the Great Assembly. "...an absence of historical records would lead to the assumption that nothing worth recording had happened. Can such a thing be imagined?" (p. 350). This view of the traditions leads to his hermeneutic principle:

> Since everything speaks in favour of, and nothing against, the historical existence of the Great Synod, a veritably scientific method cannot reject the Talmudical reports as untenable; but must rather be at pains to explain the difficulties that present themselves. (ibid.)

Most of the writers have addressed themselves to this task. These difficulties include, how many members did the Great Assembly have, what was their chronology, and are they to be identified with other groups such as the *soferim*? The identification of the Men of the Great Assembly with the *soferim* is based on Tanḥuma, Beshalaḥ 16, Zundel edition.

The problem over membership arises from sources like b. Meg. 17b which states, "One hundred and twenty elders, and among them many prophets, instituted the eighteen blessings in the order (in which they are to be recited)," and pericopae which speak of a group of eighty-five elders (e.g., y. Meg. 70d). While none of these sources mention the Men of the Great Assembly, W. Bacher in "The Great Synagogue," *JE* 11 (1905) pp. 640-43, confidently states they are identical with the Men of the Great Assembly. He then claims "these divergent statements may easily be reconciled" (p. 641). This is done by emending the texts. Though he concedes that b. Yoma 69b, b. Ber. 33b and parallels "indicates the Amoraim did not think the Great Synagogue could be any other assembly or council than the one mentioned as the source of the prayers in Neh. 9" (ibid.), he claims an historical authenticity beyond that identity.

All the writers enter the discussion of which Simeon the Just is meant in M. Avot 1:2. H. Englander in "The Men of the Great Synagogue," *HUC Jubilee Volume* (1925) pp. 145-69, sketches the history of the debate. Following J. Neusner in *Pharisees* I, p. 58, I have stayed out of this debate since the traditions concerning Simeon the Just do not lead themselves to sound historical speculation.

The greatest assortment of speculation comes in the various characterizations of the Men of the Great Assembly. Englander cites A. Kuenen, "Over de Manner der Groote Synagoge," Germ. tr. K. Budde, Gesammelte Abhandlungen, pp. 125-60, as maintaining "that the basis of all traditions touching the ʼNŠY KNST HGDWLH is none other than the assembly described in Neh. 8-10..." (Englander, p. 145). This would mean denying an historical basis for the traditions, which Englander will not do. Instead, he argues that the term ʼNŠY KNST HGDWLH should be taken in the broad sense of leaders of the Great Community. He digresses into an examination of Septuagint and NT use of *ecclesia* and *synagoge*, and states that the latter term corresponds to KNST. Englander concludes, "If then, the term KNST in the first or second century of the common era was a designation of the community or the people of Israel, it certainly could have that sense in the term ʼNŠY KNST HGDWLH" (p. 153). He then cites biblical and Septuagint passages where ʼNŠY implies leaders, to conclude that "Men" in our term refers only to the leaders of the community. I do not understand what is gained by this free association.

L. Finkelstein in "The Maxim of the *Anshe Keneset Ha-Gedolah*," *Journal of Biblical Literature* 59 (1940) pp. 455-69, maintains that they are an institution for times of crises. He postulates that they convened at least twice, the first time for the covenant in Neh. 10, and the second, toward the end of the third century, convoked by Simeon the Just. H. Mantel, "The Nature of the Great Synagogue," *HTR* 60 (1967) pp. 69-91, attempts to strengthen Finkelstein's theory which he believes is most compatible with the sources. Mantel argues that Finkelstein is flawed by the ambiguity of two definitions of *keneset*, (1) an association of the pious, and (2) a supreme court. Mantel likens the term to Hellenistic societies and defines *keneset* as an unofficial religious association.

S. Hoenig, *The Great Sanhedrin* (New York, 1953), identifies Simeon with Simeon the Hasmonean. He concludes that the Great Assembly "was a sort of National Convention" which established the Hasmonean Commonwealth in 141 B.C.E. (p. 170). He further maintains that this Assembly is the forerunner of the Bet Din ha-Gadol.

Returning to Krauss, he identifies the Men of the Great Assembly with everyone. They are identical to the *soferim*. Based on his own midrash on a midrash the Men of the Great Assembly and the "Elders" are identical, and since "there is only a short step from the assembly of 'Elders,' ...to that body which was called Sanhedrin. Nothing more was wanted to effect this change than a little Hellenizing" (p. 375).

We thus find that with the exception of Moore, the above inquiries have fallen to a number of fatal errors. First, they have failed critically to analyze the literary traits of the pericopae; second, they have assumed the reliability of the sources as historical records of the Men of the Great Assembly; and third, they have introduced anachronistic and inappropriate analogies (*Pharisees* III, p. 366).

NOTES

THE MEN OF THE GREAT ASSEMBLY

[1]When R. Ḥanina and R. Jonathan were visiting certain towns in Judea, they came into a synagogue and observed that a reader was saying in his public prayer: "The God, great, mighty, and awful, glorious, powerful, and majestic." They silenced him saying: Thou hast no right to add words to the form of the benedictions as fixed by the Sages. Whence do we know the proper form of the benedictions? From Moses, our master, who said: *The great God, the mighty, and the awful* (Deut. 10:17), to which the Sages added the form of the benediction used by our Father Abraham, *God Most High, Maker of heaven and earth* (Gen. 14:19).

Midrash Ps. 17, trans. Braude, p. 272

Comment: The pericope is either subsuming the Men of the Great Assembly under Sages, or following a tradition that the Sages and not the Men of the Great Assembly are responsible for the fixing of the prayer form.

[2]The Scroll [of Esther] is read on the 11th, 12th, 13th, 14th, or 15th [of Adar], never earlier and never later. Cities encompassed by a wall since the days of Joshua the son of Nun read it on the 15th. Villages and large towns read it on the 14th, save that villages [sometimes] read it earlier on a day of assembly.

M. Meg. 1:1, trans. Danby, p. 201

[3]Said R. Joshua b. Levi, "In the hour they were counted [i.e., they voted] and they decided, 'Three kings and four commoners have no share in the world to come,' they desired to join Solomon with them..."

Song R. 1:1:5

Comment: Song R. presents a more polished account, though it does not identify the "they."

[4]Ch. Albeck, *Bereshit Rabba*, v. 3, "Introduction" (Jerusalem, 1965) p. 36.

[5]Ben 'Zion Lurie, *Megillath Ta'anith* (Jerusalem, 1964) p. 201.

[6]J. Neusner, *Eliezer ben Hyrcanus* (Leiden, 1973); J. Lightstone, *Ṣadoq the Yavnean* (above, pp. 49-147).

[7]J. Neusner, *Pharisees* I, p. 58.

[8]An attestation is a reference to a pericope which allows us to establish a *terminus ante quem* for a tradition. For a description of attestations, see *Pharisees* III, pp. 180-81.

[9]*Pharisees* III, p. 283.

[10]I wish to acknowledge my indebtedness to my teacher, Professor Jacob Neusner, whose criticisms and insights give me constant direction. The comments and criticisms of my fellow students, Mr. David Bellin, Professor Baruch Bokser, Mr. Joel Gereboff, Ms. Diane Levine, Mr. Jack Lightstone, Professor Charles Primus, Ms. Diane Weiser, and Professor Tsvee Zahavy, have been most helpful and appreciated. I also express sincere appreciation to my teachers, Professors David Blumenthal, Barry Levy, and Rabbi Joel Zaiman. I alone bear responsibility for errors or omissions.

BIBLIOGRAPHY

I. *Manuscripts*

Babylonian Talmud: Codex Munich 95 (Reprinted Jerusalem, 1971).

Manuscripts of the Babylonian Talmud from the Collection of the Vatican Library, Series A (Jerusalem, 1972).

Midrash Rabbah (Jerusalem, 1961).

Mishnah Codex Parma (de Rossi 138) (Reprinted Jerusalem, 1970).

Mishnah 'im Perush HaRambam, Defus Rishon, Napoli, 1492, Introduction by A. M. Haberman (Reprinted Jerusalem, 1970).

The Palestinian Talmud, Leiden MS, Cod. Scal. 3: A Facsimile of the Original Manuscript, Introduction by S. Lieberman (Jerusalem, 1970).

Talmud Bavli (New York, n.d.).

Talmud Bavli, Defus Rishon, Venezia, 5280 (Reprinted Jerusalem, 1968).

Talmud Yerushalmi (New York, 1959).

Talmud Yerushalmi According to the Venice Text

Talmud Yerushalmi, Codex Vatican, Vet. Ebr. 133, Introduction by S. Lieberman (Jerusalem, 1971).

Beer, J. (ed.), *Faksimile-Ausgabe des Mischna Codex Kaufmann A50* (Reprinted Jerusalem, 1968).

Lowe, W. H. (ed.), *The Mishnah on which the Palestinian Talmud Rests* (Cambridge, 1966).

II. *Scholarly Editions of Texts*

Albeck, Ch. and Theodor, E. (eds.), *Bereshit Rabba* (Jerusalem, 1965).

Buber, S. (ed.), *Midrasch Echa Rabbati* (Reprinted Hildesheim, 1967).

________, *Midrasch Mischle* (Wilna, 1893).

Buber, S. (ed.), *Midrasch Tehillim* (New York, 1947).

Epstein, J. N. and Melamed, E. Z. (eds.), *Mekhilta d'Rabbi Šim'on b. Jocai*

Finkelstein, L. (ed.), *Sifre on Deuteronomy* (New York, 1969).

Friedmann, M. (ed.), *Pesikta Rabbati* (Reprinted Tel-Aviv, 1963).

Higger, M. (ed.), *Treatise Semaḥot and Treatise Semaḥot of R. Ḥiyya and Sefer Ḥibbut ha-Keber* (New York, 1931).

Hoffman, D. (ed.), *Midrash Tanna'im* (Berlin, n.d.).

Horovitz, H. S. and Rabin, I. A. (eds.), *Mechilta d'Rabbi Ismael* (Jerusalem, 1960).

Lauterbach, J. Z. (ed. and trans.), *Mekilta de Rabbi Ishmael* (Philadelphia, 1933).

Lieberman, S. (ed.), *The Tosefta: Mo'ed* (New York, 1962).

________, *The Tosefta: Nashim* (New York, 1967).

________, *The Tosefta: Zera'im* (New York, 1955).

Lurie, Ben Zion (ed.), *Megillath Ta'anith* (Jerusalem, 1964).

Schechter, S. (ed.), *Aboth de Rabbi Nathan* (New York, 1967).

Weiss, I. H. (ed.), *Sifra debe Rab or Sefer Torat Kohanim* (Reprinted New York, 1947).

Yalqut Shimoni (Reprinted Jerusalem, 1952).

Zuckermandel, M. S. (ed.), *The Tosefta: Based on the Erfurt and Vienna Codices* (Reprinted Jerusalem, 1963).

Zundel, E. (ed.), *Midrasch Tanḥuma* (Reprinted New York, 1924).

III. *Translations, Commentaries and Secondary Works*

Albeck, Ch., *Introduction to the Talmud Babli and Yerushalmi* (Hebrew) (Tel-Aviv, 1969).

________, *Sheshah Sidré Mishnah: Seder Mo'ed* (Jerusalem-Tel-Aviv, 1952).

________, *Sheshah Sidré Mishnah: Seder Nashim* (Jerusalem-Tel-Aviv, 1959).

Albeck, Ch., *Sheshah Sidré Mishnah: Seder Neziqin* (Jerusalem-Tel-Aviv, 1953).

________, *Sheshah Sidré Mishnah: Seder Qodashim* (Jerusalem-Tel-Aviv, 1958).

________, *Sheshah Sidré Mishnah: Seder Ṭohorot* (Jerusalem-Tel-Aviv, 1959).

________, *Sheshah Sidré Mishnah: Seder Zera'im* (Jerusalem-Tel-Aviv, 1957).

Alon, G., *Mehqarim beToledot Yisra'el* (Tel-Aviv, 1967).

Bacher, W., *Die Agada der palästinenschen Amoräer* I (Strassburg, 1892).

________, *Die Agada der Tannaiten* (Strassburg, 1903).

________, "Die Agada der Tannaiten: Sadok," *Monatsschrift für Geschichte und Wissenschaft des Judentums*, 31 (1882), pp. 208-11.

________, "The Great Synagogue," *The Jewish Encyclopedia*, 11 (New York, 1905).

________, Review of Weinstein, I. *Zur Genesis der Agada. Revue des Etudes Juives*, 43 (1901).

Baron, Salo, *A Social and Religious History of the Jews* II (Philadelphia, 1952).

Baumgarten, A., "Scroll of Esther," *Encyclopedia Judaica*, 14 (Jerusalem, 1971).

Braude, W. (trans.), *The Midrash on Psalms* (New Haven, 1959).

________, *Pesikta Rabbati: Discourses for Feasts, Fasts and Special Sabbaths* (New Haven, 1968).

Danby, H. (trans.), *The Mishnah* (London, 1933).

Englander, H., "The Men of the Great Synagogue," *Hebrew Union College Jubilee Volume* (Cincinnati, 1925).

Epstein, I. (ed.), *The Babylonian Talmud* (London, 1935-1948).

Epstein, J. N., *Introduction to the Amoraic Literature (Prolegomena ad Litteras Amoraiticas)* (Hebrew) (Jerusalem, 1962).

________, *Introduction to the Tannaitic Literature (Prolegomena ad Litteras Tannaiticas)* (Hebrew) (Jerusalem, 1957).

Epstein, J. N., *Introduction to the Text of the Mishnah* (Hebrew) (Jerusalem-Tel-Aviv, 1964).

Frankel, Z., *Darke haMishnah* (Tel-Aviv, 1959).

Finkelstein, L., "The Maxim of the *Anshe Keneset Ha-Gedolah*," *Journal of Biblical Literature*, 59 (1940), pp. 455-69.

Freedman, H. and Simon, M. (eds.), *Midrash Rabbah* (London, 1939).

Gerhardsson, Birger, *Memory and Manuscript: Oral Tradition and Written Transmission in Rabbinic Judaism and Early Christianity* (Copenhagen, 1964).

Ginzberg, L., *Commentary on the Palestinian Talmud* III (New York, 1941).

________, *The Legends of the Jews* (Philadelphia, 1946).

Goldin, J. (trans.), *The Fathers according to Rabbi Nathan* (New Haven, 1955).

Graetz, Heinrich, *Geschichte der Juden* IV[4] (Leipzig, 1908).

Gröndah, F., *Die Personnennamen der Texte aus Ugarit* (Rome, 1967).

Halevy, I., *Dorot HaRishonim* III (Jerusalem, 1967).

Harding, G. Lankester, *An Index and Concordance of Pre-Islamic Names and Inscriptions* (Toronto and Buffalo, 1971).

Hauptman, Judith, "Women in the Talmud," *Response*, 18 (Summer, 1973).

Herr, M. D., "Lamentations Rabbah," *Encyclopedia Judaica*, 10 (Jerusalem, 1971).

Hoenig, S., *The Great Sanhedrin* (New York, 1953).

Hyman, A., *Histories of the Tanna'im and the 'Amora'im* (Hebrew) (Reprint Jerusalem, 1964).

Jastrow, M., *A Dictionary of the Targumim, the Talmud Babli and Yerushalmi and the Midrashic Literature* (New York, 1886-1893).

Kanter, Shamai, *Gamaliel of Yavneh* (Leiden, 1978).

Kaplan, Zvi, "Beruryah," *Encyclopedia Judaica*, 4 (Jerusalem, 1971).

Klein, S., "Leshe'elat 'Sefer Yuḥasin,'" *Sefer Hayyovel... le B.M. Lewin* (Jerusalem, 1939), pp. 86-92.

Krauss, S., *Griechische und lateinische Lehnwörter im Talmud, Midrasch und Targum*, Teil I (Berlin, 1898).

________, "The Great Synod," *Jewish Quarterly Review*, 10 (1897-1898), pp. 347-77.

Levinson, S. J., "The Great Synagogue," *Universal Jewish Encyclopedia*, 10 (Cincinnati, 1943).

Lieberman, Saul, *Hayyerushalmi Kifshuṭo* (Jerusalem, 1935).

________, *Hellenism in Jewish Palestine* (New York, 1962).

________, "On Persecution of the Jewish Religion," *S. W. Baron Jubilee Volume* III (Jerusalem, 1974).

________, "The Martyrs of Caeserea," *Annuaire de l'Institut de philologie et d'histoire orientales et slaves* VII (1939-1944).

________, *Tosefta Kifshuṭah* (New York, 1955-).

________, *Tosefet Rishonim* (Jerusalem, 1938-1939).

Mantel, H., "The Nature of the Great Synagogue," *Harvard Theological Review*, 60 (1967), pp. 69-91.

Margaliyot, E., "ʿIvrit Ve'aramit Batalmud Uvamidrash," *Leshonenu*, 27-28 (1963-1964).

Margaliyoth, M., *Encyclopedia of Talmudic and Geonic Literature* II (Hebrew) (Tel-Aviv, 1960).

Meeks, Wayne, "The Image of the Androgyne: Some Uses of a Symbol in Earliest Christianity," *History of Religions*, 13 (1974).

Meyers, E. M., *Jewish Ossuaries: Reburial and Rebirth* (Rome, 1971).

Mielziner, M., *Introduction to the Talmud*, Third edition with additional notes by Joshua Bloch and Louis Finkelstein (New York, 1925).

Moore, G. F., *Judaism in the First Centuries of the Christian Era* II (Cambridge, MA, 1962).

________, "The Rise of Normative Judaism," *Harvard Theological Review*, 17 (1924), pp. 307-73.

Morris, Nathan, *A History of Jewish Education* I (Tel-Aviv, 1960).

Neusner, Jacob, *Development of a Legend: Studies on the Traditions Concerning Yohanan ben Zakkai* (Leiden, 1970).

________, *Eliezer ben Hyrcanus: The Tradition and the Man*, I-II (Leiden, 1973).

________, *A History of the Jews in Babylonia* I, 2nd edition (Leiden, 1969), II-V (Leiden, 1966-70).

________, *A History of the Mishnaic Law of Purities*: I-III, *Kelim* (Leiden, 1974).

________, *A Life of Yohanan b. Zakkai: Ca. 1-80 C.E.*, 2nd edition (Leiden, 1970).

________, *The Rabbinic Traditions about the Pharisees before 70*, I-III (Leiden, 1971).

Ochser, S., "Zadok," *The Jewish Encyclopedia* XII (New York, 1906).

Pape, W. and Benseler, G., *Wörterbuch der Griechischen Eigennamen*^{2} (Reprint Graz, 1959).

Porton, Gary, "The Artificial Dispute: Ishmael and ʿAqiva," J. Neusner (ed.), *Christianity, Judaism and Other Greco-Roman Cults: Studies for Morton Smith at Sixty* IV (Leiden, 1975), pp. 18-29.

________, *The Legal Traditions of Rabbi Ishmael* (Ph.D. Dissertation, Brown University, 1973).

________, *The Traditions of Rabbi Ishmael*: I, *The Non-Exegetical Materials* (Leiden, 1976).

Rabbinovicz, R., *Variae Lectiones in Mischnam et Talmud Babylonicum* (Reprint New York, 1960).

Ranke, H., *Early Babylonian Personal Names* (Philadelphia, 1905).

Ratner, B., *Ahawath Zion WeJeruscholaim* (Vilna, 1901).

Schwab, M. (trans.), *Le Talmud de Jerusalem* (Reprint Paris, 1932-1933).

Sperber, D., "The Great Synagogue," *Encyclopedia Judaica* 15 (Jerusalem, 1971).

Strack, H. L., *Introduction to the Talmud and Midrash* (New York, 1965).

Szold, Henrietta, "Beruriah," *The Jewish Encyclopedia* III (New York, 1902).

Weinstein, N. I., *Zur Genesis der Aggadah* (Göttingen, 1901).

Weiss, I. H., *Dor Dor VeDorshav* I (Tel-Aviv-Jerusalem, n.d.).

Wuthnow, Heinz, *Die semitischen Menschennamen in griechischen Inschriften und Papyri des Vorderen Orients* (Leipzig, 1930).

"Zadok," *Encyclopedia Judaica* 16 (Jerusalem, 1971).

Zlotnick, D. (trans.), *The Tractate Mourning* (New Haven, 1966).

Zunz, Y. L., *Haddreshot Beyisra'el*, ed. and trans., Ch. Albeck (Jerusalem, 1954).

INDEX OF BIBLICAL AND TALMUDIC PASSAGES

BABYLONIAN TALMUD

GENERAL INDEX